MONEY:
The Banks of the '80s

MONEY: The Banks of the '80s

$

DIMITRIS N CHORAFAS

PBI
a petrocelli book
new york princeton

Dedicated to the memory of my mother.

Designed by Diane L. Backes
Typesetting by Backes Graphics

Printed in the United States of America

1 2 3 4 5 6 7 8 9 10

Library of Congress Cataloging in Publication Data

Chorafas, Dimitris N.
Money: The Banks of the '80s.

Bibliography.
Includes index.
HG2491.C53 332.1'2'068 81-15705
ISBN 0-89433-182-5 AACR2

Contents

Forward

During the past two decades natural social and economical evolutionary forces have literally transformed the banking function at the personal and corporate level.

At the personal level, the bank is no longer seen as the place where money can be deposited or withdrawn when needed. The public today is demanding the presence and assistance of the bank at all times and all places: during the evening social hours, on weekends at the seaside or mountain resort, during the week at the supermarket or the local grocery store, to cite only a few cases.

Likewise, at the corporate level, it is no longer sufficient to provide the customer with the money when it is needed. It has to be in the right amount, in the right currency, at the right time and in the right place. It is further necessary for the bank to provide the customer with highly automated tools to minimize the inertia of funds.

Furthermore, for both personal and corporate services, the banking organization must be able to provide detailed information about the status of an account, a product, a service or a transaction any time and any place it is requested.

To satisfy these conditions, the back office operations of a modern banking organization, formerly staffed with eye-shaded operators, has undergone a radical transformation. Industrial engineering techniques and practices are being adopted by operations, while front-line personnel (account officers) are frequently leaving the comfort of their carpeted offices to visit potential customers. Banks today are adopting an increasingly aggressive approach to marketing of new banking products and services.

What we are observing is the transformation of a service function of the industrial world to an industry in its own right, where banking products and services are conceived by specialized teams, packaged by the assembly line and sold by the marketing unit. In short, we are seeing the emergence of a *banking industry* with its own products and markets, adopting industrial concepts in its management perspective and industrial engineering approaches in its manufacturing processes.

When considering the complex interrelationships among the various forces (social, economical, managerial, technological, etc.) affecting this new industry, it is not surprising that while individual aspects are often covered in specialized publications, few attempts have been made to present a global perspective.

Professor Chorafas has tackled this problem head-on in his book, *Money: The Banks of the 80s*. A distinguished career as an educator and consultant in the industrial and financial world has enabled the author to present the *practical* aspects of the day-to-day problems within the context of the *theoretical* infrastructure which is the confluence of the social, economical, technological and managerial forces affecting the banking industry.

This book should be mandatory reading to all those dynamic and forward looking bankers who are charged with the responsibility of solving today's problems while planning tomorrow's environment.

Dr. Carmine Vona
Vice President
Bankers Trust Company

Preface

Banking today is a far cry from what it was thirty years ago. The slowly but firmly established concept of a *banking industry* has deeply influenced the ways and means of doing business. The large scale integration of data processing, databases, and wideband data transmission completely transformed routine operations. Even fifteen years ago, banking was a relatively simple business. It involved collecting money in deposit and savings accounts, exchanging money, financing industry, commerce, and handling individuals who asked for loans. The more credit accounts a bank had, the better off it was in its ability to lend money and make profits. But things have changed.

In relations between banks and their clients there is these days a reversal in values and, therefore, in the criteria used in making banking decisions. In retail banking, the debit accounts of individuals may give the bank a better opportunity for profits than the credit accounts. In foreign operations, the risks of money exchange exceed any other risks banks have faced in the past. In corporate banking, the need for investments and for modernization by business and industry make apparent greater financial outlays than the banking sector could satisfy. Banking management must not only reexamine its credit policies, but also participate in the direction of the investments themselves, in a sort of extended subordinate debentures. The tendency is clear; in corporate banking, the banker has an increased responsibility towards the client, with unification of different loans, advisory services, several phases of management action, and vertical integration of the products offered by the bank to the firm. If the larger banks already have the human resources to do so, the smaller must acquire or develop them in order to survive.

Technology has been the moving gear behind the new banking concepts. There has been a steady proliferation of new, helpful, sophisticated financial services. With telecommunications, banking is no longer bound geographically. A bank in New York can pay freight bills for a customer in Rome as promptly and efficiently as it could were it actually located in that city. Competition has taken a totally new aspect. Banking automation accomplishes in fractions of a second tasks formerly measured in terms of man-hours or even man-months. It reduces errors which exasperate customers and necessitate time-consuming corrective action. It heightens productivity; and this can only lead to profitable operations. Services based on computers and communications are also becoming very important for the income they generate. Such fees can play a significant role in the growth of profits and thus of retained earnings.

Both for corporate and for retail trade, the modern bank must tool-up for permanent presence at the workpost. This includes ATMs (Automatic Teller Machines) open 24-hours/day and allowing queries on balance, transfer between accounts, and cash receipt and cash dispenser operations; it involves electronic money transfer mechanisms; and it calls for the implementation of a network of point-of-sale equipment installed in supermarkets, department stores, hotels and other businesses—and working on-line with the bank's own computer.

Classical ideas, ways and means will necessarily evolve or change altogether in this process. The idea of using the teller as a predominantly manual work-post must be radically revamped. The teller's office should be a consulting center to the clientele. The quality of the tellers must be increased; the person-to-person contact improved; the manual jobs automated. These are no supplementary considerations, but the very heart of the banker's job. Computers and communications will only help the financial institution which has a strategy to profit from their use. Companies and persons which are attracted to the bank by a single specialized service, very often broaden their relationship subsequently. This means potential market growth; and a bank would profit if management both knows and wants to exploit the potential offered by automation.

By multiplying the products which are offered to the market, and improving the qualifications of its personnel which come in contact with its clientele, the bank transforms itself. The modern banker must be trained not only in the understanding of the needs, but also in the actual skill of advising the client in such diverse issues as the stock exchange, the risks of the foreign exchange, real estate promotion, retirement plans, and the law concerning different types of companies, as well as taxation and financial advantages given from time to time through the legislative action of the state.

The modern banker will not abandon the classical role of handling money. What we just said are the new qualifications which he must acquire. His skills must become all-purpose, and his knowhow must cover both the national and the international scene. Computers and communications and the functions of marketing are just the opening aspects of a swift development which involves an increased role in human relations and the ability to plan and advise on the redistribution and employment of the available resources. In the past, it seemed more rewarding to sink our teeth into problems of immediate concern and leave the big-picture issues for tomorrow. The same could be said of sticking to aged procedures rather than scouting for new ones. However, we now know by dearly acquired experience that answers to the larger questions are a prerequisite to sound decisions in the day-to-day business, and that the wait may be frustrating. Banking history is replete with examples of failures because of old, "time-honoured", and obsolete practice. Even forceful and energetic approaches may become counterproductive when the banker loses sight of the cutting edge of technology. Then, the result is often the opposite of the intention. Ironically, such failures may not be due to lack of effort but rather be the result of it. It is the direction of the effort which sometimes fails. If this text does nothing else but show its reader the new directions, it will worth the while of reading it.

Let me close by expressing my thanks to everyone who contributed to making this text successful—to the presidents of the banks I worked with, for their drive to develop better systems; to my colleagues, for their advice; to the financial organizations I visited during my research in the United States, Japan, Southeast Asia, Latin America and throughout Europe, for their insight; and Eva Maria Binder, for the many typings of the text, the drawings and the index.

Dimitris N. Chorafas
Valmer and Vitenau,
October 1981

PART I

The Banking Industry

The Next Ten Years

1

During the last quarter century the tendency among financial institutions in the United States has been to refer to themselves as the "banking industry." This is more than a new terminology; it reflects nothing less than a new philosophy of management. Yet, in furthering the aims of banking as an industry, American financial institutions face the problem of applying industrial management techniques to banking. Five aspects are most frequently mentioned:

1. The institution of *marketing*.
2. The definition of *product lines*.
3. The *new banking services* made possible through information systems.
4. The calculation of *profitability* to be obtained from the products offered to the market.
5. The fact that banking has become a *knowledge-intense* industry.

These are aspects of the same problem: furthering the aims of banking as an industrial enterprise. It becomes, therefore, understandable that faced with industrial management perspectives, the incentive for banks to develop improved methods for penetrating markets and competing more successfully with each other is all the more urgent.

Business is where the markets are. Today's and tomorrow's successful banking institutions will be based on their ability to *market* rather than on their ability to *invest*. The evolving information technology will be radically transforming banking.

The careful student of banking management is confronted with widely differing opinions—from the past as well as the future—about the way banks view financial performance. And the financial markets call for new perspectives. Interest rates are moving upward; inflation has had its impact; sophisticated cash-management techniques have appeared and matured; computers have made possible new accounting methodologies; mathematics has been introduced into banking; corporate treasures have trimmed noninterest-bearing balances to the minimum necessary; a consistent effort has been made to establish new profit lines.

These trends have led financial institutions to develop a corporate strategy as a means of pursuing a comprehensive, coherent policy for taking advantage of business opportunities. Electronic funds transfer (EFT) has emerged on the scene; correspondent banking has been given a new mission; and bank-holding companies are expanding. Along with developments have come new risks. The number of loan defaults has grown; there has been an increase in risk ventures such as real estate trust funds; questions have been posed concerning bank profits and the adequacy of bank capital; and the development of expensive new services has led to a formalization of feasability studies renewing interest among banks in assessing their profitability, in terms of both accounts and products. The force most directly responsible for the acceleration of this process is computer-based information technology.

The standards of the past have cracked long ago. On one hand, bankers maintain that customers can use the same balances to compensate for both loan and activity services, while on the other, corporate treasurers argue that the laws governing bank profits put undue pressure on their firms. In a sense, both views are valid, since banks have tended to cost and price only a small group of standard activity services while offering others without charge.

Furthermore, bankers of all nations tend to speak primarily about conditions in their own banking system. This is proper. But at the same time it should not be forgotten that banking is an *international* activity. The transfer of money is one example; the presence around the globe of United States, English, German, Japanese, French, Dutch and Italian banks in other countries is another.

If American banks—say, in England—follow a course that remains within the limits set by the national banks, that course will inevitably have an impact on the British financial market. It is in the interest of the local banks to be prepared for this impact. By the same token, if West German banks set up branches in the United States from coast to coast, United States banks, which are restricted to relatively small regions of the country, will necessarily feel the pinch.

This internationalization of banks, and banking, is not the only example of a changing strategy. Advances in electronics technology, and the way in which these advances affect banking (as the technology already has in the United States), will profoundly affect the banking industry throughout the Western world. We saw this in the 1950s, with the advent of computer mainframes, or maxicomputers; in the 1960s, with the real time and time sharing systems; in the 1970s, with minicomputers, distributed intelligence and the money transfer networks. Banking strategy should not be determined within the limited context of national boundaries. It is therefore necessary for even small financial institutions to reconsider their strategies, both from the perspective of technology and from that of international finance.

CHANGE IN THE 1980s

The change many experts see coming in the mid-1980s will likely be much more far-reaching than anything seen during the past three decades. That is why it is so important to call attention to the movement that is already underway: the electronics revolution in banking.

One aspect of this revolution is the profits to be realized through use of Electronic Funds Transfer technology, due to the significant reduction in the number of employees needed at bank branches, and the conversion of the branches themselves to automation: from ATM (automatic teller machines) to banking at home (Figure 1.1). This is the next frontier of the banking industry. No lesser authority than Frank E. Morris, president of the Federal Reserve Bank of Boston, speaking in 1979 at a banking symposium held by the Financial Analysts Federation, suggested that, of the 32,800 banking offices currently in the United States, there may be as few as 8,000 by 1989. This is a reduction of seventy-five percent within a single decade. Had an ordinary citizen said that, one would reply: "That's nonsense."

Less than three months after Mr. Morris made his revealing statement, Bankers' Trust of New York announced that it had reached an agreement whereby twenty-eight of its branch offices would be sold

FIGURE 1.1

to Barclays, sixteen to the National Bank of North America (itself a subsidiary of the National Westminster Bank of London), and eleven to the Bank Leumi Trust Company. The sale of still another thirty-four branch offices was at the time still being negotiated.

Why did Bankers' Trust, one of the leading institutions in New York City's money market since 1903, wish to sell fifty-five of its branch offices? There had to be a reason. With $23 billion in deposits and an international network, Bankers' Trust has an operation that is solid; it is surely not short of cash. But management had reasons to decide otherwise. For example, retail banking is not as profitable as it once was. Personnel costs are too high, as is office space. For many financial institutions, the expense of operating branch offices now begins to exceed the benefits.

Let's look at the profile of this operation. Of the (1979) deposits of $23 billion, only $650 million came from the branch offices. Bankers' Trust is predominantly a "business" bank. That is, it serves primarily businesses, not private individuals. This, however, was not the basic reason for the change in policy. The basic reason was that a careful management evaluation of costs versus benefits showed that the cost of doing business in the future would force banking to change. Therefore, to remain profitable in retail banking, Bankers' Trust (like any other institution) had to make a huge investment in automation, and that was not considered a sound course in view of the predominant business of Bankers' Trust.

When we talk of a banking industry, the criteria are no more the same as in the past. As we will see in a subsequent chapter, investments—good investments—must be made to improve the management of cash. Choices are necessary to give priority: to the retail or to the business (wholesale) clients. If wholesale banking dominates management strategy, then the retail banking side would have to make do with less of the available resources. This, of course, is a choice faced by the management of practically all companies, whether financial or otherwise.

Is this an exceptional situation? It definitely is not! In the years ahead we may see something of a reversal in the way the branch offices of banks are viewed—just as we have seen other areas of banking change over the past ten years. In the past, the more branches a bank had, the larger and more solid it was considered. Before long, however, the criterion may be the opposite: the fewer manned branch offices, and the more automation it implements—the better off is the bank.

The frame of reference is changing, and it will keep changing for some time to come. Of Mr. Morris's conclusions, the first is self-evident, but all three are important:

1. A reduction of the number of bank employees will have a great impact on personnel costs.
2. The competition ahead will be in fees and pricing rather than convenience of location—which will be served through automatic devices.
3. Through technology, United States banking will move into interstate services more rapidly than it will through legislation or regulation.

Regarding the first conclusion, the point was made that banks should start immediately to adjust their staffing plans to meet the coming situation. This is necessary in order to prepare the personnel (the *right* personnel) for automated services. Current knowhow will not be sufficient, given the rate at which technology is advancing.

Why is the number of branch offices expected to shrink to less than a quarter of the present number? Because self-service banking will make unnecessary services that have long been a traditional part of banking, such as handling DDA and savings accounts. This brings us to the second conclusion, which, in turn, calls for stating goals, in terms of fees, pricing, and new banking services. The impact on personnel is evident. EFT will almost certainly allow workers to become more efficient. But they must first be trained.

THE MANAGEMENT OF CHANGE

The new banking services that will be made possible by technology pose problems for the management of change. Because change is so rapid, it must be planned for; the management of this change is a challenge. Banks must expose themselves to both the change and the planning for it. If management does not, it will not be able to provide the services that will be demanded and that are even now possible through technological innovation. Nor will these banks be able to reap the benefits. Finally, to ensure the management of change, the communications gap must be closed.

Computer and communications specialists are not always knowledgeable about the financial side of banking. Although they know about computer hardware and software, they have little understanding of the intricacies of their clients, the bankers. A similar statement can be made about the computer and communications knowhow of bank employees: this knowledge is thin or nonexistent. Yet computer-based communications are the veins and arteries of business. Financial organizations—or any business organization, for that matter—can no more operate efficiently and profitably with poor communications than the human body can function with clogged arteries.

Speaking of the new banking services, one need not view American banks as "superinstitutions" that know everything and can do everything. In Bourg-en-Bresse, France, for instance, the Banque Regionale de l'Ain (BRA), a medium-sized institution, began in February 1979 an experiment that could make cash obsolete.

In about fifty commercial locations, such as supermarkets, pharmacies, and gas stations, miniterminals have been installed, which are online to BRA. "Debit cards" have been issued to 10,000 customers. When a customer makes a purchase, the merchant inserts the customer's card in a terminal, the customer punches in a "PIN" number, and the amount of the purchase is automatically withdrawn from the customer's account.

"Innovatron," another cashless system, is being tested in Britanny. Instead of circulating cash, the customer carries a charge card containing coded monetary units. As the customer makes purchases, the card is gradually used up. (Figure 1.2)

FIGURE 1.2

The new approach to a payments system for retail banking requires:

1. a microprocessor card, and
2. a memory cartridge, which is embedded in
3. a remote POS terminal.

The debit affected on the microprocessor card is credited on the merchant's cartridge by the transaction terminal. When the cartridge memory is full, its contents are transferred on the merchant's account. The retail microprocessor card contains: the ID (identification) of the holder; his bank and account number; the authorized credit level. A similar, medical microprocessor card may include ID and all basic medical information concerning a person: blood group; vaccination record; prescribed medicaments; and other issues on which particular attention should be paid. Another microprocessor card (telepass) can guarantee encryption capabilities in a person-to-person communication:

- User ID
- Authorization for access to a given network
- Authentication for file access (read, write, add, delete)
- Coding/decoding of messages
- Encapsulation/decapsulation (for security or other reasons)

Such a card can also be used for access to broadcasted encapsulated information. Such devices designed to propel the banking and other services which will be offered to the consumer are key elements of the transaction processing capabilities which will characterize the latter part of this decade.

By the mid-1980s, plastic cards should begin to replace cash, paper identification documents, and even keys in the pockets of the ordinary person. On these cards, special magnetic strips containing codes will give their owners access to computers, both large and small. Plastic cards will perform a variety of tasks that will make them far different from the typical credit card of today. For one thing, cards will have to be much more secure than they are at present. The cards that operate automatic tellers today rely on magnetic strips to provide access to the bank's computer and to the customer's account. The drawback is that this information can be altered. Anyone with the proper equipment can erase and rewrite the information on a card's magnetic strip (by investing in a magnetic head reader and a visual display unit.) Once this person has gained access to the computer, he or she can find the way to alter data.

A new process, known as watermarked magnets, has been developed for dealing with this problem. The process involves encoding a magnetic strip when the slurry, or iron oxide, on it is still mobile. At the same time as the particles are being oriented, information is input digitally. Because it is impossible to "unfreeze" the particles, cards encoded this way are virtually tamperproof. More sophisticated approaches are envisioned; for example, the Innovatron card with its own microprocessor and solid-state memory to which reference has been made.

If the new local-access mechanisms provide greater ease of use, more alternatives, and increased security and protection than did the old, they also pose problems of data transport that can be met effectively through networks. Since 1975, both large and medium-sized banks have become enthusiastic about Distributed Information Systems (DIS). For instance, Sweden's PK Banken has projected a far-sighted distributed-information system in which the bank considers three parameters in making its choice: the need to equip a branch office with locally installed, computer-based services; tariffs on the Nordic Data Communications network; and a search for cost effectiveness to augment the productivity of the banking employee through computer support provided locally.

For more than a decade, the emphasis has been on the bank teller's function, and rightly so. The teller is a salesperson selling bank products to the bank's customers. But too much routine does not allow him to sell the banking function effectively. This teller needs the support of computers.

Once "intelligent" microprocessor-based devices have been installed, the teller is gradually moved out of routine and into sales-oriented functions, the customer is put in touch with the computer, and a user-friendly environment is developed. This has been happening in the United States, Japan, England, West Germany, Sweden, Italy, Switzerland, and France—and it has been based on efficiency.

SELF-SERVICE BANKING

Computer-intelligent devices interfacing with customers and answering their needs help substantiate a new concept of banking services. Self-service banking is coming because economics, technology, and market forces are creating a place for it. The ideal do-it-yourself transaction system is one in which the customer originates the transaction data. The data then flow through the electronic transport and processing mechanism, creating the proper debits, credits, and controls.

An idea of how such a computer-based system may work is given by the pay-by-phone procedures adopted by some banks. To make a payment, the customer simply calls the pay-by-phone number and gives the telephone teller the appropriate information. If the customer wishes to make more than one payment, he or she gives the additional merchant names, codes, and amounts.* Voice-recognition units and voice synthesizers will record the message, repeat the customer's information (to ensure accuracy), and pass the data on to the computer. The information system will then total the payments and report the total to the customer—just as a teller does today, but with greater efficiency.

After the customer has finished, the transaction is processed by the computer. Each payment, or vendor code is verified to ensure that it is a valid number for the customer. If it is not, the transaction is rejected. The customer's name and account number with the payee are picked up and added to the transaction data for reporting the payments to the payee.

Each customer's account is examined and it is determined whether sufficient funds are available to make the payments requested. Again, if the answer is no, the transactions are rejected. Transactions are sorted according to payee. The total amount credited to the payee is computed and the payment data are prepared.

Pay-by-phone accounts are debited for the total payments made. Transactions that cannot be processed because of invalid payment codes or insufficient funds are reported and processed by the pay-by-phone staff the next morning. Through the telephone line and TV set, "Information Providers" on the British Viewdata system such as Barclay's Bank have brough direct banking capabilities to many homes (see Figure 1.3).

The technology is ready. What is needed is the incentive. The basic economics and the ease of service will provide it. With reference to the latter, the attractiveness of banking from one's own living room, using such common instruments as the telephone and the television

*For a technical discussion of this process see Dimitris N. Chorafas, *Interactive Videotex: The Domesticated Computer* (Princeton: Petrocelli Books, 1981)

THE BARCLAYS GROUP 494111a Op

BARCLAYLOAN

For home or garden improvements
for owner-occupiers

- From £200 to £3000 with no security
- For 12, 18, 24, 30 and 36 months *and* for loans of £300 or more, for 48 or 60 months
- Aged 18 but not yet 61; but not yet 59 for loans for over 36 months

True annual interest rate: 21.34% approx.

Press 0 to return to Barclayloan index
1 for repayment examples
9 for an application form

FIGURE 1.3

set is self-evident. For example, in terms of economics, Tandy has introduced to the American market an intelligent TV set which can handle interactive videotex (Viewdata) for as low as $15. per month. And the user who is willing to pay $25. per month receives a free personal computer for his use as the beginning of a home information system.

Can the results be predicted? Barclays, for instance, which has been experimenting with at-home banking via the Viewdata system (Prestel), believes that as experience spreads, this approach will become more feasible and thus more widely used. The aim is to bring about growth in retail banking without a corresponding increase in the number of branch offices and the cost of personnel. This, incidentally, justifies the Bankers' Trust decision to divest itself of its branch offices, as far as its bread-and-butter operations are concerned, such as money transfers, balance inquiries, and bill-paying. It leaves open the question, however, of more complex activities such as lending beyond a certain threshold.

To answer the legitimate question of the extent to which this service will be accepted, we have only to look at the current practices of some representative American banks, particularly the small ones, which have adopted touch-tone data input and pay-by-phone services. According to my information, customers like the service. At a small bank that started with an online service using teller interfacing, the number of pay-by-phone accounts has grown steadily, in one year reaching 2,055, with a total balance of $3,560,000 and an average balance of $1,732. In the opening phase, the average number of payments cleared during a month was 7,328, the average number of payments per account, 3.6, the amount of payments cleared, $826,500, and the average payment amount, $117.70.

The bank has noted that some customers, primarily young people, are heavy users of the service. Meanwhile, approximately seventy-five percent of all bills received by strong pay-by-phone users are paid that way. Another bank has installed "Money Answer" terminals in nine of its branch lobbies. These terminals provide customers with answers to eleven different questions about their savings and checking accounts. Inquiries have been running at more than 400 per day.

Computer-based, financial information systems—coupled with telephone bill-paying, automated teller machines, and do-it-yourself check-guarantee terminals (such as Boston's Money One)—are making self-service banking a reality. Self-service in the tangible goods area has been around for some years. Why not apply it to banking? With the advent of the microprocessor, self-service systems are rapidly being developed. Thus communicating with them becomes more and more convenient.

DO-IT-YOURSELF

Two of the most popular do-it-yourself financial services today are cash dispensers and check-authorization systems. In both cases, the appeal is based on convenience and saving time. Pay-by-phone transactions have already begun; with Interactive Videotex entering more homes and small businesses, the payment of bills using a TV video display could be the next step. Connecting telephone and television sets to interactive computing systems makes possible a personal service with tremendous potential. A person can thus do virtually all of his or her banking at home rather than go to a branch office and wait in line. As for the bank, this technique eases the problem of staffing for routine transactions.

To a large extent, the success of electronic service depends on enough new services being available to make the service attractive. New banking services should be designed to enable customers to replace their traditional way of handling money with new ways.

Major growth in the area of self-service banking is expected in the early 1980s. The use of home computers and telephone services will grow: the sophistication of ATMs will increase; debit cards will come into general use; food and gasoline will more often than not be dispensed using self-service; card-activiated machines and check-guarantee terminals will gain acceptance, as will the networks for handling them.

Based on experience with early pay-by-phone accounts, we can predict that banks will before long master data-transmission systems, incorporate computer programs, provide their clients with terminal services, and mount public relations campaigns to win over the public to their use.

The composition of the banking population will also change. About seventy percent of deposits in self-service accounts will belong to individuals who were not customers of a particular bank when the bank switched to the new type of accounts. Many of these customers will be young adults. In the United States, the median age of pay-by-phone customers is thirty-six, while for some banks, the median age of depositors is around fourty-nine. Young people will be attracted by online communications, and especially by their application to banking.

Bankers believe that most pay-by-phone customers have checking accounts and that the bill-paying service will not replace the checking account in the immediate future. Given the growing range of banking services, however, and the growing desire for twenty-four-hour, seven-day-a-week service, a well-designed, self-service banking system becomes a necessity. Plans for the future of pay-by-phone are flexible. Not only banks but department stores, insurance companies, credit card companies, small retailers, oil companies, educational institutions, service firms, utilities, finance companies, real estate management firms, charities, and clubs are interested as well.

PROJECTING NEW BANKING SERVICES

To meet the challenge of providing new banking services, management must study both the market trends and the technological trends. Then they must try to determine how these trends will affect banking. Management must, at the same time, keep in mind that trends are only that—trends—and not plans of action.

When these studies have proceeded far enough to enable planners to discern the general shape of the banking services of the future, it should be possible to predict that there will be a proliferation of automatic banking offices. Most will be located in such places as existing shopping centers, large factories, and major office buildings. Some will be staffed by only one employee, who will use remote terminals to process routine deposits and withdrawals. More complex banking will take place in large, regional centers staffed by personnel specializing in lending, investment counselling, foreign operations, and other nonroutine services. Most banks will have aggressive, new-product-development policies and information systems that will play a key role in the banks of the future.

The competition for customers will be fierce. One-account banking will spread, and the leading financial institutions will borrow a leaf from computer companies in "locking" customers into their account systems. Single-statement banking will increase dramatically, giving banks that use it a competitive edge over other banks.

The use of distributed information systems will expand greatly—in two ways. First, microprocessors will make it possible to put computer power on every desk. When we speak of *power* in this context, we mean power comparable to that of an IBM 370/135 in the early 1970s. Second, the individual user, whether a private customer or a business, will have direct access to a bank's database.

This calls for the creation of regional databases, to be located closer to users. Between now and 1985, banks will have to gear up for this. Models for judging banks' performance—by branch, area, function, and client—will be widely used, as will production-management, cost-accounting, line-balancing, quality-control, client-mirror, and risk-exposure techniques. More studies will be made of costs and benefits in a manner that resembles the studies long used in manufacturing.

Front offices will be served through distributed intelligence, while other areas of an operation will become heavy users of telecommunications. Microcomputers will be firmly established in such areas as fund management, foreign exchange, foreign trading, securities handling, and trust management—all backed by minicomputers and mainframes. System inquiries will be made via interactive devices, for example, using visualization, color, and graphics. Printed output will be reduced to a bare minimum. Magnetic cards will no longer be acceptable for personal identification. New, full proof (and fool proof) techniques will be required, such as the laser-cut "Magic Stripe" used by Citibank. Vendors of banking equipment will have to provide penetration-resistant hardware. Techniques for more secure personal identification numbers (PIN) will be needed as well. Voice printing is one possibility. A practical way will have to be found to control access and identify parties that wish to access databases. Finally, for all financial institutions, the cost of conversion will be fairly high, and much of the cost will be due to staffing and personnel development. The three top problems with the new system now in evolution are: *people*, *people*, and *people*.

The Bank of The Future

2

To offer novel and advanced services to people, management must change their way of thinking, their approach to employee training, their attitude toward the problems of their customers and clients, and their way of thinking about solutions to the problems confronting them.

In Chapter One we saw that the most fundamental factor involved in providing new banking services is *change*, and that change occurs because of two forces, the first of which is people. When people alter their attitudes and start looking at the world in a new way, change is inevitable. People-directed change results from several things—initiative, whether foresight or fear; education, understanding, appreciation; or emulation of successful efforts in the past. The second force involved in change is structure. If a structure, or system of doing something, is removed or altered significantly, people are forced to change accordingly. In banking, we see both forces—people and structure—operating simultaneously.

Only the least significant part of the process, however, is revealed through better understanding. In the case of banks, the key to determining the effect of change on structure is the bank's services. The following criteria should be borne in mind in evaluating both a market and the rate at which it will change:

(1) relative advantage

(2) new services to customers

(3) compatibility with existing services

(4) cost to customers

(5) the bank's costs and profits

The complexity of new services, the ability to experiment with new services, and the ease with which the services are implemented are all involved.

IMPACT OF NEW SERVICES

A bank must be thoroughly familiar with its customers and their needs before its management can make the right decisions about new services. This knowledge of customers and their needs is the basis on which to decide whether the latest information technology is advisable, to what extent it should be implemented, at what cost, whether it should be in collaboration with other financial institutions, and, finally, when to implement the services.

How have the leading banks met this challenge? For one thing, the banks themselves have changed—in profound ways—organizing their services so as to best accommodate their customers' changed requirements. This reflects the feeling that in the years to come, greater intellectual effort will be required to solve problems that were once relatively simple and on a smaller scale. This renewed effort means a change in both the structure of banking and in the banking industry's approach to new bank services.

The operation of a bank must be divided into its logically constituent channels. Then it must be examined with a view to automation. This is what Citibank did. Citibank broke its operation into seventeen well-defined channels, the following eleven are an example:

(1) letters of credit
(2) foreign exchange
(3) lock boxes
(4) current accounts
(5) collections
(6) commercial loans
(7) general ledger
(8) wire services (interbank money transfers)
(9) funds transfers
(10) corporate accounts
(11) MIS

Citibank's management held the philosophy that the reorganization of management was necessary. Citibank's management held the view that "a bank is essentially a factory that processes client orders." To help employees help the bank's customers, management focused on ways to give managers control of what goes on in their areas.

Leading banks actively plan for change by instituting the facilities needed to reach this goal. Several examples come to mind: Bank of America, Chase Manhattan, MHTC, Bankers' Trust, PNB, BFCE, and the Société Générale de Banque. Banks classify current and potential customers according to the degree of sophistication required to serve them. This classification yields a profile of what the banks call a *customer base*. The customer base indicates the technological level a bank should strive for the best serve its customers and to help management perform more efficiently and effectively.

The operational demands on banks in the 1980s will come in the form of a sharp increase in the number of online applications, in a significant increase in the sophistication of computer programs, in graphical presentations of reports, and in line-maintenance capability as systems become too complex for the use of manual procedures.

Because of the speed required for transferring money, the shrinking supply of good clerical labor, and rising costs, this development will become mandatory. The impact on both society and the labor force will be tremendous. In *The Informatization of Society*, Simon Nora and Alain Minc predict that over the next few years, as many as thirty percent of the jobs in banking will be eliminated because of irrelevancy. And a study recently conducted by leading German Financial Institutes has given similar results.

The work place is changing radically. Paper as a record-keeping medium will be sharply reduced. This applies to everything—ledger cards, reports, and so forth. The electronic files to be maintained at a typical financial institution will be in the billions of characters.

A good approach to studying both the direction and extent of change needed within a financial institution is that of determining which customers will be moving to new stages of *service development*, and thus increasing their needs, and those whose needs are likely to remain at their present levels. The value of doing this is obvious; no solid bank planning can be done without taking market forces into account.

An analysis must be done to determine whether the bank is currently offering the technology warranted by the customer base. As a result, both the kind and extent of client service and of decision support services must be reviewed regularly. Furthermore, investigations help project the best time to develop technology for each group of clients. Once a relatively good schedule is determined—indicating the shifts that are likely to occur, when and how broad they will be—it is easier to time the introduction of the new banking products and the support technology needed. In short, the goal of the entire project is to compare the likely growth of the customer base with the science—and capital inhouse plans being made by management.

Few banks realize how dependent they have become on the efficient functioning of information systems. Yet a study conducted in 1980 by leading financial institutions of the West Coast revealed that a bank which is deprived of its computer services for three consecutive days is no longer competent to handle the needs of its clientele.

Figure 2.1 brings this simple fact into perspective. The shaded areas suggest the relative degree of computer support leading banks are now in the way of achieving in four of their key operational areas. This is no "average" figure: it is reflecting the best which is now done—and yet a bird's eye view suggests impressive areas of improvement particularly in the offering of automated services to the client base.

Once a bank has analyzed its customers and the technology now offered, the bank can make a decision as to whether it will be "pro-active" or "re-active." Depending on management's overall objectives, it might be desirable to use technology to increase the pace of change, for instance, through customer education. Indeed, banks are now offering customer education programs that had not even been thought of only a few years ago.

GEARING UP

The first prerequisite for banking management is to decide how to go about organizing for the changes to come. Structure and people—human resources—must be considered. Strategy must be planned and concrete proposals advanced for discussion and subsequent decision. In terms of priorities, the policy to be followed over, say, the next five years bears no resemblance to the slow-moving plans of the past. The pace is accelerating, and plans must be examined in the light of prevailing trends and requirements.

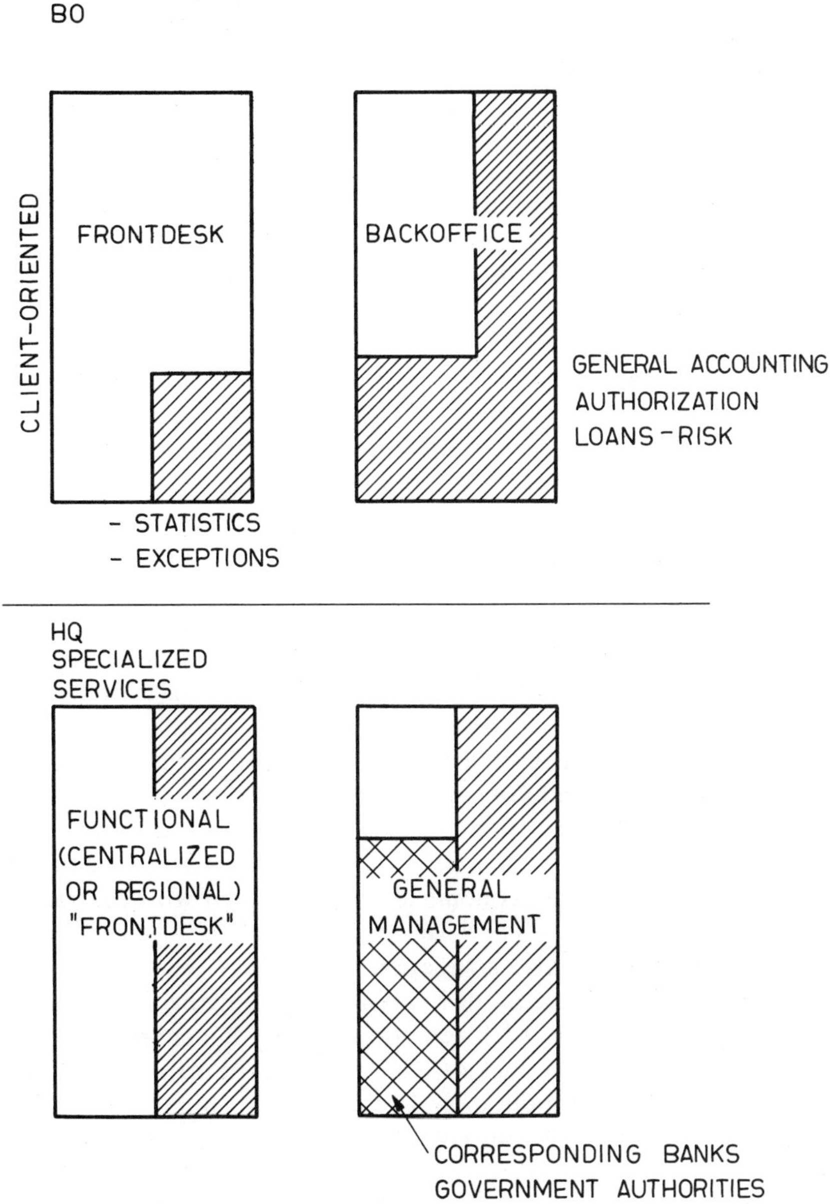
BO
CLIENT-ORIENTED
FRONTDESK
- STATISTICS
- EXCEPTIONS
BACKOFFICE
GENERAL ACCOUNTING
AUTHORIZATION
LOANS - RISK
HQ
SPECIALIZED
SERVICES
FUNCTIONAL
(CENTRALIZED
OR REGIONAL)
"FRONTDESK"
GENERAL
MANAGEMENT
CORRESPONDING BANKS
GOVERNMENT AUTHORITIES

FIGURE 2.1

The directives to be given affect every aspect of banking—from the structure of the central information file (CIF) for clients, to the way tellers should talk, to customers and the online support the customers should be given; to the eventual replacement of tellers by automatic machines. The systems built in the early 1980s must meet not only the requirements of the present but the future requirements of bank management, with regard to handling clients and maintaining steady growth. First, for all their accounts, banks will be forced to integrate into their computer programs a new account structure capable of providing for planning the client base and controlling it. Second, banks will convert from batch to interactive applications, from centralized to decentralized computers, and from mainframes to minicomputers and microcomputers. Third, banks will discontinue their current practice of memo posting via realtime, switching to network processing and direct access to databases. Fourth, management will strive to simplify clearing, by sending only magnetic supports and keeping all paper where it was deposited. This means that the branch where clients' checks are deposited will be responsible for transcribing them on magnetic support media, including amount, date of issue, date of transcription, bank and B.O. number, and running (handling) number.

Installations of minis and micros, first at the B.O. level and then (for micros) at every desk, will be designed to supply local intelligence in order to simplify financial operations—administratively, socially, and financially, as well as security operations, while attempting to reduce costs, increase flexibility, and keep options open.

Distributed information systems (DIS) will be the order of the day, as changes to meet developing local conditions become easier to handle and much more economical with DIS than with centralized solutions.

Granted, this is also a function of topology, volume, and the type of work being done. Studies conducted during the last five years have identified the need for different types of equipment to serve both the front office and the back office. For the front office, equipment must be designed to handle discrete forms. Such equipment must be modular and include a front-feed unit; a printer (120 characters per second for general use, sixty cps for high-quality use); a video (soft copy) unit; and a keyboard (light, thin, and movable).

For the back office, it will be sufficient to have one integrated unit capable of handling continuous forms. This unit should be programmable, with memory-extension devices as an optional feature.

Another optional, but necessary, facility is "recognition capability"—signature recognition, fingerprint analysis, palm (mesh) of the hand analysis, voice recognition, badge with photo, and personal identification number (PIN) units.

In terms of memory attachment (for this size unit), diskette and minidiskette are no answer. Bubble memories can better serve in small machines while the now developing, fairly inexpensive optical media are ideal for greater storage.

THE EVOLVING ENVIRONMENT IN BANKING

Future systems are a continuation, or extension, of those currently available. If one wishes to name the three outstanding developments at the close of the 1970s, most likely the following would be mentioned:

First, banking became cost-conscious in terms of production facilities and bank "products" (both old and new), which were to enhance their marketability.

Second, computers became an integral part of virtually every bank's operation, with EFT making feasible new delivery systems for traditional services.

Third, about eighty percent of all American households now have checking accounts, up from forty-six percent ten years ago; furthermore, eighty percent of all households have savings accounts, up from fifty-four percent in the same period.

The market has broadened; services have been amplified and demands on banks have increased. The same is true of opportunities. The credit card offers new potential for business (if not for profit), with thirty percent of all households possessing at least one card. There have been usually large loan losses because of a world wide recession, however. Also, government regulations have added a significant nonproductive overhead. Just the same, the many government regulations have had an impact on EDP.

The new banking environment is the result. Because of the factors just mentioned, some of the traditional rules of operation no longer hold. The management of American financial institutions particularly stress that commercial banking, both retail and corporate, has entered an era in which automated customer services are a requirement of doing business. Credit will surely remain the mainstay of banking profit, but support services for it will be far more extensive than they were in the past.

Because they face stiff competition for deposits, banks must look to services as a means of attracting and holding the deposits needed to fund credit. This should be viewed in the light of the projection that the corporate customer would then use more services at one bank and thus not share his business with other financial-service institutions.

The lesson to be learned here is that a supportive organizational structure is needed. Bank management must become more "mobile." It must become easier for young managers to move from operating areas to specialized staffs, and vice versa. And they must be trained in the use of electronic support media to the full extent.

This message should be carefully recorded: for the modern bank, farsighted management and performance means, in large measure, doing a good job preparing today's business for the future. This is an area in which measurement of management performance—or at least an appraisal of it—is a good way to increase sensitivity to both current and future requirements.

Statistics help underline the extent of structural change in the evolving banking environment. A documented study by the Federal Reserve Board of Boston demonstrates that among well-equipped institutions, the current accounts post is more intense, in terms of money spent in capital investments, than is the average position in industry. This has been known by many bankers, but during the 1970s, the proliferation of equipment in Western banking has resulted in an increase in the number of skilled—and expensive—personnel. Now, however, banks are beginning to realize that advancements in technology should be projected and implemented so as to require fewer, not higher, skills in the work place. The common term for this new trend is *user-friendly environment.*

Because the user-friendly environment is more technology-intensive than ever, let's look into the possibilities science and technology are likely to open to us in the early 1980s, with "intelligent" machines accounting for most of the user-friendly image of banks.

THE MICROPROCESSOR: FRIEND OR FOE?

Microprocessors and memory units are the crucial part of intelligent machines. Their logical complexity doubles every year. It is now projected that by 1983–84, the power of an IBM 370/158 will fit on a chip the size of the palm of one's hand and that it will cost only a few dollars.

The annual usage of logic gates, or bits of memory, has increased 12,000 times from 1960 to 1980. In 1960, approximately 500 million transistors were produced; in 1980, an estimated six trillion equivalent functions, or bits, were manufactured and shipped. It is expected that more than twice as many bits and gates will be produced in 1982, a pace that will almost surely continue into the 1990s.

Disc-drive capacity has jumped from five megabytes in the early 1960s, to 600 megabytes in 1979; and 2.2 gigabytes in 1981. The price per megabyte has decreased more than a hundredfold during the same period. Handheld calculator costs have declined a hundredfold in ten years. Memory (RAM) prices declined thirty to forty percent annually between 1971 and 1980. The extrapolated values indicate a coming cost per component at the 0.0001 cent level: with one million components or bits per VLSI (very large-scale integration) circuit now viewed as a distinct possibility by the mid 1980s.

In four to five years (1985–1986) we can expect greater performance by three to four orders of magnitude from Josephson (tunnel junction) technology. This is at the switching level, of course, it is not the result of computer speed. But one hundred fold improvement in performance over current levels should be practical in the late 1980s. This should be sufficient to change the "style" of management.

The impact of the technological advances I am describing will be felt at all management levels. It will be felt in the area of particularly profit and loss. Successful and unsuccessful financial institutions will be distinguished by the use they make of technology. Let nobody forget or fail to realize that the time to apply studies for implementing the new technology is *now.* It will take years to implement the major changes in organization and structure, systems, procedures, and the human mind that the effective use of the new technology will require.

The next five years in the computer field will bring major changes for all users. The *user* will become *coinvolved*, hence, accountable for what he does with the computer power at his disposal. Bringing computer power into the work place will increase user involvement with machines.

Not only must users be prepared, trained, and equipped to cope with this new environment, with its challenges and requirements, but computer specialists must be taught how to provide relatively painless migration paths for moving current applications—for example, programs, data files, and reports—to the new systems without upsetting organizational procedures and people.

As a result of the coming information revolution, people and organizations, not technical issues, will be the dominant problem users will face in the coming years. In the information-systems field, change is of the essence, as we strive for continuing productivity improvements. Today this is just as true of the banking profession. The manager who cannot cope with change, plan for change, or produce continuing change will not be effective. This role will be a new and different one from the traditional roles of management.

TECHNICAL TRENDS AND THEIR IMPACT

The semiconductor revolution now going on in the United States is changing the shape of organizations, both financial and industrial. It is making available facilities unheard of before, such as the IBM 370/135 *on a chip* that has already been announced by Intel, and the ten-times-more-powerful 370/158 is expected to be announced during the next few years—also on a chip (Figure 2.2); while mid-1981 saw the introduction by Intel of the 32-bit per word "micromainframe" on a chip.

Let us recall that the total computer power of medium-size banks was once that of a single IBM 370/145, or 370/135. When this is understood, the significance of possessing such power, not just at a central location but distributed at every executive's desk, can be appreciated.

Distributed information systems, or DIS, are no longer the issue. DIS is a subject that no longer has any force. Now we must look to

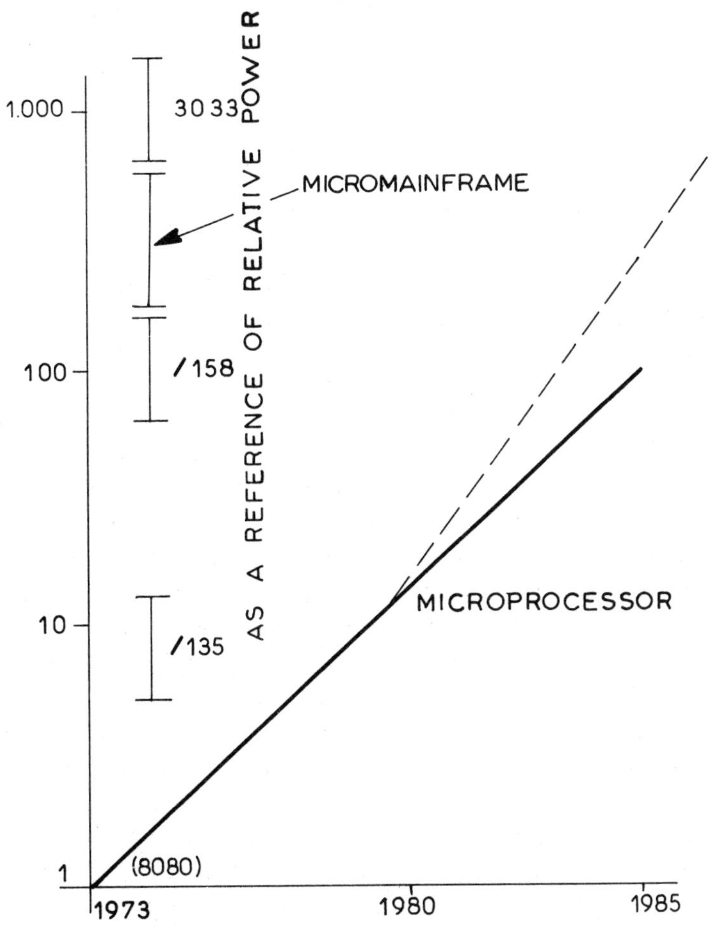
AS A REFERENCE OF RELATIVE POWER
1.000
100
10
1
3033
MICROMAINFRAME
/158
/135
MICROPROCESSOR
(8080)
1973
1980
1985

FIGURE 2.2

the future, not to the past. In the opinion of leading experts, by 1985, one-megabit chips may be available. How will we use them? At what cost? By 1983, the cost will be moving towards one one-hundredth of a cent per bit. That's an order of magnitude less than the cost today. As the "Willis Ware" rule aptly states: when something changes by a factor of ten, fundamental new effects will be presented and management decisions will change. Such changes will be reflected in every part of banking life in terms of costs, speed of handling, and facilities.

We can do many things with this capacity. Here is what leading bankers think will be possible:

1. Having the data-handling load distributed at a single desk level.
2. Bringing the CPU (central processing unit) to the problems, not the problems to the CPU.
3. Going beyond database management in computer resource management as a whole, which calls for work on networks, both local and remote.
4. Applying new communications technologies based on packet switching, assuring online transaction processing applied in every banking operation.
5. Placing emphasis on problem-solving, using computer resources to attack imaginative problems, rather than doing routine postmortem jobs.

To become a reality, item five will require much organizational effort, including skill in applied mathematics. Management theory and quantitative analysis will again become focal points (see chapters five and six).

In 1980, and for the five years before that the chip was king. The primary emphasis was on applications that revolved around the microprocessor, the memory system, and the database management system (DBMS). But for the mid-1980s, the pivotal point will be "executive appliances" that incorporate logical and organizational features. What I am talking about is not a single piece of equipment but a complete solution involving strategy, structure, and network systems. Network systems will be devoted to data transfers, DBMS's, and voice communications—moving toward all-digital management.

The services to be provided to the banker are vital to competition. They range from decision support, to global communications and office automations with current computer applications, the seven-eighths of what is feasible has been denied to the user. Yet these services will be a competitive weapon no financial institution can forego without losing its market share.

Mass storage is another key to banking in the 1980s. The need for it has been brought into focus by the ever-growing requirements of databases. A mass storage system will include automated self-storage; for data centers, it will handle, online, large libraries and provide support to text and image processing.

Computers are heading for *text usage*, which eventually may swamp data usage. Eventually, *all* banking documents will be stored in databases and will be accessible online. Such requirements will create a need for trillion-byte storage. Because these large memories will mean an increase in access time, financial institutions will almost certainly show greater interest in projecting the management of very large databases.

Programming challenges must also be faced. Micro-level languages might lead the way, by creating hardware-resident statements. The same is true of analysis languages based on solid-state software. Other language developments will come from DBMS. To be successfully implemented, however, DBMS must be accompanied by a language that is user-friendly.

Strategic Planning in the Banking Industry

3

Strategic Planning in financial institutions is evolutionary. At Chase Manhattan, for example, David Rockefeller started it in the mid-1960s, and it took a decade to be structured. Why should banking management be concerned about strategic planning?

Strategy is a master plan to be used against the competition. Plans are financial; they concern human resources, as well as products and services. They involve market orientation, market penetration and share, and operational-tactical characteristics. Strategy involves the longer term, whereas plans are coordinated within a given time frame. Strategy is never in black and white. It can, however, be read through the lines of decisions, actions, and pronouncements. To deduct strategy from decisions, facts, and actions, we must study these decisions, facts, and actions carefully and analyze the background factors.

This is what the banking industry is doing every day. Banking management is greatly concerned with the solutions to salient problems. What is the true significance of product strategy? What will our bank do in twenty years' time? Where will the profits come from? Should we be a product leader in every field of endeavour? What are the costs? The risks? Many soul-searching issues are of an organizational nature. Who are the product strategists? What are their functions? Should our bank develop all products through its own forces? Should it buy a package? What are the effects of competition? What are the opportunities? Is there enough management skill to handle the new product lines?

To observe and implement a given strategy, we need resources; we need to make decisions on how to use them; we need procedures (to attain objectives) and priorities. In all this range of decision and action, the prime mover is management's ability—and that can be developed. Modern management requires more thinking than did classical approaches of the past, particularly, analytical thinking. It involves faster reactions, and to achieve them, computer-aided decisions are a must.

SETTING GOALS

A critical, and difficult task is to establish objectives for the future. Then come the strategies for meeting them. Management-by-objective is a new development in banking. The process begins with an examination of the current organization.

Visibility in management decision is increased when the following exist: a statement identifying each major business and market served, a clarification of the current objectives and strategies of each unit, and a critical evaluation of markets, products, and services. Many times an entirely different and revealing perspective results from stepping back and asking: "How does the user of our services view us?"

Identification of the strategic issues, assignment of planning goals, and the creation of a corporate planning staff of bankers and industry experts, are among the fundamental building blocks of a master plan. Such a plan should interact with the major departments and major branch offices of the bank. Stress is placed on the earnings impact and the way in which the evolution of the marketplace influences the bank's way of doing business. Lead time is vital. It takes some seven years of effort to establish strategic planning procedures. Broader acceptance by the organization takes another two years.

Once established, the strategic plan must be implemented through program management.The plan must accomplish the following objectives: balancing the time required for planning and marketing; integrating into the plan the various plans made by individual departments; providing a tracking mechanism for deviations; monitoring the implementation of management reviews; and defining the steps to be taken.

Strategic planning goes hand in hand with financial planning. In several major banks, the managers responsible for both report to the president through a member of the executive committee responsible for all planning processes, for example, setting goals and objectives and sharing responsibility with the board for planning policies, including their proper definition. The lack of a clear planning process—and of the premises on which the process is to be sustained—can kill it. Hence the need for a program-management procedure. Let's look into some examples on how plans are influenced by environmental factors.

A good example is international banking, as seen by American financial institutions, precisely, the evolution of European banks, from 1973 until today, into international entities with expanding international operations, that touch base with correspondents, that have an impact on the market. "The twenty-year monopoly ends," said the senior vice-president of a large American financial institution. "We have to react to this change. We must now rethink . . . our product." This led the bank's management to realize the need to examine its network. As the senior vice-president remarked: "We must make it more realistic. More responsible. For each subsidiary, business was in its country. Now we must make the people think in terms of a network, as part of an institutional approach to marketing. The German subsidiary must, for instance, benefit us in Brazil".

MANAGING A BANK

The basic factors that determine the character of a bank and the image it wishes to project are: customers, competition, products, employees, investments in productivity and new services, and suppliers. The procedure involved in this line of thinking can be expressed simply: take a channel (a product or service sector); rethink what the product is, under steadily developing conditions; and examine the network—its topology, knowhow, bank penetration, and hold. Then present management with documented facts so that decisions can be reached in the most expeditious fashion possible. The problems may vary in nature, but the procedural thinking of financial institutions can be quite similar from one to another. Most often major changes in the way banking is conducted are a direct result of technological evolution. This has been the case with computers, data communications, and electronic transfers of funds. Until the new business opportunity is clear, however, a bank's strategy must be flexible. Its master plan must take into consideration all alternatives. The bank should study these alternatives and be ready for them.

If management has not decided on a strategy, every proposal must be examined and evaluated as an entirely new proposal, requiring a decision. Strengths, weaknesses, business opportunities, and threat of competition must be studied. Salient problems must be identified, and responsibility for resolving and implementing the planning are very important points. The next step in strategic planning is to formulate existing objectives into a concise, consistent statement covering financial issues, market position, innovation, management, personnel, and organizational development. This statement, communicated and applied to daily activities, constitutes a powerful guiding force for the financial institution. As the vice-president of a leading United States bank remarked: "If we can come up in our minds with the best product for the future and dress it with the new information services, we can expand nationally and internationally through a profitable facilities service. This way, the 'ABC' Bank of Denver will still be in business. The client will deal with the 'ABC'—but *we* will be doing *all* the back-office."

ELABORATING A STRATEGY

The value banking management places on information systems as a strategic issue is best assessed by considering the possibilities electronics offer in establishing a network for nationwide banking facilities, as well as the alternatives different major institutions have chosen in pursuing this goal.

—Citibank, Morgan Guaranty, and the Bank of America pursued, from 1975 to 1980, a lone-wolf strategy, using cititellers, mortgage banks, and similar facilities. The "Edge Act" permits establishing branches in United States cities for international trade, but international trade that is *broadly* defined.

—The First National Bank of Boston got together with some two hundred other New England banks and formed the Money One network for do-it-yourself check verification.

—Chase seems to favor the "Europartner solution"—associating with other major institutions in the United States on a partnership basis.

Facilities management is another strategy for offering new EDP services to small banks that lack the skill. Citibank, for example, purchased several S/1 minicomputers, programmed them with DDA and other applications, and offered them as a complete service (hardware, software, and facilities management) to smaller banks—against a payment based on the transactions being performed.

By and large, whichever master guidelines are chosen, the way a bank formulates its strategic plan largely reflects the following phases:

First, the *correspondent operation* is the most important. "As the oldest bank in country, we are the tenth largest in correspondent business—but the seventeenth in size", said the First National bank of Boston.

Second, a bank must make a choice of *retail* or *corporate* banking as the mainstream for business and profits. No bank, not even the largest, can be a leader in every sector.

Third, *computers and communications strategy*. "Basically with I.S., we talk about reducing paper. *Paper is the most expensive thing we handle*." Thus stated another major bank, adding: "but paperless products carry [with them] a host of other opportunities".

With EFT, the B.O. is projected to become a two- or three-man operation, for example, that of a real estate office. Management thinks: "All money will move through the supermarket, the department store, the transport center. . . . Retail banking is not profitable, because of the high cost of servicing the consumer. . . . We must automate this job".

NEW PRODUCT STRATEGY

By and large, bank management has started paying attention to this issue. The references made point in this direction: "To become large, we *must develop a unique service*. . . . We look to Money One as a unique service. Not necessarily a system that we suggest to every bank. It is a high risk operation, but, if successful, it will help the bank well. . . . Electronics is a way we expand services around the limitations imposed by the law."

Management also pays great attention to profit and performance strategies. Here are typical quotations: "We calculate what each one of our departments earns. The bank must earn twenty-five percent on that . . . . Department services can only spend up to seventy-five percent of what they make . . . . A manager can 'buy' and 'sell' services inside the bank, but the prices have to be competitive."

Choosing a strategy, and the subsequent process of strategic planning, call for an inventory of images on which we can build a plan.

From basic images to market impact, we necessarily need to implement the capabilities technology can offer. From the products we would support, (and their specifications), to the marketing structure needed to carry these products and the sales objectives to be achieved technology is a basic ingredient. (Figure 3.1).

Strategies, particularly alternative strategies which themselves bring the need for evaluation and final decision, cannot be made in the abstract. Not only do they require the attention and support of top management but they must also be supplemented by the proper understructure. We must know *where* we wish to go, as well as *how*, *when*, and *what* resources will be required to reach our goals. We must know ourselves and our organization, its strengths and its weaknesses. We must learn as much as possible about our opponents.

MANAGEMENT PLANNING

Planning is a systematic approach to improving a bank's performance, increasing its profitability, and establishing future directions. Its benefits derive from its process and the orderly thinking it implies, even more than from the plan itself. Dwight Eisenhower once said: "The Plan is nothing. Planning is everything."

Planning is a state of mind. No matter how well balanced the bank might be regarding its hierarchical levels, its ultimate success still turns on the inclination of senior management to devote the proper amount of time to broad issues—to synthesis and evaluation. There is an excellent method for determining quickly how well management is performing in this area. All one need do is examine the questions management is concerned with. If the top problems faced by the management of a financial institution are loaded with action words such as *perform*, *locate*, and *apply*, the focus may well be too narrow. If words such as *infer*, *deduce*, and *analyze* are used, the interests probably are much wider.

Over a period of time, a study of words used to pose questions can be an invaluable aid in diagnosing the thinking of an organization

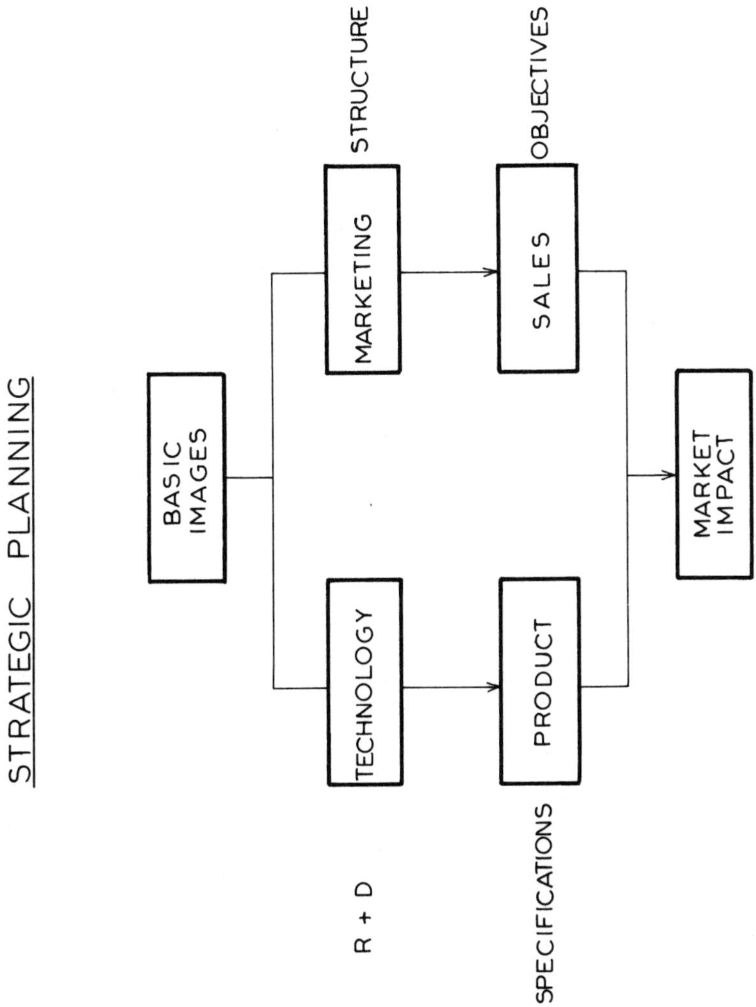
STRATEGIC PLANNING
BASIC IMAGES
MARKETING
STRUCTURE
SALES
OBJECTIVES
TECHNOLOGY
R + D
PRODUCT
SPECIFICATIONS
MARKET IMPACT

FIGURE 3.1

and the value of the concrete actions that follow. Here are some basic fields identified by leading American banks, on which the planning effort of financial institutions should concentrate.

EFT DEVELOPMENT

Many bankers have never looked closely at the benefits that might accrue from an industry-wide move to an automated payment mechanism. Thus we find an odd situation in which marketing officers are devising strategies to sell preauthorized debits though electronic fund transfers, while their own banks have no aggressive program for selling internal preauthorized debits for such things as instalment loan payments.

The rationale for not developing an in-house program is that the transition costs are too high when compared with the anticipated volume. A careful analysis of the overall payment mechanism, however, might reveal that costs could be significantly reduced in an automated payment environment. Asking only the cost of the initial involvement, and only within one's bank's context, is simply too narrow; hence, it is misleading.

COMPETITIVE IMPACT

Far too many banks tend to view competition only in terms of the other bank in town. Needless to say, this is an erroneous approach. Computers and data communications have changed the horizon of banking operations and international banking has been given a still broader dimension.

It is true that more attention than ever is being given to nonbank competition. But when action is called for, management often reverts to reacting to the latest move by the bank down the street. Today some potentially great opportunities are offered by cooperative ventures. Recent research conducted by financial institutions clearly demonstrates that the consumer sees considerable benefit from shared automated facilities available in many locations. Likewise, corporate treasurers are waiting for schedules and interregional exchange mechanisms. In this case, the broader question of future services, retail and corporate, is clouded by what are essentially interim hurdles.

GOVERNMENT REGULATION AND LEGISLATION

Here is a classic example of thinking only in the short term. Banking has changed dramatically in the past ten years, and pending legislation has the potential of creating even more drastic alterations in the way banks can do business.

The reaction of management is usually to comment only when the proposed rules affect their bank directly. The larger challenge, however, is to review the viable options with an eye to the potential risks and benefits. The services that are developing offer new options with advantages over old lines of thought, but the element of risk has not been eliminated. If anything, it is even more prominent. Product pricing is a good example. As banks expand their services, a growing penalty is being paid for not developing a rational pricing system. The new concept among American banks is "rational pricing," or "cost plus." It may ultimately prove essential in the highly competitive world of retail banking.

What these examples underline is that the reaction to regulatory and legislative proposals must be examined from the broadest possible perspective, including the pricing structure a bank plans to adopt for its services. This helps quantify decision issues which otherwise might remain largely qualitative.

ECONOMIC DEVELOPMENTS

Economic developments have to do with the evolution of the marketplace. On the American scene, for instance, ever since the deep recession of 1973–75, significant shifts have been occuring in the financing patterns of major corporations. The commercial paper market has become a prime source of funding for some of the largest and most creditworthy corporations. In the face of this trend, and with all indicators predicting that it would increase, most banks have focused on creating ways to increase loan demand.

Only recently have we seen banks acknowledge the changed environment and offer credit services that are competitive with the commercial paper market. Such examples make it clear that many kinds of planning will be needed in guiding the modern financial institution, both today and in the future. Planning is required by all levels—units, individuals, and specialists—to weld an organization into a functioning whole. This task is complicated by the fact that banking has not yet developed a literature of planning, nor has a unique planning style emerged.

There is no commercial bank planning model that can be lifted from the shelf, say, from a successful bank, and implemented as a planning system in another bank. Each bank must develop a planning philosophy and assemble the planning skills and techniques that best match its needs. It should be unnecessary to add that each institution must find its way.

THE PLANNING CYCLE

As is true for any other basic managerial responsibility, the establishment of proper procudures for planning is the cornerstone of the edifice. Procedures must be established that spell out the task to be completed and that assign the roles and responsibilities necessary in completing the planning cycle. The following should be thoroughly explained:

1. Why a plan is needed.
2. The results expected.
3. The relationship of the planning staff to line management.
4. The organization of the planning effort.
5. Feedback and control of results.
6. The corrective action to be taken.

The planning cycle embraces all basic functions of management: forecasting (a prerequisite of planning), planning, proper structure (and the prerequisites this involves), staffing, executive (or directing) and controlling.

Forecasting takes place within an information environment that is highly unstructured (Figure 3.2). Nobody has tomorrow's newspaper today, but if he knows how to read between the lines, he can preconstruct some of the news—not only by making educated guesses but also, and mainly, by using the computer-supported quantitative management tools available today. Morgan Guaranty has a department of twenty-four high-grade professionals dedicated to such studies.

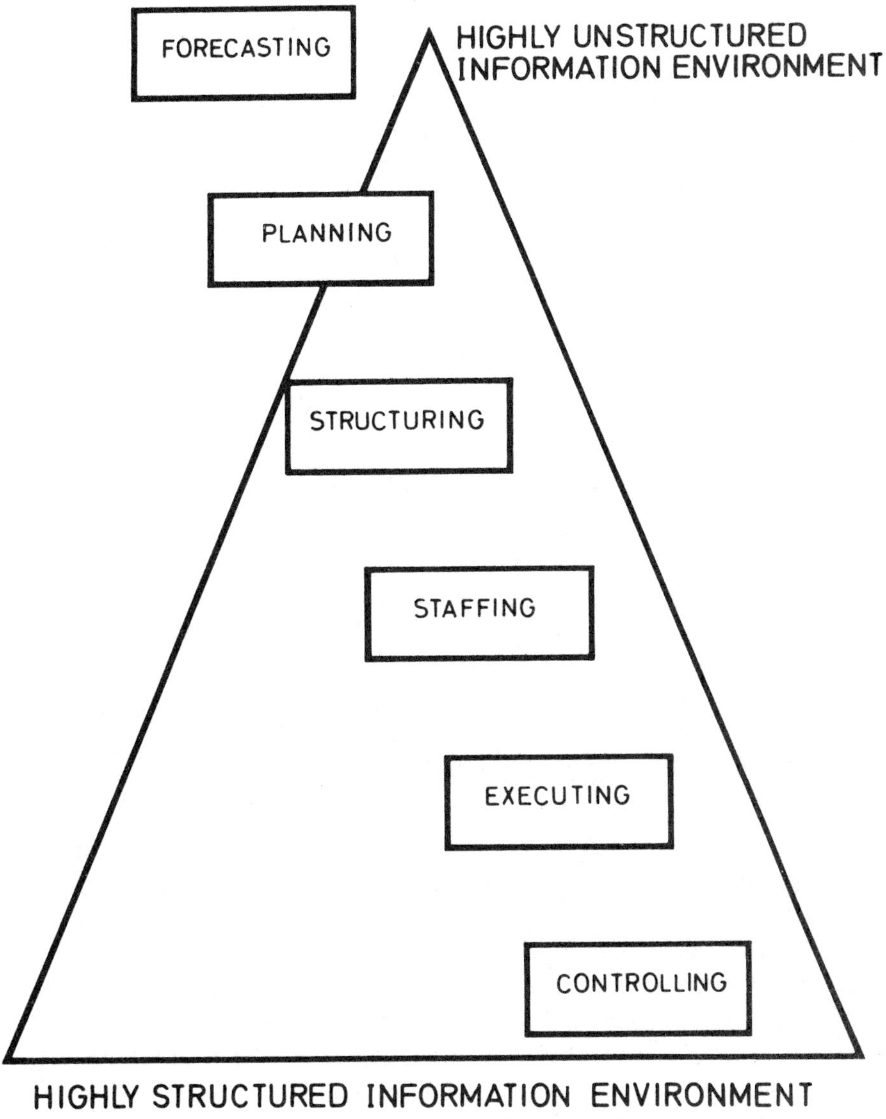
FORECASTING
HIGHLY UNSTRUCTURED
INFORMATION ENVIRONMENT
PLANNING
STRUCTURING
STAFFING
EXECUTING
CONTROLLING
HIGHLY STRUCTURED INFORMATION ENVIRONMENT

FIGURE 3.2

Control on the other hand, occurs within a highly structured environment. Things happen; they are recorded, measured, and evaluated and action is taken. There is no uncertainty here as there is in forecasting.

Looking back to the six basic functions outlined above, we can see that the basic principles of managing responsibilities do not vary from one financial institution or industrial firm to another. The issues to which the most attention should be paid, however, are quite definitely a function of the situation and of the special problems presented by the situation. For each planning cycle, it is necessary to establish objectives and record any changes in procedures and emphasis. At each planning level, whether organizational or procedural, the planning results should be formalized in accordance with the policy that describes the process of planning as well as that of operations. Objectives, strategies, programs, and budgets must be detailed, and examples provided. The planning manual should establish time frames and important checkpoints of progress. These are needed to guide the specific cycle of planning. Properly constructed, the planning manual can become an important teaching tool for bankers; it can enforce planning as a management style for the entire organization.

To help banking management in its planning, the first basic reference is *business opportunity.* The way this is done in modern banking is to first establish the opportunities and threats that lie outside the financial institution's control yet which influence it by their impact on the market. Business opportunity reports must identify a consistent set of assumptions within which planning can proceed. Statements of assumptions and guidelines for planning are formulated by executive management on the basis of what the environmental analysis shows about the economic climate, anticipated social and political changes, technological developments, legislative and regulatory changes, and the expected competitive pressures. This leads to an appraisal of the situation that is concerned with the bank's ability to perform the essential tasks of the businesses in which it wishes to specialize. The situation appraisal must identify strengths and weaknesses—and do so in terms of the results established by the situation appraisal. Some major areas to be examined are:

1. management
2. organization

3. product lines
4. geographic presence
5. pricing strategy
6. human resources
7. systems support

Each area must be examined for efficiency, integration with the organization, and external image created. Each department and division must determine where it stands and how its position was achieved. Data should first be developed on such major categories of assets and liabilities as loans, deposits, total assets, and equity. Data collection begins with aggregates (to provide history) and then proceeds to such simple analytical measures as rate of growth and stability. Mathematical models can be used advantageously in this effort, as we will see in the chapter on quantitative methods.

The basic problem is to develop a way of measuring market share. One way to do this is to build a comparative database from a panel of banks considered competitive in various markets and products. The position of the bank in each major area for which financial objectives have been established must be evaluated. Overall performance, specific effectiveness by geographical sector, and impact on each service or product offered by the bank must be calculated and considered. This requires internal research, research that can be helped through the use of cost-analysis programs. The calculation also calls for environmental studies and competitive situation appraisals; these results should be assembled in a set of statements describing the current position of the bank.

The Marketing Organization

4

The planning organization in a financial institiution must be given two main missions, each with its own requirements: (1) corporate clients (both domestic and abroad), and (2) retail banking (marketing). It is difficult to strike the right balance between the two. In some banks, the former is more developed. This is true of commercial, or business banks, which are usually cash-hungry because they need more capital than their own network can collect. In other cases, retail banking is more developed than are corporate accounts. Savings banks and loan associations are a classic example; popular banks are another. Whatever a bank's orientation or goal, though, always at a premium are the management of customer accounts, the keeping of customer statistics, research in market development, and generally, tools which allow management to perform its functions in an able manner. Like all organizations, a bank goes through different marketing periods, or cycles. This is not new; the problem is how to achieve change within a marketing framework, and this calls for procedures that are both flexible and that reflect the basic requirements presented in different marketing approaches.

Banks merge. In the late 1950s, one of the most celebrated mergers was that of the cash-rich Guaranty Trust Company with J.P. Morgan, which, since the time of the great banker who founded it, had invested heavily in corporate accounts. Because of changes in the law, services not allowed in the past became possible. The Debre law in France, which allowed business banks to engage in retail activities, made it possible for the Banque de Paris et Paysbas (Paribas) to take advantage of a business opportunity that had not been available before. Furthermore, as banking became more aggressive, it took on many of the characteristics of other traditionally aggressive industries in the market place. Market research has thus become an integral part of the process, and it must be given the importance it deserves.

Another boost to marketing policies comes from the new products policy. Many questions have to be answered before a final decision to launch a new product can be made: the future for the economy of the area; the growth in personal disposable income; the growth in the number of households; and the competition, including such statistics as how many branches other banks have and the strengths and weaknesses of each.

Answers to these questions have to be determined, both qualitatively and quantitatively. After the facts have been established, and if things look promising, a detailed marketing plan can be drawn up. This plan must ensure that developing a market approach, providing for ways to evaluate and offer services is valid, if not necessarily unique.

MARKETING BANKING SERVICES

Banking services can be marketed like any other product. It is to the advantage of a financial institution to establish an efficient marketing plan with the aim of providing necessary support to branch offices in launching new customer services and improving the bank's share of the market. Furthermore, since most of these services are information-intense, it is necessary to closely coordinate the approach with computer operations.

In industrial organizations, including banks, the concept of marketing is particularly significant. Organizations that are growing seem to be concerned less with *pulling* than with *pushing* the market. They move because of involvement in goal-seeking and because of intense engagement with external forces. Generally, however, such organizations reach a point where they seek to control, to the greatest extent possible, themselves and their environment in *the future*. This is the point at which the complex and intricate interaction of resources, products, and clients takes on the familiar aspects of marketing. (Figure 4.1)

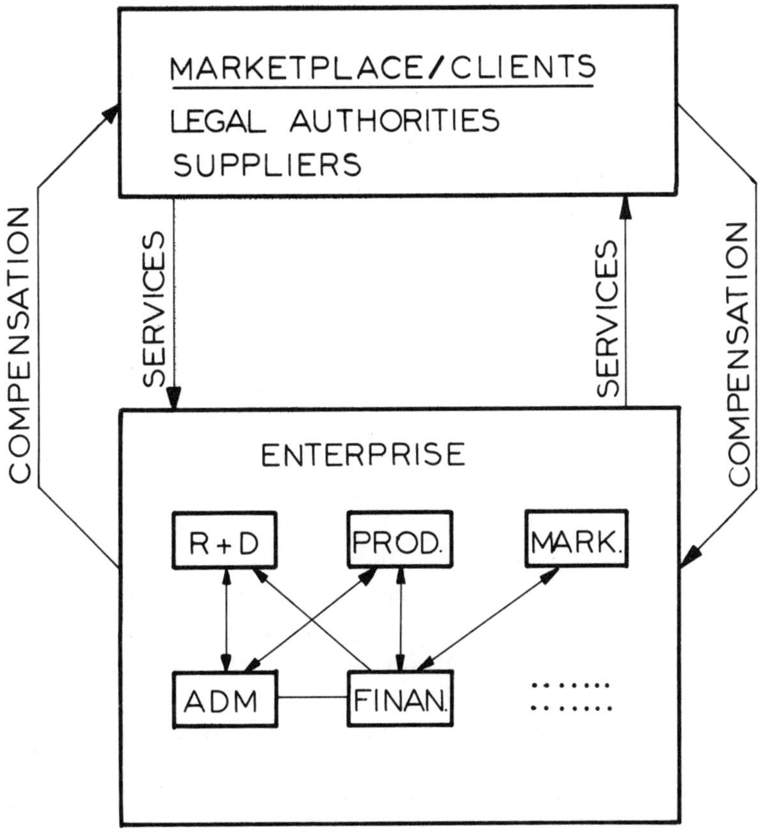
MARKETPLACE/CLIENTS
LEGAL AUTHORITIES
SUPPLIERS
COMPENSATION
SERVICES
SERVICES
COMPENSATION
ENTERPRISE
R+D
PROD.
MARK.
ADM
FINAN.

FIGURE 4.1

Banks frequently approach this point overly concerned with techniques and procedures and thereby tend to become bureaucracies —organizations that institutionalize the past, making what was learned a fixed reality rather than moving dynamically forward. Bureaucracy is no answer to the need for marketing. If anything, it is its negation.

A fundamental problem in marketing management is how to overcome the past through techniques employed in the present so as to develop marketing in the future. To achieve this goal, we must understand the history of the bank's organization and its marketing drives over the past few decades.

A bank, like any other organization, is a living organism. As such, it has a distinct personality, the personality of an organization shaped by years of practice, management drives, market forces, environmental constraints and opportunities, and, quite often, the iron hand of its presidents. Organizational personalities, like those of individuals, can evolve over time. Like sailing, however, abrupt turns of the steering can cause loss of speed and sometimes upheaval. Change has to be gradual, and the best way to preserve the marketing punch and guard against obsolescence is to implant the spirit of perpetual change in the minds of executives and employees.

In marketing banking services, one must be extremely sensitive to environmental evolution; to the means put at one's disposal for facing challenges; to ways of offering new products, their correct timing and pricing; and to market forces. This sensitivity is not typical of yesterday's banking organizations, which often held sacrosanct a particular market approach, failing to remember that the banking world is cluttered with dead organizations which, at one time, were highly successful.

Perhaps more than for any other industry, banking must merge tradition, imagination, innovation, and creativity in creating the most efficient marketing. Very few financial institutions, however, show evidence of genuinely understanding this need, and even fewer appear able to come up with an approach.

Can a banker be both creative and innovative and still work within the confines of tradition? Can this banker combine a real entrepreneurial attitude with a steady policy? The answer is definitely *yes*. One of the most important prerequisites is the creation of a climate of entrepreneurial initiative—but, at the same time, a climate with well-implanted parameters of self-control.

A FRAMEWORK FOR MARKETING STUDIES

I have just emphasized the role of human capital. The question was once posed to Andrew Carnegie: "If you had to lose all your factories *or* all your people, which would you chose?" Carnegie answered: "I would rather lose my factories because if I have my people I will build the corporation once again."

Whether they are in steel or banking, people are the most vital resource. As we will see in Chapter 8, however, people can become obsolete, just as any resource can. This dramatizes the requirement for lifelong training in banks at all levels of management. In a survey of three hundred Virginia bankers in 1976, fifty percent predicted that their colleagues would be obsolete by 1980—that is, within four years' time.

Clearly, these trends emphasize the need for making a concerted effort to achieve excellence in overall bank management, as well as in marketing. How can this excellence be achieved? First, a product-and-market-development climate must be established in the organization. The essential point is that top management be committed to market development. That is, top management must be profoundly interested, both in the exploitation of the market's potential and in the human assets to be committed to marketing. Furthermore, senior officers must become involved in recruiting, thereby demonstrating the bank's desire to obtain first-rate people.

Second, in the management of products and services and the handling of market sectors, responsibility must be formally delimited and accountability defined. Management ability is a highly individual art. No two managers do their work the same way. Most learn by actually managing. To manage well, they must know the limits, goals, and policies involved in putting forward a marketing program while preserving the traditions and reputation of the bank. That's why marketing results in *all* banking sectors should be measurable, and individuals be held accountable for them, the more so as we move from old "established" banking products to new products and services.

Third, accountability must be enhanced through concrete measurements supported by *cost-accounting procedures.* It is not sufficient to sell products and services; the bank must also make a profit. This can be done adequately through industrial-type cost accounting and the implementation of feedback procedures based on corresponding job descriptions and results achieved. A case in point is the cost-consciousness of the marketing strategies followed by management—and the tactical tools used to implement them. Fourth, for feedback purposes, decision-making, and client service, there is a steadily upgraded requirement for improved management information. Computer systems must become a generic part of professional life, not an esoteric function performed by a system specialist.

SALE OF BANKING PRODUCTS

The sale of banking products, and the profits to be derived therefrom, are the objective. Rapid replanning and resetting of strategies are called for. The ability to flex with a fast-changing economy and market requires different management and organization than in other, more stable periods. It is therefore important to assess how well prepared a bank is for a period of change—in media, concepts, services, and income base. We must drive to increase productivity. And this means increased reliance on technology to serve customers and train staff. Maximum use of an increasingly cost-effective technology is one answer. But this cannot be achieved without proper clarification of the bank's role and its markets (Table 4.1).

It is becoming increasingly difficult to compete across a broad market; to be everything to everybody. A careful definition of role will thus be immensely helpful in making equipment choices, establishing staff-training schedules, implementing new services and making marketing decisions. Banks that take the time to plan for the future, to project themselves into the 1980s, foresee increased specialization in banking products. It is also projected that there will be a growth in specialty financial service institutions which will focus on particular market segments. This attention will place emphasis on each bank, further clarifying its role in the various markets. With this will come the necessity of *selling* banking products.

The art of selling banking "products" has not changed, but the selling environment has evolved dramatically during the last fifteen years. New banking products have been developed and should be marketed in a profitable fashion. That is why, given today's environment, sales training should be an integral part of banking.

Table 4.1

JOB DESCRIPTION FOR A NEW MARKETING MANAGER

Establish yearly; review every 3 months	1	2	3	4
Responsibility	Develop marketing organization	Hire able persons	Open marketing perspectives	Establish share of the market
Indicators	Establish exact objectives per area of operations	* Set up a marketing function in the main branch offices * Set up sales support center for the branches	* Communicate with government authorities * Penetrate major districts * Take an industry marketing approach * Handle public relations	Product I "U" % Product II "V" % Product III "W" %
Objectives	Complete missions within "X" weeks from start	1) within "Y^1" weeks 2) within "Y^2" weeks 3) within "Y^3" weeks	1) immediately 2) within "Z^1" weeks 3) within "Z^2" weeks 4) within "Z^3" weeks	Perform strength and weakness analysis: "ours" vs "competitors" Give definite figures and evaluate progression quantitatively

To answer a possible question by skeptics, in a broad sense, any organization that concentrates its efforts on the market can be defined as a sales organization. For the most part, however, formal sales training in American banking has not amounted to much.

The new services banks now offer—and will offer at an increasing pace in the future—require a new approach to handling clients, and with this, a well-timed training of the bank's own staff. Let's look at a recent example, one involving not a mammoth financial institution but a relatively small bank.

City National Bank & Trust of Columbus, Ohio has been building "autobanks"—minibranches combining automatic teller machines, each with space for one teller—to serve drive-in and walk-up customers at self-service gas stations. The units can be installed for some $65,000 and can be built off-site and moved to the stations. Is this service sellable to clientele without first selling it to the bank's own staff, in terms of the wisdom and potential of such a service? No, it is not! City National therefore first instituted a program designed to sell this automated solution to its own staff.

Faced with changes in competition because of automation and market evolution, banks feel that the need for quality sales training is at an all-time high. It is not enough to emphasize the need for increased sales. Proper electronics supports and timely sales training programs must be put in place to help banks meet their objectives. What is important is that, regardless of the rate of change and services offered, most banking services will continue to be sold on a personal basis. Thus the ability to deal effectively with clients will continue to be vital.

In upgrading human resources, and banking sales programs in general, significant emphasis must be placed on the changing technologyof the client-oriented deliverysystems.Telephone lines, computers, and terminals allow commercial banks trying to attract more business to extend their services well beyond former limits. Along the way, though, these banks must not forget that banking essentially is a people-to-people relationship.

Not only must we take notice of the need to balance people and machines, but we must also be aware of the average banker. That can be done only through training. Otherwise, banks will be condemned to employ more people than ever before—at a time when a sharp reduction in employment is forecast for banking. What's more, banks will need more people to handle complaints from customers caused by malfunctioning computers and mishandling of clients.

More than ever before, bank employees must be taught to use the new services available to them, as well as to respond effectively to changes in media, banking laws, customer demands, and competition. At the same time, there will be greater profits through increased selling. Banks must now aggressively sell their services, something they have not been accustomed to doing in the past.

RETAIL BANKING

Before it can know what to offer in the way of services, a bank must study in detail every product offered or projected by all other financial institutions in its market area. This is particularly important in retail banking. Banks compete for clients' deposits and loans with other banks. As bankers know, however, individual clients do not move their accounts to other banks unless they become especially unhappy with the present banks, in which case, they find it convenient to make the change, possibly because the "other banks" offer services by more competent, courteous, or well-trained staff.

Intelligent marketing decisions presuppose a thorough study of the competition and its services. Another basic requirement is the development of the marekting techniques needed before launching a product. These techniques are not static, nor can they be standardized; they are a function of the market, the competition, and the characteristics of the product.

W. H. Parks, president of Community Bank in Greenville, South Carolina, gives a good example of how he used successively longer banking hours as a marketing strategy. Four of the seven banks in Greenville closed between 1:00 and 3:00 P.M. None offered either drive-in or lobby banking before 9:00 A.M. or after 5:00 P.M. except on Fridays. When Community Bank opened its first office, Parks opened the drive-in at 7:30 A.M. and closed it at 5:30 P.M. Mondays through Thursdays and at 6:00 P.M. on Fridays. He opened the lobby for full-service banking at 9:00 A.M. and did not close until 5:00 P.M. Mondays through Thursdays and at 6:00 P.M. on Fridays. Including

Saturday banking, his bank was open to the public fifty-four and one half hours a week. He advertised these convenient banking hours extensively, with very good results.

A similar policy was instituted at Credit Mobilier de Monaco, in Monte Carlo. The branch was kept open during lunch hours, when the other banks closed, with similarly good results. Add to this a real-time service for demand deposit accounts (DDA), the first to be offered in the area, and the advertising fallout this had in the early 1970s, and it made a small bank look big among the giants in the city.

Longer hours, although helpful, will not meet all requirements. A database on retail banking operations, by area and type of branch office, is important. This is equally true of associated market-development statistics. Management must be able to document the evolution of each branch in its respective operating area.

Tracing profit and loss by the company or private customer with whom the bank is doing business is a valuable management tool. Here, the "client mirror" is important at both the single-customer level (for selected cases) and the group-customer level. A client mirror reflects all costs and profits related to a client account, by branch and by total bank operation.

To be helpful in determining market orientation, a marketing report must show statistics on people, by profession, social stratification, geographic distribution, age, and sex. Just as helpful in retail banking is the periodical tracing of credits, by branch of industry or private individual (type of employment, age group, sex, income bracket). The same is true in periodically tracing deposits by branch and by profession, age, or sex. Cross-indexing should be provided on savings and deposits, savings and current accounts (DDA), and so on; statistics should be presented to management in a form that allows effective action to be taken. Decisions will be more accurate if the bank uses market-planning models.

This discussion makes it clear that, to be successful, retail banking must have prerequisites. Some of the examples given above are client-oriented, but there are also other structural requirements, for instance, a short chain of command. Bank employees in charge of client accounts should report directly to an executive with decision-making authority. Such a reporting system does not violate the span of control. The breadth, or span of control, of an individual manager depends on his capacity as well as that of the supporting structure. A short control span allows faster operation. In addition, with one person handling multiple but related responsibilities, there is less need for coordination. Communications move faster if the chain of command has few levels.

FULFILLING THE PREREQUISITES

Five basic characteristics underlie the strength of a well-organized operation in marketing banking services. The first is *direction*—the goal of providing central and branch-office management with information that will enable it to take the proper steps in achieving the bank's goals. The second characteristic is *timely coordination*. All the bank's marketing activities must be adjusted to support and complement rather than antagonize each other.

The third basic characteristic is *promotion*. This includes implementation of new services to clients; product development; advice for branches; and the planning and control of money deposits, investments, credit programs, and payments. The fourth characteristic is a *longer range* one and includes general customer- or group-oriented measures; training of advisory service people; sales support for branches; assistance for special customer groups (for example, federal, defense, and migrant workers); cooperation with the advertising function; and awards to employees.

The fifth characteristic goes under the general name of *adaptability*. The aims are to keep pace with development in banking, with services continually drawing on supplementary sources of new knowledge, and to ensure that information channels permit the proper transmission of new information.

Marketing plans should go beyond the normal scope of the "profit center" unit, to ensure multifunctional responsibility and to guarantee the continuation of business. To perform these tasks ably, marketing management needs a significant amount of information, which must be processed jointly with the information-system division.

The marketing database should include indexes that facilitate cross-referenceing of account information so that all relationships between bank and customer are visible. In introducing the concept of a marketing information system, a gradual approach to account cross-referencing is prudent. Generally, this system must interface with other existing computer applications within the bank. Many marketing requirements of a dynamic financial institution are evolutionary, something that is true of demand deposit (checking) accounts, time deposits, savings, personal trusts, fiduciaries, and corporate trusts, where the bank maintains shareholder records and acts as an agent for stock transfers.

In every field of banking activity, it is necessary to identify and analyze effectively all information about bank-customer relationships, to consolidate the significant data into a direct-access database. Underlying such requirements is the need for communication with stored information to provide marketing management with factual, documented action. The organizational approach to establishing a database is important. The broader a database, and the more it is used as a planning and control instrument, the greater the need for a thorough study that takes into consideration all the requirements for marketing information.

Still, market planning can be well supported by computers. The interdependence of product markets and resources that characterize any sales activity can be expressed in plans. Formal definitions lead to fulfillment of objectives, and thus enable management to take advantage of business opportunities. Table 4.1 presents job descriptions of responsibilities, indicators, and objectives. To achieve the greatest efficiency, such goals and plans must be supported by people who are conscious of the available technology, who seize opportunities and establish goals.

One imperative in market planning is to make sure that profits are properly safeguarded. Profits can be achieved only through greater efficiency, through revised plans, reorganization, replacement of personnel, and overhaul of control techniques. Emphasis must be placed on market planning *as a system*. It is the methodology that is important, not a specific market plan. Plans can change; a methodology, if it is correct, evolves slowly. That is where computers come in: the automation of much of the planning work.

Decision Support Systems

5

In discussing strategic planning and organizing the marketing effort in banking, I have referred to computer-supported tools designed to enhance the planning process. I have spoken, for instance, of a customer-oriented mirror of deposits, savings, investments, and foreign operations capable of reflecting movements in accounts and giving the resulting costs and profits to the bank.

Some of the ways designed to help bankers make decisions involve the ability to conduct research on masses of deposits, savings, and portfolios in order to discover significant events and new business possibilities. Most valuable is the analysis of a credit profile, which can enhance the sales-promotion efforts of the bank and the customer advisory services. This analysis is in line with a policy several modern banks have adopted: having a customer served by one advisor and bringing in specialists as necessary, depending on the needs of the customer and the special services required. In designing decision-support systems, therefore, a major effort should be made to promote strategic planning and product-marketing services.

This effort can be broken down into three parts. First, isolate the "critical fact" on which the success of the business depends. For any bank, this fact usually breaks down into four to six key issues representing activities or aspects of the business. These issues have a major impact, not only on short-term profits but on long-term growth and competitive strength. The kind of factors we are discussing here are of such continuing significance that the failure of any one of them over a sustained period can impair both earnings and industry position. The salient problem facing the bank—that is, the one management should pay the most attention to—will most likely be associated with one of these factors.

The second part of the effort involves exploding each factor into its profit-making components, which are important performance elements that must be controlled individually if satisfactory overall results are to be achieved. Typical components are market penetration, share of market, profitability of banking services, and the strength of the branch-office organization.

In the third part, develop computer-based decision-support tools. This means primarily a well-organized database and the mathematical models necessary for making decisions about analysis, simulation, optimizing, and reporting. As we will see several times in discussing information systems policy in a banking environment, these solutions should not only be online but interactive for all authorized executives.

WHAT DOES DECISION SUPPORT MEAN?

Knowledge of the types of error committed is needed to improve performance. Analysis of errors provides a basis for evaluating both individual employees and the internal control system; overall compliance with prescribed criteria, in the case of the former, and the way it is managed, in the case of the latter. Controls effected by establishing standards and supports in a decision-making process offer advantages. Control procedures:

1. Allow management the opportunity to balance programs for meeting objectives.
2. Conform fundamental principles of management in planning and controlling operations.
3. Ensure that functional managers have the necessary information—in the right format—with which to better program activities.
4. Permit management, at all levels, to focus on problem, or high-risk, areas.
5. Give analysts general guidelines in their search for the causes of out-of control situations.
6. Help managers judge whether discretionary costs are adequate or excessive, thus enabling them to allocate resouces more effectively.

7. Increase the visibility of business opportunities that might otherwise escape attention.
8. Reduce uncertainty by making available information that will enable decisions to be made rapidly, precisely, and with little disruption of business.
9. Force managers and employees alike to realize that there are both upper and lower limits to their ability to reach objectives.
10. Use statistical data for quantitative evaluation, something that, in the past, was either unavailable or difficult to obtain.

Standards of performance may be affected by the emphasis on control provided by the measurement process. As we will see in Chapter 7, when we speak of management by objective, managers and employees should become part of the standard-setting process so they can understand the purpose of the proposed standard and therefore accept it more readily. Standards would also require revision of goals and objectives as data from controlled activities became available. Computers, communications, and decision-support systems ensure that within a banking environment, decision-making can be significantly more scientific and predictable than it was in the past, by establishing proper procedures, planning tools, and management controls.

Having a computer on every desk, an idea American banks now ascribe to, will increase the emphasis being placed on decision-making. In the past, a well-founded decision-making process was mainly a process advanced by senior management people. Peter F. Drucker tells the story of Alfred P. Sloan, Jr. of General Motors. Sloane once said at a board meeting: "Gentlemen, I take it we are all in complete agreement on the decision here." When the assembled executives nodded their assent, Sloan said: "I propose further discussion of this matter until out next meeting to give you time to develop disagreement and perhaps gain some understanding of what the decision is all about."

The principle enunciated by Sloan, a distinguished businessman, is equally applicable in banking decisions. In fact, probably no aspect of the entire process is more important than assembling information or controlling results. If we don't know all the alternatives, our choices will be needlessly limited. If we don't know the deadline for making a decision, we may end up having it made by default. If we fail to heed expert advice, we will unnecessarily limit the scope of our understanding. If we do not establish proper controls, we will never know whether the action taken was in accordance with plans.

Some decisions involve little risk or uncertainty. Other decisions involve substantial risk and uncertainty and therefore must be weighed, both in terms of our ability to sustain a decision that goes against us, and in terms of being able to gain the potential reward. What all decisions require is *planning.*

By and large, the aim of decision-support systems is to establish a framework within which management can make the maximum use of its organizational capabilities. Decision tools help top management plan such special staff activities as profit, product, and manpower. They can also be invaluable for line personnel. Because they are based largely on computers and mathematical models, decision-support tools help management foretell possible courses of action, thus enabling them to make future-oriented decisions. They draw attention to the implications for the future of contemplated management decisions, by simulating expected results. They also help measure the results obtained through the proper analysis of feedback.

A BROADER PERSPECTIVE

It should never be forgotten that the first syllable of management is *man*. Support systems, whether in banking or another industry, are no better than the men using them. In practical terms, this means viewing decision-making from the perspective of managers. The following points characterize the decision-making environment and underlie the need for adopting a broader perspective in the management of financial institutions:

1. The shorter span of time involved.
2. The intensifying competition between banks.
3. The information systems services offered by banks.
4. The growing complexity of lending.
5. The need for a higher return on assets.
6. The realization that the global scope of the monetary operation affects everyone.

The shorter span of time involved.

Today, a banker often has only a day to reach decisions that only a few years ago could be reached in a week, or ten years ago, in a month. Although acceleration has its positive aspects, it also entails greater risks—unless information and decision-support tools are readily available.

The intensifying competition between banks.

Banks are moving aggressively in numerous marketing activities, and competition is mounting, particularly in the more lucrative areas. Throughout the United States, banks, and sometimes savings-and-loan associations, install point-of-sale units in grocery chains and stores. In France, the Société Générale de Banque speaks of determined efforts to exploit "les grandes surfaces." In Italy, the big competition at the moment is in new accounts, opening mini-BOs in factories to serve employees. All over the world, competition in foreign trade mounts.

These examples not only point to increased effort in the marketplace, they identify the growing importance of the third area of endeavor:

The information systems services offered by banks.

These services will be a good money-earner in the years ahead. American banks indicated that after 1985, as much as fifty percent of the yearly earnings of a financial institution may come from the sale of information systems services. Today there is a great discrepancy among banks as to how they view the matter. Services range from direct access to a bank's database by authorized clients to payroll, billing, factoring, and other routines, including the sale of EDP services to other, smaller banks. There are also specific reasons for better management of a bank's bread-and-butter operations, due to:

The growing complexity of lending.

Mathematical models and computer applications are necessary for making an effective loan analysis. Risk analysis and computer-assisted studies have been given impetus by the modern generation of bankers. After several failures—for example, the mortgage and real estate fiasco—many realize that, in contrast to the prevailing view, accounting is far from a science. Also, many bankers have been misled by postmortem accounting practices.

The need for a higher return on assets.

This return is necessary to satisfy capital needs, to safeguard the property of the bank, and to ensure the bank's survival. This is equally true of the firms that banks finance. Bankers traditionally sat on the boards of the companies they financed. Today, as industries encounter the cutting edge of competition, some—as has the Chrysler Corporation —are getting deeper into debt. They require the highest caliber of management skill, and good information supports, to turn around the situation.

The realization that the global scope of the monetary operation affects everyone.

The bank, even in the remotest areas, is not isolated from money rates created by national and international monetary transactions. These trends point up the increasing pressure on bankers to become competent financial experts in many areas, not just that of credit. Clearly, bankers have a great impact on decision-making. They require decision-making tools that increase their ability to face challenging situations as they develop. Because of these trends, there is a need for strenuous effort to achieve excellence in bank management. A bank's top management must be committed to developing a decision-support foundation and to eventually putting a microcomputer on every desk that will be linked via a network to databases, that will work interactively with mathematical models and use them (as we will see in the next chapter).

Equally important is the need to delimit responsibility and define accountability. The manager of a bank must know beyond doubt the area for which he is responsible. This, together with training, is a prerequisite for every banker who wishes to acquire an in-depth knowledge of the functional area he manages.

Finally, management ability is a highly individual art. No two managers do their work in the same way. Managers learn by managing.

Therefore, they must at times experiment in making choices on the job, including choosing people for management positions. In dealing with human beings, we need to recognize that there is merit to experimentation and that the failure of an experiment is not necessarily a demerit or cause for punishment. A bank with a good management climate should be able to try out a person in a position. If the decision was not a good one, and the individual did not work out, then the person should be reassigned without the accompanying trauma that so often happens today.

THE MECHANICS OF DECISION SYSTEMS

Managers use formal authority to organize, direct, and control the operations for which they are responsible. Authority is power over others; it is also decision power on whether to undertake activities deemed appropriate to the realization of the bank's goals. Decision power requires a broad perspective with which to allow the decision process to mature. It also calls for the finer mechanics of a system that allows bank managers to view a situation through a "tableau de bord." Two computer-supported aids that help managers make decisions are graphics and algorithmic expressions. Their able presentation calls for system studies capable of ensuring compatibility between the bank's aims, the overall information system structure, the communications solutions to be adopted, the processes to be run on the bank's facilities, the databases to be handled, and the information elements contained in the databases and their relationship. Furthermore, as we will see in the chapters on information systems, planning for a decision-support system is inseparable from planning for integrity. This includes error reduction, journaling for statistical and recovery purposes, and the all-important protection of security. To achieve instant response, a management-oriented computer system must support media. It must involve algorithms, which should be designed for *directional* rather than *positional* data.

The bank will be better off if the specialists who design its management-information system plan for the integration of goals between decision-makers and information-providers. Coordination is vital. Design aims must be capable of responding to the information needs of users at all levels. Because this aim will be *new*, information-systems designers must ensure that the transition to new systems will be easy. Current structures should not be upset until they are replaced. One recommended way to develop a computerized interactive system would be:

1. Have a time series-oriented data storage facility.
2. Accommodate data sources, external and internal, coming from either manual or automated systems.
3. Provide for narrative and statistical sets of data capable of residing in the database, with a catalog of available information.
4. Ensure flexibility of analysis, including spontaneous and scheduled types.
5. Make provision for graphics, preferably color.
6. Have an output facility capable of office-size individual output displays.
7. Be interactive and directly accessible by people with problems provided they have the necessary authorization.
8. Enable users to communicate directly and quickly with data and to evaluate alternatives, making full use of the system's analytical aids.
9. Provide features that allow decision-makers to pose and respond to questions considered crucial in making decisions.
10. Incorporate facilities that make the system easy to use.
11. Be adaptable to a changing environment through an accommodating system architecture.
12. Anticipate an evolutionary development cycle. A modular approach is suggested.

Typically, user modules will consist of a series of related decision options and decision processes. The need for decision-making information will grow more rapidly than most data systems can effectively provide this information. Properly designed, computer-assisted decision modules can act like a prototype of the decision process by allowing quick response to the needs of management. These modules will access a common database and display information tailored to the decision-maker's style and patterned to the environment to be managed.

By and large, the interactivity I have been referring to will be of the "menu selection" variety, in which the banker choses a frame of reference, just as a menu is chosen. This procedure has an important aspect; it makes possible choices for visualizing the alternatives to be analyzed for decision. Based on the concept of utilitarian decision-making, menus enable decision-makers to select from a table of earlier choices or to develop new approaches for examining the factors relevant to making decisions. Evidently, such a structured approach calls for much preparation. Here is where the real challenge will be.

FITNESS OF THE INTELLECT

I have emphasized my belief that the banker of the future will be better at his work if he knowns computers and can work interactively with computers and information. Decision-support tools not only help in day-to-day operations and long-term projections, they can also help develop intellectual proficiency by providing the understructure necessary for the exercise of the intellect.

Computer-run simulation studies are a powerful tool in experimentation. Simulation is a working analogy. By altering the variables of a model, we can obtain, in compressed time, results that permit us to look into the effect of decisions and adjust the decisions accordingly. (This has long been the goal of business games, an area that attracted considerable attention in the late 1950s and early '60s.) Simulation studies, however, even if managed by computers, will be of academic rather than operational significance if there is no realistic, up-to-date database to support them. And that calls for specific measurement of banking operations implemented through cost-accounting procedures.

Cost accounting is used to compare costs with revenues. Also, in distinguishing between fixed and variable elements, it helps a financial institution work out efficiency controls and the optimum expansion strategy. One dynamic financial institution, having noted that the fixed costs of its current accounts was extremely high, compared to its variable costs, launched a "family budget" campaign. Furthermore, by providing cost-accounting information to each branch, the branch's staff can be given an incentive and a branch balance sheet and profit-and-loss account can be set up. The information thus provided can then be used to establish objective criteria for opening new branches.

Similarly, in cost accounting for individual customers, the principal aim is to evaluate objectively the marketing tactics that can be applied. Exact, detailed data permit the consideration of each client as an entity. The aim is to discover the profitability of customers, something that could have considerable influence on bank management's policies toward their clients.

The intellect, enhanced by computer studies, should be used to develop among bankers a cost-consciousness of banking operations in general and of marketing strategies in particular. For its marketing policy, a bank must necessarily rely on the data provided by its cost-accounting system. In addition to supplying data to assist in decision-making, data processing is an essential tool in marketing policy. In many banks, when a campaign is to be launched, data processing is placed in the "front line."

The result, on one hand, is the selection of many criteria to which customer accounts are submitted for statistical or marketing purposes, and, on the other—a greater extent—the defining of operations in which data processing plays an important part.

This leads to the unescapable conclusion that a steadily improved management-information system is required by every financial institution. Good operating principles, a modern dynamic accounting system, and an intimate knowledge of computers and communications can be used in this development. A good information system is based on statistical data and on mathematical models to exploit these postings. Banking management uses this information to measure performance. Each banker is well advised to become familiar with this information. The same data are also valuable in making projections.

Until a manager develops a scanning technique and the ability to interpret and act on all the information available, the manager's decisional moves will be characterized by inappropriate proposals and plans and by fairly drastic corrective maneuvers that place undue stress on an organization. Another way of saying this is that, unless marketing managers become students of banking dynamics, their proposals and projects will always be in danger of being out of phase with the bank's resources and policies. To become students of banking dynamics, they must work interactively with the computer and use the various decision-support tools as they are developed.

Daily Business and Quantitative Tools

6

The yield on earning assets does not vary greatly with bank size, but the percentage of earning assets to total assets does tend to go down as a bank becomes larger. Therefore, quantitative tools are necessary in helping managment make decisions through increased visibility. To fully review the yield on earning assets, we must analyze yield on loans and securities, as well as the distribution of loans and investments. In examining individual banks, however, we find situations where management overinvested in tax-exempt securities to the point where taxable income was not great enough to cover the exempt interest, causing some part of this interest to lose its favored status.

The proper running of a daily business, or taking the long-term perspective, do not happen accidentally. Next to management skill, the most important factor is the availability of timely and accurate information. The right information, at the right time and place, complements management ability and enhances the quality of decisions.

The computer can be instructed to do what the manager might have been doing if he had the time (and inclination) to go through the thousands of necessary calculations and file searches. Management still has the last word: the mark of skill in decision-making is the ability to get to the heart of a problem. Presented with a problem, the skillful bank manager selects a few key elements from among the thousands of possibilities confronting him. That's how the good decisions are made. The manager's decision will be qualitative, not quantitative. To be factual and to document decisions, however, requires quantitative tools. Measurements help in the evaluation of alternatives, as well as in the choice of approach that best satisfies a bank's requirements.

A good, regularly updated database can assist the banker in the identification of alternatives. A model of the quantitative relationships of different factors affecting the problem can also be of invaluable assistance in the manager's choice among the alternatives. Defining the problem, developing specific cost and statistical studies to supply measurements of the unknown quantities, preparing a mathematical description of the problem area that relates the problem elements to the objectives, evaluating alternatives by testing them by means of models—all are operations in which a computer expert and a mathematician can help. It is up to the bank manager, though, to describe qualitatively what workable alternatives exist.

Returning to our example of loans, the banker, from his knowledge of the installment business, must formulate such questions as:

> Do we turn away too many applicants who would have proved good risks?
>
> Do we have too many losses for the number of loans made?
>
> Do we waste time pursuing defaulted loans with little chance of recovery?
>
> Do we make too many small loans that don't "pay their way"?

Together with the computer specialist, the banker must quantify the factors involved in the decision process. This is a cooperative approach based on a standard of excellence.

KEY RATIOS: AN EXAMPLE

Bankers have been using quantitative approaches and mathematical models without always knowing it. The study of critical ratios is a good example. They are part and parcel of everyday business life. Where is the accountant who does not know about the acid test?

A key ratio in evaluating bank performance is the break-even yield. This measures the minimum yield on earning assets necessary to cover all expenses, including interest paid. In formulating the ratio, we subtract all noninterest income such as that from a trust department and service charges on deposit accounts and other service charges and fee income. A low-value ratio indicates high performance, in the sense that the bank has apparently been able to control its expenses and put into effect an adequate service charge schedule, thus enabling it to break even at a lower yield. Given a low break-even yield and a relatively high yield on earning assets, a bank should show a reasonably good profit picture.

In a nutshell, here are the key ratios as outlined by United States banks:

1. *Net income*. As reported in the consolidated report of income at the close of the business year. This includes domestic and foreign subsidiaries of the bank.
2. *Average total assets*. The average of the four yearly reports on condition, submitted to the bank's federal supervisory agency. In cases where a bank has foreign assets, the assets are included as reported on the bank's consolidated domestic and foreign report of condition.
3. *Net return on average assets*. Net income divided by average total assets.
4. *Net return on average equity capital*. Net income divided by average equity capital. Equity capital includes any contingent reserves, surplus, and undivided profits, but it does not include capital notes and debentures.
5. *Tax equivalent yield on earning assets*. Income on:
   (a) earning assets including interest and fees on loans; interest on balances with other banks; federal funds sold; and United States treasury securities
   (b) the obligations of other United States government agencies
   (c) the obligations of states and political subdivisions on a fully tax-equivalent basis, as well as other bonds, notes and debentures
   (d) dividends on stock and income from direct lease financing. All this is divided by average earning assets, including securities, interest-bearing balances with other banks, federal funds sold, loans, and direct-lease financing balances.
6. *Break-even yield*. Total operating expense, less noninterest operating income, including trust department income, service charges, and other operating income, divided by average earning assets.

Several other ratios should be used in any overall analysis of a bank's performance. These are subsets of the foregoing key ratios. They involve growth perspectives, for instance. Growth ratios will show the progress a bank has made over a period of several years. Similar statistics will indicate the bank's ability to sustain growth in earning and assets.

Furthermore, the use of percentile values within "peer growth" enables a bank to plot its trend line through the use of ratios. By following the trend line, management can quickly get an overview of the bank's performance, measured against similarly sized banks in the same or comparable areas of operations.

PROFITABILITY ANALYSIS

The stress on ratios as a criterion of management performance is no idle mental exercise but a good way to force banking management to think in terms of profitability. The bank is a service institution, and a service institution shares in common with manufacturing, sales ability, product quality, and profit requirements.

Banking profits don't just happen; they are based on studies of business opportunities. As new banking services are designed, they should be aimed at a specific market segment. It should also be remembered that each market has somewhat different expectations for service quality characteristics. Often, a focus on costs or profits leads to the neglect of "quality," which, while seldom measured, is still an important part of successful management.

Designing a banking product to develop a high level of service generally increases the cost. Designing toward low-quality service can create customer dissatisfaction. Either can cause a total or a partial failure in the performance of the financial institution.

Service suffers when easily measured characteristics overshadow the real purpose of the institution. Every serious banker strives for greater efficiency, but this should be accomplished within a large framework. We should never permit the goals of cost reduction or cost justification to obscure the real goals. In this vein, many American banks are now working on the development of *quality measures* for data processing, audits, trust operations, new client services, response to consumer requests, money transfers, and other services. Such banks have recognized that until the industry has a quality standard to go along with quantitative work measures, management will be trying to analyze and improve its operations with only half the scope.

Having stressed the need for quality services, let's now look into the standard profitability-analysis criteria. Here, the key issue is the goals to be met, as the main reason that customer-profitability analysis is not more widely used is that many banks don't understand it. Management may believe in profitability analysis, but if the loan officers, the men and women on the front line, do not, it will not be used. Still, the front line is where profitability analysis has to work—in negotiations between loan officers and borrowers, between tellers and clients at drive-up windows. To right the balance, management should establish the right perspective. Historical data and mathematical tools are of prime importance in this task. One of the best results that can be expected from an historical analysis is to identify the most profitable third of the bank's customers and the least profitable one. We should, then, compare the profiles.

We should *not* expect to fine tune such studies to do all the rate setting, or to distinguish between two customers of average profitability. That is why it is useless to wait until we get "better data" on costs, float, balances, and activity before starting to use profitability analysis. Opportunities to improve the bank's performance will be passing by. If the available information is used to feed well-designed mathematical models, surprisingly accurate loan pricing can, for instance, be achieved. The key is to start with simple approaches. There are six steps to a successful study: (1) select the customer relationship you wish to analyze; (2) assemble all the available information about this customer; (3) project the future activity in the relationship; (4) determine the funds needed for future activities, as well as your future profit goal; (5) calculate a profitability index for each selected customer relationship; and (6) use the index to improve loan pricing and increase bank profitability.

PRACTICAL RULES IN LENDING

Some basic statistics derived from experience can be important. This is the case of the "80–20 rule," which states that eighty percent of the loan dollars are borrowed by twenty percent of the customers. This leads us to think of the wisdom of analyzing the bigger borrowers. Through stratified sampling we can also take into consideration some of the remaining eighty percent, and generalize about the profitability of this population.

The next step is to identify the complete customer relationship. A rough definition of a customer relationship is "all the business a customer could take away from us if he got mad at our bank." The major value of profitability analysis is that it brings together in one place all the facets of a customer relationship. (Here, an integrated "basic code identification system" can be helpful in presenting management with an integrated picture of client accounts as a function of topology and of the type of account.)

Similarly, we should determine the balance and the activity and servicing costs of the entire relationship. Then we should project these statistics for the year ahead. The critical question is : "What will we do for the customer and what will the customer do for us next year?"

A *future cost of funds* and a *future profit goal* are essential for making profitability analysis a working tool. If we use historical costs and historical data on the relationship, all that we can find out is that we made a mistake when we last priced the loan, or else we got lucky and priced it right.

But loan pricing should particularly involve the future perspective of present decisions—not the past. The customer will pay in the future; the profits will be earned in the future. The factors used in the analysis must definitely relate to the future.

Although service costs are a vital factor, it should be clear that there is little need to worry about inadequate information on service costs and other relevant inputs in a profitability analysis. The cost of funds is the big expense item. There is no need to be more precise in any other input that in estimating cost of funds six months or a year ahead. Calculating the profitability index can be a simple matter once the rest of the information is available. Many formats can be used, but they all come down to a simple income statement for the borrower's relationship with the bank. The profit is compared to funds used or capital allocated to determine a profitability index. The index allows loans of different sizes to be compared with each other and with a profit goal.

Minicomputers, or microcomputers, dedicated to a given banking field can ably serve the outlined functions. As an example, let's look at an "income-and-expense" application developed and operating at a small American bank. The bank used a minicomputer-implemented format of accounts that follows the regulatory reports. By doing this, the minicomputer is grouping similar types of assets and liabilities and income and expense. This, in turn, makes the compiling of reports relatively simple and the internal reports that are generated more meaningful. A procedural solution was chosen because it has no subsidiary ledgers; they are all part of the general ledger.

Each investment, bond, or stock is a separate account. All income and expense accounts are subaccounts of the undivided profits. This means the undivided profits account is up-to-date daily, and no closing entries are necessary at the end of the period.

By setting all these types of accounts as individual accounts and by putting detailed information into the basic record, the minicomputer automatically pulls off reports of all types. Such reports include: monthly income due from stocks and bonds, showing the detail on any individual stock or bond; monthly operating income and expense on an accrued basis; monthly operating income and expense on a cash or tax basis; maturity schedule of the bond portfolio; and, on a monthly basis, actual creation and posting of accruals of stocks and bonds income and accrued and prepaid expenses.

All this is accomplished without mainframe support, big DP budgets, and expensive technical personnel. The minicomputer actually does fit on top of a desk. It occupies an area thirty by forty-eight inches. If a person can run an adding machine, that person can learn to handle the general ledger in less than half a day.

INFORMATION ELEMENTS FOR MARKET PLANNING

Quantitative tools can be applied most effectively in the marketing function considered in Chapter 4. Among the information elements we can use for this purpose are:

Analysis by bank area.

Observation of market development; both overall and regional market sharing; the competitive situation; market research forecasts.

Supply planning.

Study and development of new services in various types of business, for private and corporate customers.

Location and distribution planning.

New branches (location planning); new distribution channels; overall sales organization for banking services.

The application and use of quantitative approaches in market planning must be operations-oriented, not just an annual paper exercise. This requirement can be met only if each line manager formulates clear-cut goals for the manager's area and is helped in devising action programs to reach them. An important complement involved here is that the potential uses of and limitations on marketing plans be clearly understood, and that management at all levels act accordingly. The necessary guidance and coordinating action means that performance and measuring profitability results must be anticipated and taken into consideration in making plans and setting sales objectives (Figure 6.1).

The use of quantitative models in relation to market plans facilitates a consensus for goals, methods, and the framework in which financial resources are employed. The market-planning mechanism to be created must: provide for the integration of functional management decisions into a comprehensive structure; quantify estimates on outcome of decisions given the commitments made on resources by the different divisions or departments; enhance the ability to measure resources allocated and results achieved; and offer a unifying effect and coordinate aspects, with the aim of increasing skill and cost-effectiveness.

Because the choice of time range is important, the most frequently used time range coincides with the overall management planning of the bank.

Short range:

Twelve to eighteen months, often called the "rolling year," synonymous with the classic budget period.

Medium range:

Usually two to three years.

Long range:

Five years, varying with the institution; sometimes extended beyond the five year period.

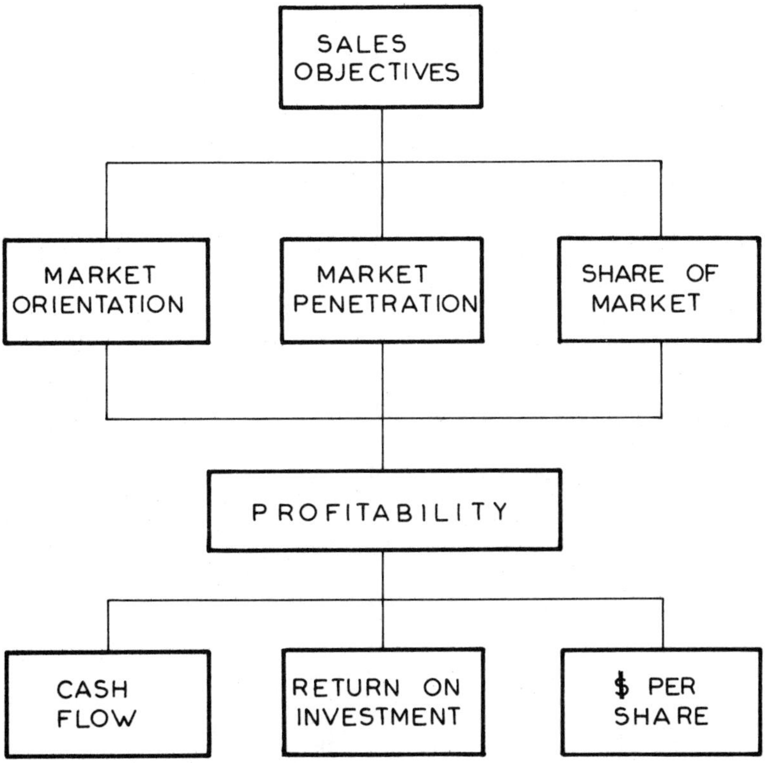
SALES OBJECTIVES
MARKET ORIENTATION
MARKET PENETRATION
SHARE OF MARKET
PROFITABILITY
CASH FLOW
RETURN ON INVESTMENT
$ PER SHARE

FIGURE 6.1

Far out:

Up to fifteen years; this is the most recent, aiming to answer the question, "What should this bank be doing at the end of the century?"

In the background of long-range planning lies the requirement that management must recognize the possible implications of commitments. When making firm commitments, the logical course of action is to establish subgoals so that there are clear stepping-stones. Marketing subgoals may be established through such precise measures as share of the market, annual growth, and profit margin by area and customer group. Corresponding measures in finance are return on investment, cash flow, and profit margins. Objectives are needed in every area where performance and results directly effect the survival and prosperity of the bank. There is a tremendous importance in identifying the key factors. The imagination and depth of thinking with which it is done will largely determine the quality of the market planning process.

The specific length of the planning period for developing formal, comprehensive market plans is relatively unimportant. What is important is that this period, once established, be observed. The choice of time range will invariably reflect itself on the structure and the content of corporate plans, the latter influencing all segments of the banking organization.

FEEDBACK

The meaning of what we are saying is the necessity to use quantitative approaches, both in the day-to-day business of our bank and as a means of developing, evaluating, and implementing the objectives and strategies that will guide the bank's future. To help in terms of goals, resources, and performance appraisals, quantitative data relating to the bank's operations must be databanked, and available interactively to qualified executives.

The elements in the database, and the algorithms written to help in their retrieval and visualization, should be designed to give a comprehensive, consolidated presentation of corporate objectives. A rational presentation of a statement of objectives begins with the *mis-*

sion. The statement of the mission provides important guidance. It delineates the fundamental business and thrust of the bank. It relates the segment of the lending market to be emphasized. Each time the planning process is undertaken, important businesses, principal markets, and management philosophy should be reexamined in detail and restarted. This exercise provides an opportunity for management to steadily evaluate its position and achieve a new commitment to principles. It also helps produce the financial plans, as budgets should be based on projected actions.

Action plans should be communicated to the organization through assignments that identify specific projects, short-term goals, resources requirements, authorized expenses, and time for accomplishment. Action plans call for precise resource allocation that can be quantified through a budget. A budget is a financial plan. As such, it offers a detailed schedule of expected income and expenses. By being quantitative and specific, however, it also helps financial and profitability goals.

Budgets are prepared by a profit-and-cost center, the lowest organizational level subject to formal planning procedures. These centers should be organized so as to allow the measurement of performance. *Performance can be measured only against standards.*The same is true of corrective action undertaken.

Measuring and evaluating performance is difficult if there are only assumed conditions underlying the action plan, and not clearly stated ones. Furthermore, plans must be dynamic. Because budgets change, management must be capable of adjusting goals and financial allocations to match current conditions.

To track performance accurately, a sophisticated, flexible accounting system is necessary, and this should clearly be reflected in the budget. Financial plans must have built-in mechanisms which allow reorientation of the thrust of each level of the organization. The preparation of the financial plan generates the opportunity for detailed schedules of resource requirements. These are needed to carry out the objectives and strategies of the financial institution at higher levels.This system results in a response from the basic organizational units as to their collective ability to achieve corporate objectives, given resource and market constraints.

Opportunities for change in the organization are recognized by noting the existance of a gap between the ambitions of top management and the response from responsibility centers. Based on these criteria, we can look on indexes of bank performance. In reviewing bank performance, the key measure is the return on assets. Two ratios—operating income and net income (after securities), and gains and losses—are basic references. Ratios, yields, gains, and losses—the whole reference to performance—exemplify the feedback mechanism necessary to any effective system (Figure 6.2). Planning will be an abstract exercise if we do not have the capability to compare the results to the plan, provide for changes, and give the means to management to effectively exercise operational control.

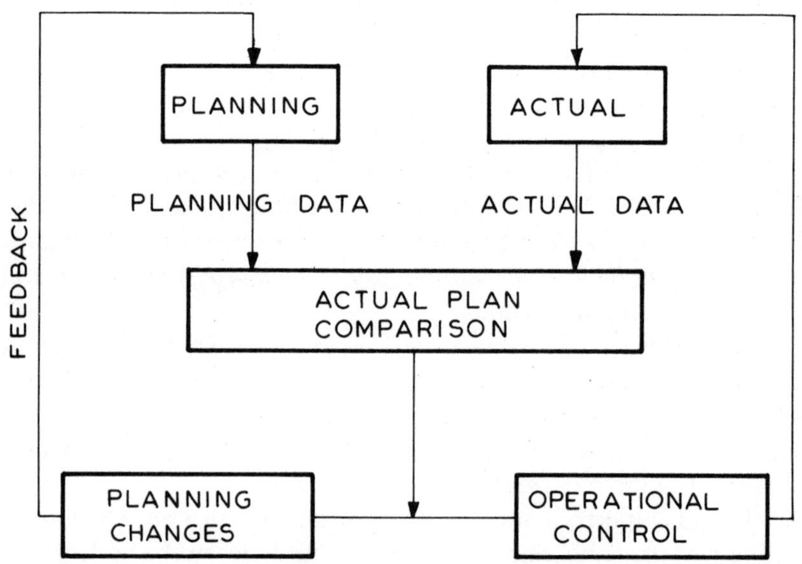

FIGURE 6.2

Management Objectives and Control Charts

7

What has been said on profitability analysis as a valuable tool in banking identifies a new philosophy of management, one based on objectives. A bank employee can work more effectively if he knows the exact objectives he is trying to reach. He will work harder toward an objective if he has had a voice in setting it. And he is more likely to perform well if he feels that he will be rewarded for performing well.

Furthermore, an employee's performance will be improved if he plans his activities according to a specific time schedule. Management-by-objectives (MBO):

- assigns responsibility for efforts
- forces development of specific goals toward which efforts can be directed
- provides a systematic approach for integrating actions, to help support and reinforce each other
- aids in motivating employees
- offers standards for measuring employees' efforts
- by quantifying, permits computer-based assistance for employees and managers

MBO is a dynamic process because the original objectives are always subject to change. Improved information about customer needs, more competition, new processes, and new products underlie the requirement for regular reviews. Many attempts to implement MBO are not successful because subordinates see no real link between results and rewards. Yet such a link helps them overcome the problem of different standards among managers. Objectives can be set in many areas of activity. They will require a fair amount of planning. But MBO can be effective only if appropriate control tools are provided and enforced. An integral part of MBO is to help employees make up their minds quantitatively.

What is different about the new tide of decision-making knowledge is that theoretical models are being devised which encompass all sorts of questions—from the most routine decision to the most complex business decisions. Here, the distinction between making decisions and solving problems is valuable. When we attempt to solve a problem, we look for a correct answer. When we make a decision, we look for a correct method. A correct method is no guarantee that the outcome will be a desirable one. It does, however, help us make sure that, over a period of time, our decisions are more likely to be the right ones. That is why correct methodology is so important.

CONTROL CHARTS

To help visualize the sense of planning and control in banking, some American banks have recently moved into graphic presentation through statistics, which long has been the domain of business. This is accomplished by means of *control charts*. Control charts apply to a variety of situations, including collections of receivables and cost of operations. They can be used successfully in such budgetary problems as programming, budgeting, and cost control. It has been demonstrated through specific examples in financial institutions that charts used to control the quality of output of manufactured goods can serve as a useful management tool to supervise discretionary activities or operations proper to banking. Control charts are particularly useful where measurements are statistical. Controlling losses from uncollectable accounts is one recommended area for their use. Management sets an acceptable average loss, plus and minus tentative upper and lower control limits. Actual losses are plotted on a control chart. Losses in excess of the upper control limit indicate that credit selection has been too lenient. Losses less than the lower control limit indicate tough credit selection standards which adversely affect revenues. Upper and lower control limits, above and below a tentative average, can be changed to statistically determine control limits once sufficient historical data of the controlled activity become available.

Observations outside the control limits signal an out-of-control situation requiring a search for the cause. Action can then be taken to correct the situation or remove the cause of unacceptable results. The frequency of reporting—whether daily, weekly, or monthly—depends on the activity. Statistics must be posted to the control chart to visually display the result and determine whether it is within the control limits. Out-of-control results require analysis to establish the cause and then correct them. This is both quantitative and qualitative work. The control chart points to possible causes of out-of-control situations. But offenses and offenders call for careful analysis of the individual breakdowns in internal control that allowed the defalcations to occur. The study of offenses helps uncover weaknesses in the internal control structure.

Internal control is the first line of defense against defalcations. Control limits can be determined statistically once sufficient data from controlled operations are available. The goal is to limit the risk of errors and irregularities. Errors above allowable limits require a careful audit by type and cause, to determine proper corrective action. Error rates below the lower limit cause concern about mistakes not discovered, and therefore not corrected. But charts will not help management if the objectives have not been spelled out:

Do we know what our bottom-line net is for each dollar invested in loans?

Have we looked at our income from all types of loans to determine the percentage of gross income this produces, relative to our total gross income?

Have we included interest and all fees from the loan operation (late charges, mortgage application fees, prepayment penalties, and so on)?

How can we relate loans to overall bank operations as a potential profit center?

Control charts help the management of lending. To do this, however, we need the right procedures and the proper supports. The requirement is simply to initiate a mangement program that stresses responsibility for performance, monitoring and evaluating results, providing feedback to make sure the results are maintained, and allowing the study of trends, which makes possible estimates of the future.

THE PERFORMANCE CONTRACT

We have taken an example on lending; but like lending, any banking operation can and should be managed quantitatively. The basic principles are simple. The first act of management is to set objectives. These should be written, measurable, verifiable, and obtainable. The objectives constitute a *performance contract* between the bank and its employees and managers. This should be executed within a given time period.

Critical questions should be asked when devising objectives. If, for instance, a new banking service is being launched, some relevant questions are:

For which market?
At which cost level?
What do we expect in sales?
What do we expect in profits?

The basic process starts with *quantitative fundamentals*. These exist in every business, but they are not always observed. Cost, timing, and performance are integral parts of good banking management. The entire process can be classified into routine, development, and interlocking objectives. Interlocking objectvies should be subject to reevaluation and joint evaluation by the departments concerned. It is crucial that individual managers—in all departments and branch offices of the bank—realize the need for and effect of a joint effort and measurable goals. Wherever interlocking objectives exist, they lead to joint accountability.

Management-by-objectives is no substitute for sound judgment. It should not be bogged down by rigidity. The goal is to ensure that banking managers know their jobs and that they appreciate what's to be done to improve performance—within the broad perspective of the strategic plan set by top management. To achieve this, we must make sure that human resources are ably managed.

The fundamental contribution of management by objectives is to help develop a realistic action plan. Action plans in banking must answer specific questions. What do we want to happen during a certain period? If we want to achieve profitability, we must be specific: How much do we make on each loan? If it is penetration, we must consider the following questions:

What is the market?
Do we want new customers?
What about the quality of the loan portfolio?

It is necessary to specify, but not to overquantify. The best way to specify is to provide steady feedback. The important thing is the work—the methodology, the discipline. Through evaluation and quantification, managers get to talk among themselves, and that is much better than giving flat orders. Every time we move a function muscle, we weaken the organizational body.

WHAT IS A MATHEMATICAL MODEL?

Management-by-objectives is a qualitative approach to directing the operations of the bank (both daily and longer term) which can make profitable usage of mathematical models—both for planning and for evaluation. Mathematics is a formal game of signs and rules, formal in the sense of applying a well-defined, complete, noncontradictory system of laws and postulates. But what is a mathematical *model*?

A model of a system under investigation is essentially a simplified abstraction of reality. It eliminates the irrelevant and unimportant details of the real system and concentrates on the fundamental elements, variables, and relationships. While seemingly complex to the uninitiated, the language of mathematics is a precise vehicle for expressing in a concise and unambiguous manner the structure of the problem being investigated.

Why use models in banking? Of the many advantages that models offer to the problem-solver, perhaps the most important is that models furnish a perspective of the situation in which all the fundamental assumptions are explicitly formulated—therefore objectively examined and, if necessary, altered. The model reflects the assumption the banker has made; then it handles that assumption in a very efficient manner through computers.

Open-eyed bank management harnessed mathematical models some time ago. At Morgan Guaranty, the Midlands Bank, and the Belgian Société Générale de Banque, to take a few examples, engineers and mathematicians have been added to bank staffs to analyze the technical issues involved in industrial loans and design and program new computer applications to help management make decisions. It is thus recognized that computers are capable of doing much more than the routine data-processing tasks usually assigned to them.

Successful model-building, in banking as in industry, starts with defining the problem. First, it is imperative that one become aware that a problem exists. Next, the probable bounds and location of the problem must be delineated. Although the need for this might appear obvious, there have been many situations in which management was trying to remedy what in fact was only a symptom, or even worse, that it simply did not know which problem it faced, and kept on fighting false problems.

There are certain common characteristics of problems to which mathematical analysis has been fruitfully applied:

Alternative courses of action should exist, and a choice must be made among them.

Quantification and measurement are not only possible, but can also be done in a reasonably accurate manner.

Alternatives to problem-solving can be formulated; the possibility exists that problems can be evaluated and measured.

It is possible to analyze the effects of the decision after it has been implemented and feed the results back to the model, thus improving it.

In his approach to a decision problem, the mathematical analyst should help the decision-maker separate the problem into its quantitative (i.e., numerical) and judgmental elements. The quantitative aspects of the problem may then be explored in a set of mathematical equations: the mathematical model. The mathematical model does not represent every conceivable facet of a problem. If it has been well specified, however, it will reflect the key features of the problem.

Models can be used to forecast the influence of decisions on a bank, especially in terms of risk and profit. Possible alternatives can be tested on a model at relatively low cost instead of in actual practice, where they might disturb the position or the operations of the bank. The great significance of mathematics in financial evaluations and in the preparation of decisions must be explained to executives if the total effort is to be well integrated into one coordinated action program. Many banks recognize this fact and therefore start with a teaching program.

Many management seminars by leading banks are intended to reach all levels of management. The systems approach, and the way mathematics help management meet objectives, is the focal point of such programs. Four areas in particular are of the utmost importance: (1) risk evaluation, (2) liquidity analysis, (3) credit calculation, and (4) investment potential. Following is a short list of mathematical-analysis studies conducted by financial institutions: evaluation of credit risks for loans; development of a credit scoring system; analysis of cash flow; selection and evaluation of branch office force; medium- and short-range forecasting, using regression analysis; analysis of accounting and auditing procedures; distribution of claims, using sampling techniques.

PUTTING MATHEMATICS INTO BANKING

Chapter 6 begins with reference to a long-standing practice in the banking industry in terms of calculating and using financial ratios. Now let's see what sort of adjustments can avail handling by a model. Say that a model should be made to calculate income and cash-flow statements. This model will interact with another model for cash-flow forecasting. A series of timeshared computer programs, including a linear programming algorithm, will be available online to assist the manager in controlling and monitoring the daily money transactions among his cash accounts, his account at the Federal Reserve, and incoming funds from correspondent banks.

Typically, the linear programming model will use the short-term forecasts of sources of funds, fund requirements, and interest rates to develop a cash-flow network that sets various cash balance targets, say, for the coming week. This model schedules the cash coming from the correspondent banks, maintains the required reserve balances, and selects an optimum plan for the purchase and sale of short-term funds. This example is not an abstract hypothesis. The system in question has been operational for many years at the Mellon National Bank & Trust Company. An online comparison between his actual balance and his target balance allows the banker to allocate income and outgoing cash more efficiently, on an immediate basis.

The forecasts obtained and the associated probability distribution of forecast errors make up the information structure on which a decision model is based. A decision model can be run in different time frames—day, week, month, or as requested. The database is more critical. The underlying information must be revised between successive decisions; otherwise, the next trial will not give better or fresher results.

The assistance models offer to the banker is self-evident. By analyzing the forecast errors within each reserve period, an optimal decision policy can be obtained. Performance can be evaluated, for instance, through simulation of reserve decisions. That is what several banks have done. Over the years, such performance has been found quite reliable. Let's take two examples of, at least so far, outstanding aids to decision. Among banking models in reasonably widespread use, we distinguish *balance and profit calculation* and *prime interest rate by time period*. Balance and profit calculation takes into consideration the monthly balance statistics according to the policy of the central bank, the profit-calculation procedure itself, interest income calculation of the user bank, and the prognosis requirements for medium-range liquidity planning. In prime interest rate by time period, the positions are separated by the balances at the beginning of the planning period, by the cost of money, the intervening policy, and the balance in disposition. Data preparation by accounting programs must be made in a timely and accurate manner if this model is to give good results.

Generally speaking, typical models for decision-making under uncertainty involve the enumeration of alternatives, the evaluation of consequences for each path, the expectation of each outcome, the evaluation of outcomes, and finally, the decision. An additional, important feature is the ability to quantify the importance and value of key factors. If the level of bank deposits determines certain decisions, it is important to know the range of these deposits for which exactly the same decisions would be made. Thus *sensitivity analysis* provides an indication of how accurately we need to determine our key variables. Sometimes sensitivity analysis tells us that an intelligent guess is sufficiently accurate for our purposes, that a long forecasting cycle would not produce a more accurate result.

For example, the First National Bank of Boston implemented these concepts in its price determination, investment strategies, and financial planning. In most cases, several closely related alternatives are determined and the evaluation of consequences is rapidly provided through computer simulation.

Credit optimization does require an explosion of the loans currently considered by economic sectors. A similar statement can be made about the analysis of factors affecting mortgages. Four different areas are usually considered: industry group; range of loan; interest rate (taken as different from the prime rate); and geographic area. Several mathematical models center on investment decisions. Even when an investment plan is formulated for a company, the problem of determining the corresponding optimal activity remains. In numerous cases, this problem can be solved, using linear programming techniques, even if in making an investment choice, the optimal investments to be realized are not known and must be determined, largely through guesswork on the banker's part.

Proper attention should also be paid to the presentation of the model's results to cognizant bank executives. Different methods are used to request and present data. Account inquiry is a specific, snapshot-type method that is individualized, whereas a request for management information is a decision-oriented method involving numerous accounts. Management information should be related to objectives. Clear objectives are set through experimental procedures; this calls for investigation at greater depth to be enhanced through simple mathematical formulas.

As the managerial planning and control aspect of the information system begins to be emphasized, the contents of the database, no matter how well suited to individual-account inquiry, will have to be supplemented with information that enhances its usefulness for analytical purposes. Such data is environmental, for instance, *demographic* (consisting of census and other population statistics); *competitive* (including, at minimum, each competitor's profit-and-loss figures and, where possible, the competitor's share of market) and *economic* (comprising a variety of seasonally and locally adjusted business and economic indicators).

A bank's management-information capability should prove increasingly powerful as the system matures, with managerial benefits continuing to rise. The central-file picture of the bank's overall operations and position must become complete as details are added. If the system has been well studied and properly implemented, each new class of file data, regardless of its importance in terms of accounting activity, helps advance the system by amassing sufficient data to drive a meaningful bank model. The goal is to ensure documented assistance to management.

THE AUDIT FUNCTION

Databases, mathematical models, and quantitative approaches help management-by-objectives, not only in setting goals but in performing crucial control activities. No better example can be found than the all-important audit function. Auditing concerns information. As such, it requires databases, models, and computer support. Auditing also has much to do with decisions. The data an audit would provide may change the course of a bank—or at least of some of its operations. On the other hand, once detailed, timely, and accurate data have been collected for auditing purposes, they can be used in other decision-making areas as well.

Among American financial institutions, the original statement of the establishment of internal auditing defines the basic purpose of this function as being the prevention and detection of loss. That definition has evolved over time to include the bank's control systems. The internal-audit function is better perceived as one that independently evaluates the control system and the way it works. Thus the ultimate purpose of internal auditing is not merely to prevent and detect loss. Nor is it that of evaluating the control system in an absolute sense. It has a much broader purpose. Internal auditing serves the same goal as self-examination at the individual level: self-improvement. That is why "effective auditing" must be defined in positive terms. Effective auditing does not merely evaluate and recommend proper controls and review compliance with laws, regulations, and policies, as auditing might have done in the early 1960s. It must also:

Yield constructive recommendations for improved policies, procedures, information flow, and profits.

Create a demand for independent advice from internal auditors in the design of decision and control systems.

Obtain acceptance, demonstrated by management action, in accordance with recommendations offered.

Many bankers consciously or unconsciously do not look to internal auditors for an evaluation of all aspects of their institution's internal control. They would have a different attitude if they answered for themselves and their institution such questions as: What is the difference between internal control and internal audit? What should management expect from internal audit and the internal auditor? What should the internal auditor expect from management?

It is just as important to keep in mind that bank management has always been concerned with the safcty of assets in an industry with a high degree of risk and the exposure of negotiables. In that environment, audit's responsibility is to verify accuracy, particularly of the financial statement, as well as ensure financial integrity through cash count, statement reconciliation, income and expense ticket review, and loan-proceeds-disbursement control.

In a bank that exploits computer and computer-based procedures properly, this work should be done through sampling inspection by means of terminals. I cannot repeat too often that computers are a control mechanism. Databases are the source of information to be called on to straighten out problems. And the approaches must be interactive.

REPORTING ON EXCEPTIONS AND DEVIATIONS

Both organizational and structural contradictions have existed in the past in relation to the audit function. In many instances, the internal auditor takes part in the performance of operational tasks that he was later asked to verify for accuracy. In other situations, audit is a part-time staff function intended to fit in after primary line duties have been completed.

Many auditing departments report to the senior financial officer of the bank—the comptroller, treasurer or cashier—inasmuch as audit is considered a purely financial activity. This is wrong. Audit is essentially a control function, with the auditor the prime part of the continuous control necessary to all financial institutions. The scope of audit responsibility must extend into operations, administration, and finance. The internal audit department should conduct functional, organizational, special management, and compliance reviews, as well as ensure financial integrity. This department should also complement any review conducted by outside sources rather than simply do the groundwork for the review.

All this work must be done in the manner of a highly professional, multidisciplined management tool, one used properly with an adequate staff. It follows that the internal auditor must be a person capable of meeting those objectives. This person should understand the scope of management's objectives and the reasons for decisions. The internal auditor should also be conscious of and report on procedures that are working well, in addition to negative situations that develop.

The words *exception* and *finding* can be used for both positive and negative reports, coupled with proper documentation. The internal auditor should be innovative. His methodology should change with the audit objective. Perception is another attribute that the auditor should possess. He should be able to relate to management the cause of problems, not just the effect. Empathy and sincerity will help.

The most important characteristic bank management should expect from its internal auditor is management perspective. Asking for the internal audit department to be a part of management is not enough; the internal auditor must think like a manager in order to relate to management. By proposing the placing of internal auditing on the control side of the decision-making level, I am advising against the self-imposed limitation in many banks of treating only those measures that safeguard assets, that corroborate the accuracy and reliability of accounting data and verify compliance with policies relating directly to financial records.

Quality, cost, and the use of time and quantity controls other than those incorporated in the financial reporting and accounting systems must be vital parts of an audit. Computers and communications are no exception. To take a constructive view, the content, objectives, and procedures of internal audit must be considered from at least two standpoints. The first is the view that auditing serves to record and present the financial effects of transactions and check records, to measure income and other financial results for the information of those interested in the fortunes and progress of the institution, especially the owners, investors, and governmental supervisory bodies.

The other standpoint is that auditing management, the data resulting from this function and the procedures guiding it, are a matter intimately connected with the operation and management of the bank —at all levels of the organization.

The foregoing is exactly why auditing is a part of management. To ably serve this goal, the auditor must have access to the books and records of the institution, even those concerning top management. The records are not sacred cows, and banks or management that consider them such have something to hide.

The data on which much of the fact-finding associated with managerial decisions is based are largely accounting data. But so, too, are strategies, policies, and plans. These are seldom established without some reference to accounting records and reports made from data accumulated by the system of accounts through the paperwork and routines associated with individual transactions.

Evaluation of the results obtained in the performance of specific operations, to measure efficiency or to coordinate different parts of the bank's activities, is almost always based on data accumulated and presented through the information system. These internal data (the kind of information seldom, if ever, reported to creditors, investors, and the general public) are the basic material with which the auditor must work.

The internal auditor is therefore deeply interested in the accuracy, timeliness, and precision of the data being dealt with. As more and more, such data are stored in databases, the internal auditor should receive training in computer processing, among other things, to audit computer operations. This auditor should also be able to supervise the quality standards of the systematic collection of facts about the detailed operations within the institution, the procedures related to internal control, and the orderly handling of operational details, from the standpoint of a systematic observance of rules and regulations.

The Human Capital

8

The strongest bank today may be weak tomorrow if it falls behind in the task of developing its human capital. In the past, the thought prevailed in the banking industry that if the right intake were done at recruitment time, some of the most brilliant young people would find their way to the top after years of practice. On-the-job learning, and the maturity this brings, was and is a great teacher. But though this is still necessary, it is no longer enough.

People who know how to work the bank's systems within the demands posed by the bank of the 1980s are not available in the marketplace, and few banks so far have cared to build into their managers and employees this sort of skill. The "bankers of the eighties" must be developed. Because they will be too valuable and too costly to the institution, the span of services each individual can offer must be increased and their careers properly planned. Life-long learning is an imperative requirement, and training must be multifunctional. People-information interaction will, of course, be a vital part of any program. The low profitability of the automated services some banks have offered can be traced to a people-machine gap that can be closed only with more training. This is especially true of the new demands by information systems, precisely those of:

1. dialog and query
2. visualization (along with computer graphics and color) as a substitute to paper
3. teleprocessing and communications
4. database organization, access, segmentation, and distribution

We cannot expect bankers (anymore than system analysts) to do better than they know how to do. Therefore, steps must be taken to offer employees the skills they need through a program scheduled to run without interruptions—in a way that will cover all managers and employees without conflicting with or even delaying the day-to-day work of the bank. Not only the younger personnel but also (if not primarily) management must be trained in the new technology. Both a highlights and a skills program for management development is necessary. Its aim should be to build up operating people who can bridge the gap between customers and computer-run systems. Technology is one more reason why the traditional wall between operations and customer services must come down.

Finally, a successful program for the development of human resources is one that, whatever its other qualities, is addressed to both senior management and to the rank and file. Top management must stand by this program. Unless and until employees feel that the company president and his immediate assistants believe in the program, they will not be interested in it. No one, however, can really believe in a program if they are not investing their own time.

DEVELOPING HUMAN RESOURCES

Training is a better means than methods and procedures to make the organization work the way management intends it to be working. Executive development is the responsibility of top management; it ensures that:

1. Both today and tomorrow, the bank will continue to grow, taking advantage of business opportunities.
2. The thinking and philosophy of its people at their work place is properly shaped.
3. The needed human resources to run the banking operations projected by strategic planning are in place or are in development.

A steady, well-financed and supported personnel development program is the best guarantee against obsolescence in banking skills. In 1966, when I was doing a research project with the American Management Association, I found that IBM and AT&T were the two organizations among sixty-five I interviewed that spent the most time and money training their people. On the average, twenty-four percent of the typical IBM employee's time—nearly one day out of four not on the client's premises or at his office—was devoted to training.

Many banks and industrial companies, particularly European ones, scoff at this ratio as being "too expensive" and too difficult to support. Then, two years later, in May 1968, came the minirevolution in Paris, in which not only the students and the workers but some managers took to the streets. The reason: unemployment in their ranks because their skills had become obsolete. I was talking during these days with Dr. Ponte, then president of CSF. He told me that his greatest problem was the obsolescence of his engineers. At about the age of twenty-five, they finished their university studies and were hired by the firm. It took them another five years to convert their theoretical ideas into practical results (Figure 8.1). Their effeciency, however, peaked by the time they were thirty-five; and at forty, they became obsolete. Still, the firm had to pay them until retirement at age sixty-five.

Well, then, what can we do about it? Work people for at most about fifteen years, then write them off (while still on the payroll) for another twenty-five? Or should we invest twenty-four percent of their time in company-financed lifelong learning—say, ten years out of forty —and thus ensure that they will be top performers most of their time? A career plan requires steady management attention. Training must focus both on this job and on the next job of the individual, including the opportunity for a reasonable interaction between skills in development and the projected functions.

Training must also open up professional perspectives and horizons. The kind of experience that classically trained people tend to have is too narrow. Classical training is much too compartmentalized by area of main interest: savings, lending, foreign exchange, computers, and so on. At some point, people coming up the line become managers, but without the prerequisite of sufficient knowhow of the "other functions" they will manage.

Planning the developments of the human resources of a financial institution involves revised compensation schedules to place more stress on performance, forcing executives to begin really evaluating their subordinates, and making an overhaul of the trainee program to make sure that it is not turning out robotlike bankers. The financial institution must have a timetable capable of ensuring that certain milestones are

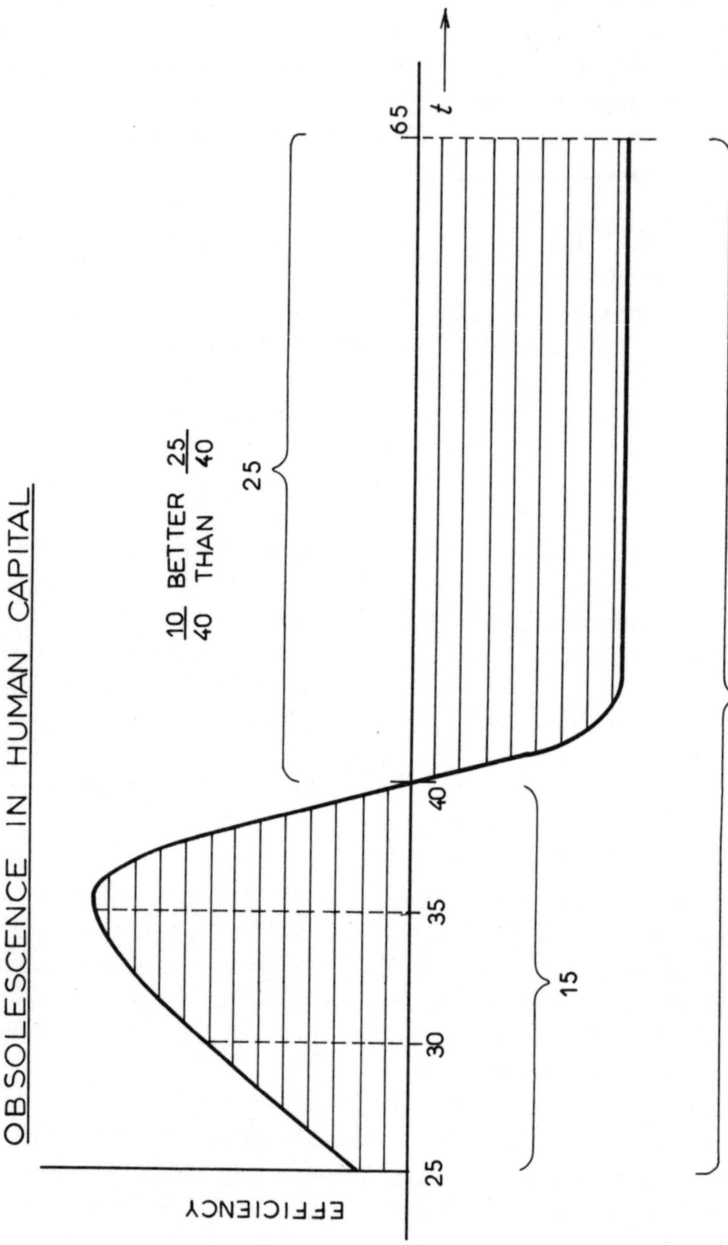
OBSOLESCENCE IN HUMAN CAPITAL
EFFICIENCY
10/40 BETTER THAN 25/40
25
15
40
25
30
35
40
65
t

FIGURE 8.1

observed within a preestablished time range. This is how Chase Manhattan faced this issue. To guarantee the proper development of human resources, the following deadlines are implied:

1. January:

(a) performance evaluation
(b) development needs outline
(c) individual career-interest evaluation

This should be done with the manager in charge of the employee (or supervisor) under scrutiny.

2. February: The process is up at the Divisional level, reviewing:

(a) performance evaluation—the top ten percent versus the low ten percent
(b) promotional capability
(c) learning ability

This policy implies consistent review, and management must constantly make an effort to get supervisors and subordinates to understand the process. The grades must graduate; otherwise they are irrelevant. Being in the low ten percent is not necessarily bad for the employee—but the manager must make this identification. There are managers who say, however, "We don't have a bottom ten percent." What is meant by "being fully satisfactory in a job"? Management must set objectives. It is good policy to set higher standards for better people. The banker must ask himself: "How do I do my job?" The answer requires making action plans and setting quotas. This is something that is often overlooked in banking. Somehow, managers hope things will fit their plans. This is not so; good results will not be achieved if standards are nonexistent.

3. March: Evaluation takes place at the departmental level.

4. April: Evaluation reaches a higher level, one just below top management.

5. May: Evaluation is done by the top management committee.

The points to look for in the structure of the right development program can be grouped into a few major categories. The first is *organization*. What are the strengths and weaknesses of our bank? How can we capitalize on our strengths? What is needed to correct our weaknesses (everybody has them) and turn them to our advantage? Does everyone understand his or her assigned responsibilities? Is supervision effective? Are the available skills effective?

The second category is *policies*. Have necessary policies been developed to guide development activities? What about operational activities and the decision-making processes? If the necessary policies have been developed, are they understood? Are they being used? Are they effective? If not, what's the timetable for action? Who will be responsible for the task?

The third category is *procedures and work flow*. How efficient are the procedures now in operation in the different departments of the bank? Have we used a methodology similar to or better than that of our competitors? Do the procedures we have adopted support operations? Marketing? Planning? The production of client-oriented services? Are they effective? If not, why not?

The fourth category is *technology*. In the fiercely competitive financial markets of the 1980s, the bank with the best technology has made a first big step toward its goals. Technology will carry the banking services further than ever before; financial institutions will never be the same again. Are we taking advantage of technology in terms of systems and of training people to use the systems effectively?

CONTROLLING PERSONNEL COSTS

The repeated appeal for training is by no means a hidden way of joining the club of big spenders. In an industry like banking, where personnel costs amount to seventy to seventy-five percent of operating costs (other than the interest on money), it is very important to keep personnel costs low. That is exactly what training, properly done, intends to achieve. (The other pillar of cost reduction in personnel is cost analysis, which, however, does not concern us in this book.) By increasing the productivity of each person, development programs help reduce the man-hours for each job, and hence, the people employed. There are enough nonproductive expense chapters in a bank, and their elimination could well pay the training program's cost.

It is encouraging that the attitude toward personnel costs is changing in the banking industry. Internal comparisons, ratio analysis of personnel costs and benefits, and measurement of the time it takes to do a certain job in the work place are becoming popular and helpful analytical tools for profit planning. In the early 1970s, a study by McKinsey of the top thirty banks in the United States indicated that absolute income growth—not people control—was the main concern of management, relative to expenses. This attitude, however, has been changing during the last couple of years. Maintaining profitability may well depend on zero population growth in banks during the next decade; some say this will take the form of personnel reduction at the thirty percent level or more for the same or higher level of business.

Tremendous pressure on personnel costs has developed from state legislation over the last decade. In 1967 there was the Age Discrimination in Employment Act, in 1968 the Civil Rights Amendments, in 1969 the Tax Reform Act, in 1970 the Occupational Safety and Health Act, in 1972 the Equal Employment Act, and in 1974 the Employee Retirement Income Security Acts.

A bank can, and must, control personnel costs. This is not quite, but almost, synonymous with increasing productivity through bank automation. The next best way is to train the human resources we now have, to bring out their latent abilities.

The savings to be realized from increased personnel utilization are considerable. In addition to lowering current and future cost bases, training programs can instill a cost-consciousness throughout an organization that will last for years to come. The fact that some areas of banking are more capital-investment intensive than industry should never be forgotten. Bank automation will certainly have a major impact on personnel costs, including salaries and such other direct-wage payments as bonuses. Keep in mind, too, that fringe benefits constitute an often overlooked or underevaluated part of the cost relating to personnel.

In many financial institutions, work-time-utilization analysis for payment for time not worked is frequently ignored. Yet this is a highly significant cost. Total hours not worked (Table 8.1) is thirty percent of total time, or 86.3 days per year. At best, a bank then, has less than seventy percent utilization of its personnel. Even this assumes that, while the employee is actually at work, he or she is doing something useful. The solution is increasing personnel utilization and productivity, something that can be done with online computers, if management is serious about it.

Table 8.1
WORK-TIME UTILIZATION

Work year	2,120 hours (265 days)
the average bank employee has:	
20 days vacation	160 hours
10 legal holidays	80 hours
sick leave (10 days in the average)	80 hours
personal leave (4 days in the average)	32 hours
coffee breaks (40 min/day x 221 days)	148 hours
Toilet (30 min/day x 221 days)	111 hours
personal calls and intra-bank office visits	40 hours
lateness, extended lunch hours	40 hours
total hours not worked	691

A SYSTEMATIC EXAMINATION OF FUNCTIONS

The first thing that calls for attention is a systematic examination of a particular bank's functions, whether productive or not. The next step in personnel utilization is to examine the organization's structure. How many levels of authority are there? How many levels of supervision? In most cases, a bank can increase the span of attention of its officers and supervisors and reduce its overhead cost. The reduction of one supervisor's job will equal several clerical positions. Another savings is the control of unwarranted turnover of personnel. To hire a new employee generally costs twenty percent of the employee's first-year salary. Management must ask how much turnover is good. Should fifteen percent be normal? How is turnover controlled?

Turnover can be controlled by establishing orientation programs and through internal personnel policies that promote training, upward mobility, and, of course, supervisory exposure. The supervisor is the key to most work habits and productivity. A factor contributing to high turnover that is frequently overlooked is boredom, and this causes considerable changes in jobs among bankers.

Another factor in personnel utilization is compensation control. The first step is for the manager to know what he or she is paying for. The job function must be described and assigned and performance standards must be explained. This requires discipline on the part of the supervisor. Surveys and common sense show that the action of employees is largely determined by work and conduct standards set by the supervisor. You cannot delegate discipline; you have to be the example.

One of the major pitfalls in bank management is ambiguity about setting job objectives clearly for managers and employees. Where clarity of job objectives has been achieved, openness, candor, and a high degree of participation can be found. The next major pitfall—one born largely of a leisurely tradition—is to leave personnel untrained and unmotivated. Little can be achieved in effective personnel utilization unless basic disciplines are established, work definitions made, job objectives set, and training and performance standards worked out and known to all. Training is needed. It should definitely include time management. Time available to do the day's work can well be classified in three categories, diffused, private, and interpersonal. Diffused time is ninety percent of one's working day. If a banker is well organized, private time accounts for another five percent. Interpersonal time is the last five percent or about thirty minutes of the day.

Diffused time is the most difficult to account for, and thus to control. Charles Schwab, a former president of Bethlehem Steel, asked a consultant to give him an idea how he could use his time better. The consultant suggested that he take a piece of paper and write down everything he needed to do that day, ranking the items by priority. Once this was done, Schwab was to begin with the first and most important task and work until all the tasks were finished. If the job took all day, he wasn't to worry; the important thing was to proceed until they were done. Schwab tried it, and his associates did the same; he finally sent the consultant a check for more than $25,000. Bethlehem Steel became the largest independent steel company in the world, and Schwab was paid an annual salary of $1 million. When he was asked why he would spend $25,000 for a simple idea, he replied: "This idea is the one that really made the difference in our corporation. Everyone in the organization is using it, and we are accomplishing things that we couldn't do otherwise."

The technique of writing things down on a pad in priority order is fundamental. It reinforces the memory. Now, with the coming banking environment where computers of a significant processing power and database size will be on every desk, the banker can nicely put *priority planning* into practice. He can construct his work schedule, develop milestones, time them, and control their execution, always making sure that he addresses himself to the salient problem until it is solved.

This kind of development in personnel resources, and the way in which employees and executives approach their jobs, will not come automatically; management must plan for it and make sure it becomes policy and practice. Top management itself should take part in training exercises that open a perspective of the future.

At Chase, top management is trained for two weeks, twice each year. Some twenty people participate in each program. The areas are strategic planning, market evaluation, and management skills. But Chase has also been deeply interested in new technologies, a key subject of which due account should be taken in top-management development programs.

During the 1980s, a major concern for any bank should be how to get its people to recognize that their jobs are changing. "How can we make our people sensitive to factors external to their jobs?" is a priority question facing bank managers at all levels. The answer to this question calls for a steady policy. It takes three to five years to implant the process of change in a banking organization.

PLANNING FOR MANAGEMENT TALENT

The making of managerial talent, and its rating, was a recurring theme in my discussions with bank directors. The search for such talent is increasing, not only to get today's job better done but also to provide for expansion and build for the future.

The main emphasis in the bank of the 1980s will be on the need for proper planning of human resources. Modern, dynamic financial institutions aim to highlight the pertinent facts of a factual, documented personnel-management system. (The approach described in this section is intended only as a reference; the specific solution to be adopted by a bank, however, should be examined and carefully planned within the framework of the bank's operations.)

Computers can be used to help in the task of managing personnel. The correct analytical approach has become more critical because this function has until recently been burdened by obsolete practices. Unlike some other applications, personal management is open to significant improvement, while continuing to observe the traditional policies of the bank. The payoff from a rational study of human resources can be measured by its success in helping bank management think ahead to make decisions about the proper courses of action in hiring, training, promoting, and sometimes discharging people. Such a study can also increase the choices before personnel are committed. Timely, accurate, and reliable forecasts of personnel availability are the cornerstone of successful management.

Purpose is implied in a forecast. In personnel management forecasting, our purpose is not to predict the future precisely but to determine the effect of needs and availabilities on the organization. A forecast should not be rigid. It should provide for identification of the probable course of personnel requirements and the best way to meet them. On this probable course will rest the development of management inventory, including expected results, timing, and cost.

Forecasts are made for planning purposes. Personnel-management planning is a process of preparing for the commitment of resources. This requires data collection, storage, and analysis; field research in personnel needs; and indicators of management development (training) requirements. Forecasts on personnel needs enhance management's ability to manage. Too often, managerial leadership consists of the effective use of four components: position, personality, character, and competence. All except position are the province of executive development. Because of their interaction, and sense of position, close observation must be maintained.

An old principle of management states that authority must be delegated in proportion to responsibility and that it defines the organization's position. For many managers, personality and character are easier to comprehend than the authority of competence. Somehow these managers confuse "authority of position" with "authority of competence," believing that a senior position and its concomitant status make competence self-evident. This amounts to a serious misunderstanding that inhibits or destroys a person's ability to keep up with change.

MANAGEMENT INVENTORY

I felt it necessary to emphasize these characteristics because the correct way to build management inventory is through lifelong training for the job. It is something every manager is expected to engage in. From the overall need of management development, executive evaluation, structural determination of needs, and managerial tests comes a synthesis that leads to efficient manpower planning. A proposed overall organization chart and replacement schedule is shown in Figure 8.2.

This approach to management inventory is expected to answer the questions, Who are the present managers? Are they promotable? When? To what positions? Who are the first and second in line for promotion? What further development do they need? How should they be given the proper training and opportunities for promotion?

To bring all the information on managing a bank together in one place, some kind of summary is desirable. It is usually more helpful to make use of a device that enables the chief executive officer to visualize the entire organization at a glance. Often only a simple replacement table or handy list is necessary. This table or list should merely list the incumbent of each management position, along with the names of the individuals considered the most promising replacements.

The detailed organization chart and replacement schedule I propose, however, adds information on age, service, and experience. As Figure 8.3 demonstrates, such a chart can be a working tool, but it must be kept up-to-date. In no way does it mean that those listed as replacements have actually been *selected* for particular jobs. Even after the company president's approaval, the chart still represents *potential* rather than *actuality*. It does, though, help ensure that suitable replacements are found for each position as the need arises.

The facilities that computer-supported, online solutions make feasible are flexible. Periodic revision becomes easy. Traits of personality, character and competence, can be quantified, and the database can be kept dynamic. Various codes can be established to indicate performance, to show when certain moves are anticipated, and to indicate when the named replacement can take over a new job.

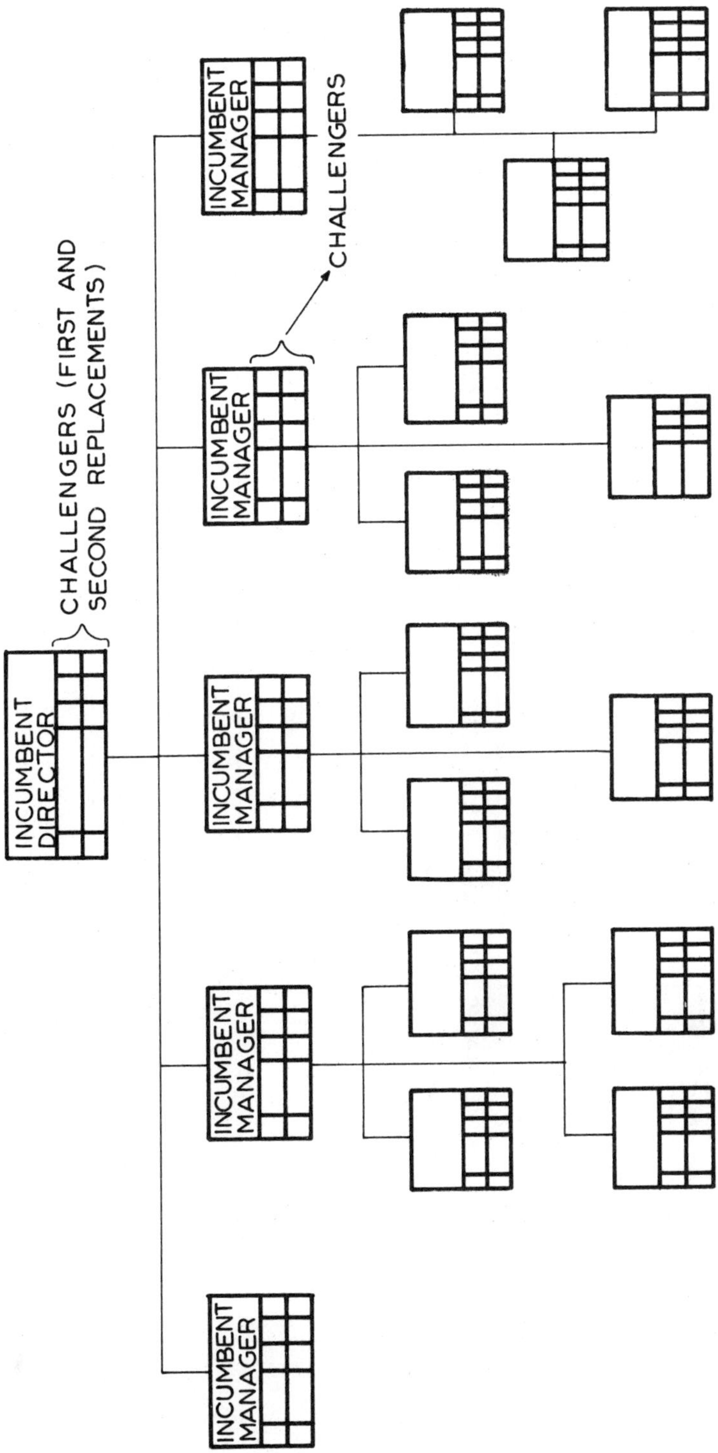
INCUMBENT DIRECTOR
CHALLENGERS (FIRST AND SECOND REPLACEMENTS)
INCUMBENT MANAGER
INCUMBENT MANAGER
CHALLENGERS
INCUMBENT MANAGER
INCUMBENT MANAGER
INCUMBENT MANAGER

FIGURE 8.2

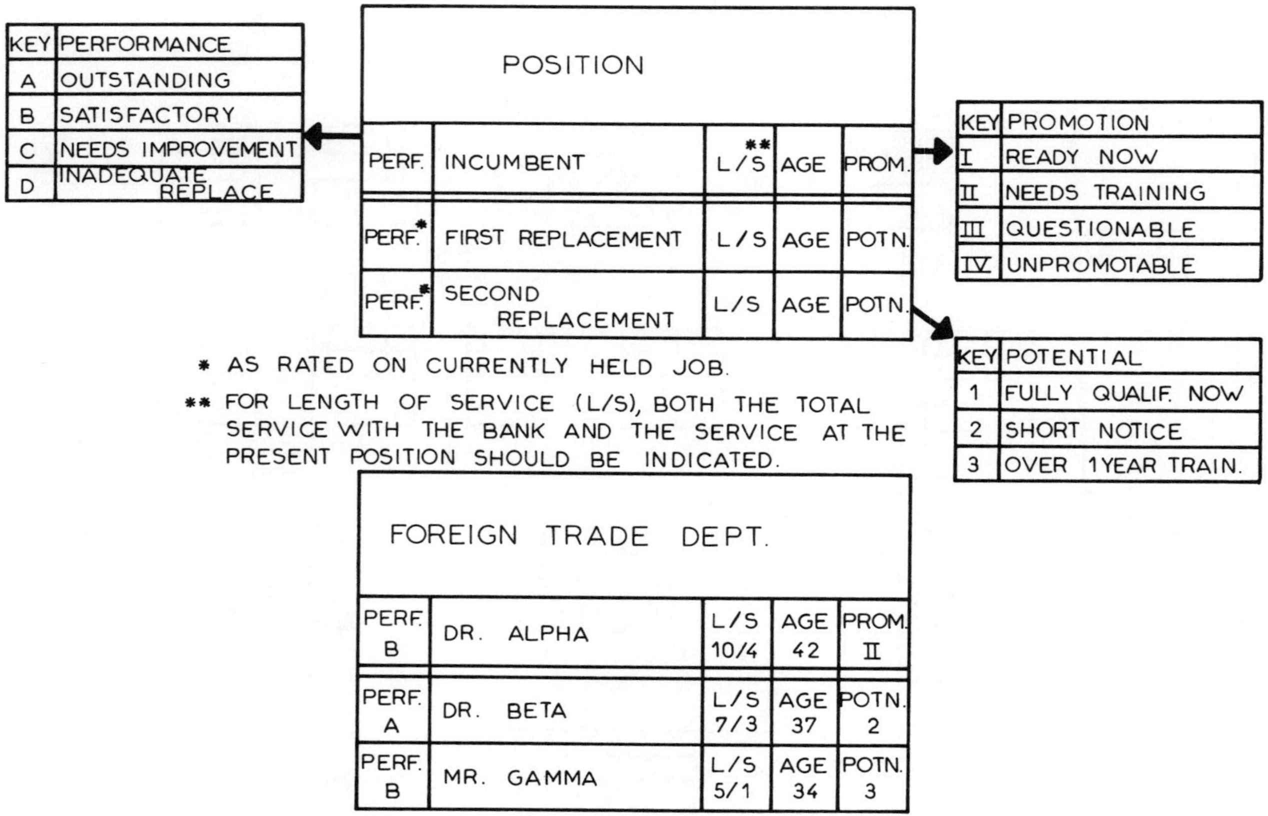
KEY PERFORMANCE
A OUTSTANDING
B SATISFACTORY
C NEEDS IMPROVEMENT
D INADEQUATE REPLACE
POSITION
PERF. INCUMBENT L/S** AGE PROM.
PERF.* FIRST REPLACEMENT L/S AGE POTN.
PERF.* SECOND REPLACEMENT L/S AGE POTN.
KEY PROMOTION
I READY NOW
II NEEDS TRAINING
III QUESTIONABLE
IV UNPROMOTABLE
KEY POTENTIAL
1 FULLY QUALIF. NOW
2 SHORT NOTICE
3 OVER 1YEAR TRAIN.
* AS RATED ON CURRENTLY HELD JOB.
** FOR LENGTH OF SERVICE (L/S), BOTH THE TOTAL SERVICE WITH THE BANK AND THE SERVICE AT THE PRESENT POSITION SHOULD BE INDICATED.
FOREIGN TRADE DEPT.
PERF. B DR. ALPHA L/S 10/4 AGE 42 PROM. II
PERF. A DR. BETA L/S 7/3 AGE 37 POTN. 2
PERF. B MR. GAMMA L/S 5/1 AGE 34 POTN. 3

FIGURE 8.3

In Figure 8.3, the projected codes and their respective meanings are identified. Top management should require—and obtain—efficient, unrestricted cooperation in establishing and managing human resources. Furthermore, these programs must show adequate knowledge and a good grasp of current needs and realities, together with an appreciation of aims and objectives.

PART II

Computers, Communications and the New Banking Services

Going Cashless

9

Both corporate and retail banking can gain from the electronics-intensive banking operations soon to arrive. The solutions to be adopted, however, are different for each of the two major markets of banking activity. The same is true of the investment to be made—with one exception: no matter which market orientation is chosen for leadership by a financial institution, the investment required will be substantial.

As is true of all business opportunities, electronic-funds transfer must first be recognized. Then a thought process must be initiated that reflects a reality other than the reality managers have known. *New thinking* is both a result of and a requirement for new directions. The perennial enemy of good management is the tendency to focus on the *process* rather than the *goal*, to think in old terms rather than in new ones.

The electronic tools needed for bank automation should meet requirements that reflect both the needs of the institution, in terms of management, and the needs of the consumer. Market orientation is thus fundamental. Without the basic choices, no clear direction can be discerned. If management does not establish the results it wants, the specialists expected to implement the new system will find themselves with ambiguous requirements, a situation that can lead to high costs and poor performance.

TRANSACTION-HANDLING

The first basic step the management of a financial institution should take in moving toward cashless operations is to decide that it *wishes* to make the move, not that it is making the move because the term is glamorous or because a competitor did so a year ago. After management convinces itself of the wisdom of making this move, it should select the market and the direction. Then the operation to be automated must be analyzed and broken down into its component parts, with each examined for possible application.

The world of securities operations comprises three main parts: the trading, or investment, area; the custody, or safekeeping, area; and the settlement area, where delivery systems are vital. Each area has its own internal dynamics and governing structure of regulations, procedures, and policies. The actions taken by settlement agents in the performance of their functions can profoundly affect the success of the overall trading or investment operation. These actions must be reflected in equipment design. In this sense, a discussion of the major technological changes that have occurred in the various sectors of securities activity can be beneficial, because they lead to new forms of investment management and transaction-handling. These forms assume major importance in the marketplace and have an impact that will be felt for years to come.

Choices must be made, choices that must reflect utility to the client, as well as return on investment. Service is at a premium. A concentrated product, for instance, enables a client corporation whose operations require numerous banks to concentrate funds in a single bank. Deposit information is collected over a national or international telephone network and transmitted to the bank, which automatically draws checks on the customer's local bank accounts and concentrates the funds in its central account mangement. This service is especially useful for companies with numerous outlets.

Another corporation-oriented example is automated financial accounting, the foreseeable ultimate in accounting services. A compact terminal in a customer's office can transmit on a nightly basis accounts receivable and general-ledger information by telephone line to the bank's computer. By morning, the customer has in hand all the data needed to monitor cash flow. This eliminates manual bookkeeping, reduces the number of inaccuracies, and saves time, money, and manpower.

Still another example is account reconciliation. Forward-looking banks offer a variety of plans to assist companies in reconciling their checking accounts—from a relatively simple summarization plan to one that completely relieves a customer of the need to perform reconciliation. Microprocessor-based machines in retail outlets (principally supermarkets) verify cardholders' checks for cashing, and customers are able (with the right legislation) to *bank* at these remote locations, to make deposits, perform interaccount transfers of funds, and make loan payments.

In retail banking, a key development for the bank of the 1980s will be the installation of self-service, customer-operated automated teller machines (ATMs), cash dispensers (CDs) online to computers and the communications network, and point-of-sales (POS) equipment. ATM installations have been stimulated by client needs for after-hours banking, as well as the desire to reduce queuing within banks. Probably the most interesting trend in worldwide payment systems, however, involves POS or *bank-retail* equipment. POS systems emphasize check authorization and verification aimed at reducing bad check losses, by placing an online hold on the customer's account by immediately processing transactions. As we will see, though, a well-planned POS can give much more.

The forerunners of true EFT/POS systems have acquainted merchants and consumers with terminals accessed by Debit cards at the point-of-sale. As demands on POS units grew, the next generation of POS systems was designed, which utilizes locally installed databases and single data entry for multiple functions. The combination of ATMs and POS involves terminals that perform funds transfers as well as authorization services. Another generation should be able to perform cash register functions. When EFT, local databases, and electronic-cash-register (ECR) technologies are merged, true bank-retail systems will be established. This will involve a higher level of knowhow, however, making possible subsidiary activities directed toward such retail operations as inventory control and sales analysis. These retail-management approaches have not yet been used to significant extent.

The demand for EFT and POS should eventually increase because of changes in the retail infrastructure and in retail front-end automation. The self-service concept is gaining wide acceptance in nearly all sectors of the retail service industry—in department stores, specialty stores, supermarkets, gasoline stations, and transportation terminals. Also, there is continuing reduction in the number of retail outlets and a subsequent increase in the size of those remaining. These trends accompany changes in the purchasing and payment habits of consumers as they move from small, frequent purchases to less frequent, large-ticket buying habits with significant impact on marketing strategy.

For consumers, retailers, and computer manufacturers, the fallout can be significant, since it is not necessary to pass through the preceding (and by now, largely obsolete) areas of bank-retail mechanization before reaching a newer, more promising perspective.

THE DEBIT CARD

From the United States to Western Europe and Japan, as intrabank and interbank systems become more sophisticated and efforts are directed to developing POS strategies, the groundwork is being established for transitional technologies at the point-of-sale. But even to begin implementing ways and means to improve the handling of noncash payments, a new concept must be sold to the consumer: the *Debit card.*

The Debit card is an efficient challenger to the credit card. To win wide acceptance, however, it must overcome several obstacles. One example is security, an aspect embraced by both automated teller machines and POS terminals. Several levels of protection are required to achieve the flexibility needed for banks to serve the rapidly developing marketplace. This is particularly true for:

1. A full fledged Debit-card operation capable of handling deposits and withdrawals, as well as transfers between accounts and payments.
2. Operations that are completely paperless and entirely online.
3. Networks shared by several banks, including the better service, cost savings and problem areas (security and protection) that such networks create.
4. Bank-to-industry (or -commerce) and commerce- (or industry-)-to-bank, online applications.

Let me add that such approaches have already been implemented selectively. Leading American banks have been experimenting with terminals at client sites, thus giving clients the ability to access directly computer memory and manage their own accounts. The results have been both interesting and encouraging, but the real breakthrough will come when home-to-bank online applications are universal, or nearly so. The telephone linked to the TV set, and not to specialized terminals, seems the ideal way to reach this goal. The true point-of-orgin is the home.

Valid approaches should stress paperless solutions in terms of transaction-processing. Consumers should not have to fill out forms or deposit or withdrawal slips. They should receive a message to be stored in local memory, showing the results of any transaction at the time it is made. The various functions and transactions that are possible from each type of terminal are shown in Table 9.1. To repeat, the true solution is *Viewdata* (Interactive Videotex).

No other means of consumer-to-bank communication presents a user-friendly environment as effectively as does the home TV set in sending messages to a bank's viewdatabase. Viewdata harnessed to computer power—that is its major contribution.* To do this, it used simple, comprehensive approaches which go a long way toward creating widespread computer utility. The wall dividing the eventual user—be it a company president, a junior employee, or a housewife—from the computer expert is gone. Anyone can use a simple numeric keypad, such as the Touch-Tone telephone; everyone can send and receive messages to and from the bank. In the same way that we communicate with an office, with friends and family, we can call on the bank's viewdatabase. Crucial to this ability is authentication.

Some forward-looking bankers are convinced that by the late 1980s, the average home will have a microprocessor-based TV that will permit all kinds of transactions and information retrieval from financial and other databases. For such projections to come true, however, current bottlenecks must be relieved and the rate of change accelerated.

THE PERSONAL IDENTIFICATION NUMBER

The use of the Debit card and Viewdata call for protection and security. The first—and, perhaps, the most important—security decision concerns the processing of transactions online and the authorization and authentication procedures associated to database access. Most other security decisions will either follow or be affected by this basic consideration.

The online EFT system concept places precise responsibility on the management of the cardholder file and the access at the bank's database. Debit cards do not contain the customer's personal identification number or the real account number. Instead, the bank uses a number that "points" to the real account number—a useful strategy for avoiding the skimming, reading, and duplication that are widely recognized as problems of magnetic-stripe technology.

* See also Chorafas, *Interactive Videotex.*

Table 9.1

PRESENTDAY TRANSACTIONS BY TERMINALS

Transactions	ATM	Retail POS	Banking Terminal	Interactive Videotex
Deposit to DDA (demand deposit accounts) and savings	x	x	x	x
Withdrawal to/from DDA and savings	x	x	x	x
Transfer to/from DDA and savings	x	x	x	x
Bank payments	x	x	x	x
Current balance/ customer inquiry	x		x	x
File inquiry—no PIN authorization			x	x
File maintenance			x	x
Merchant payments		x		x
File Inquiry-PIN authorization	x	x		x
Duplicate receipt		x	x	x
User-friendly approaches				x
Banking at home				x

The personal identification number (PIN) described in Chapter 1 is the key to Debit card usage. PIN is the four-digit number known only to the cardholder. It is entered via a numeric PIN pad to validate a transaction and is the EFT equivalent of the customer's signature on a check. Because the card and PIN grant access to the EFT system and provide basic approval for performing a transaction, it becomes necessary to secure the PIN so it cannot be obtained easily.

The central file contains the customer's PIN, the accounts that can be accessed, cash withdrawal limits and any restrictions on the card. The arrangement virtually excludes the possibility of a customer overdrawing his or her account or using a reported stolen card—a major source of loss in many ATM-POS operations.

Maintenance of this centralized database can be done periodically without affecting or changing the physical card. The bank may change client-account relationships and limits without ever needing a new card. Bank management does not need to send out or control new cards and PINs, thus avoiding expense and another major threat from interception of card and/or PIN in mailing.

The Debit-card system has addressed security problems by ensuring that the PIN carried on the card master file which is matched to the PIN entered at the terminal is in encrypted form. The encryption method or algorithm is often created and programmed outside the bank as an additional security strategy, and the algorithm is held only in the audit department, under dual control. This reasonably ensures that no insider can associate clear PIN numbers with account numbers for possible misuse. Even a memory dump by data-processing personnel will yield only a useless list of encrypted PINs. To maintain the integrity of the system, it is essential not to have the clear PIN available at the file level, even after it is entered at the terminal and transmitted to central processing for approval.

Remotely installed ATM units should be able to instantaneously verify the PIN entered by the customer at the terminal level. When a customer inserts his or her plastic card in the ATM, only the magnetic-stripe data is sent to the central processor. The card information is verified for accuracy, proper status, and whether it is unrestricted, or "hot." The encrypted PIN is then sent back to the terminal, and matching is accomplished through local intelligence.

What if the PIN test fails? The reason for incorrect PIN entries and possible failures could be that the customer forgot the PIN or that fraudulent use of the card is being attempted. In an attempt to cover all possibilities, the system keeps track of all PIN fails for that card. When the number of accummulated PIN failures exceeds a parameter established at the terminal (for instance, three), the card is restricted automatically, and no further transaction is allowed for the card.

THE PAYING CLIENT

Although the technological challenge can be met without great difficulties, there exist more factors to take into account than the advancement of science, the preparedness of manufacturers to offer cost-effective equipment, and the willingness of banks and merchandising firms to adopt them. A case in point is consumers and their pressure groups, and their impact on government.

In the United States, the National Commission on Electronic Funds Transfer said in its final report: "The future of EFT is inextricably tied to consumer acceptance. The technology must fulfill consumer needs, and if it does not, EFT is unlikely to grow beyond its early stages." Yet the commission members failed to include a single recognized consumer leader. Nor, in light of consumer activities, were the major consumer concerns adequately addressed in the final report. Let us examine, therefore, how the situation has developed in terms of the *paying* client.

First, we must return to the origin. The bank credit card has become firmly established in consumer purchases. The interchange system, whereby one card can be used in many locations, has existed for less than twenty years. Yet more than twenty-eight million active bank credit card accounts exist in the United States alone, and the total amount of credit outstanding exceeds ten billion dollars.

Even if it is noted that many households have more than one account, it is apparent that the bank credit card plays an important role in the financial affairs of American consumers. With the growth in card use, and the rates charged on credit extended via the card, usually the maximum permitted by state law, it would appear that the credit card business is highly profitable. Such is not the case.

After allowing for direct expenses, a share of overhead, loan losses, and the cost of funds, it was found that for banks participating in the Federal Reserve's Functional Cost Analysis Program, the net return on the amount of bank credit cards extended was lower than that of any other credit category. Indeed, on the average, banks with deposits of less than fifty million dollars had negative returns. Even if some arbitrariness in cost-accounting procedures is acknowledged, and it is noted that some banks may consistently outperform the averages, the picture is not one of large profits, contrary to the impressions of many consumer groups.

The reason for this lack of profitability is the manner in which bank credit card services are priced. In general, the difficulty arises because revenues and costs are generated from different sources. When a credit card transaction between a cardholder and a merchant is completed, some revenue may be forthcoming from the cardholder. However, processing costs, the cost of funds, and allowance for risk accompany every transaction.

When the merchant deposits his sales slips, the bank credits him with the amount of the sales slip, minus a sum referred to as the "merchant discount." This discount varies from two to five percent, depending on local competition conditions. Bank credit card plans, however, would quickly go bankrupt with only the merchant discount because of the tremendous paperwork generated, something that was not foreseen when the credit card system was established. Thus, for the bank, the bulk of the revenue comes from finance charges to cardholders who use the revolving credit feature of the bank credit card. The latter accounts for sixty to sixty-five percent of all bank credit card revenue. A cardholder may generate both processing costs and the cost of funds, yet add nothing to the interest income of the bank, simply by paying for his card purchases within a certain period after receiving his bill.

The customer who pays his balance within the prescribed time period enjoys the use of the funds advanced during that period, the convenience and safety of not carrying cash, and the vast, expensive processing facilities—all without incurring any charges. Inevitably, resource-allocation inefficiencies and inequities are associated with this cross-subsidization. There is also concern for the profitability of the activity.

THE CONSUMER'S REACTION

The consumer's reaction should also be taken into account, as a business opportunity study must examine all aspects. The position taken by the eventual users can, under no condition, be omitted from careful accounting practices. Following are the highlights of reactions heard so far from consumers, especially pressure groups and cooperatives.

When a new technology becomes available, it often fills a void in regulation and consumer-protection laws, which did not anticipate the technology. While this period of nonregulation affords some opportunity for innovation and experimentation, at the same time, it creates market uncertainty and the risk that consumer reaction, when it sets in, could make obsolete many of the systems installed.

To think aloud of possible situations that EFTs may encounter, we should look at the introduction of the Universal Product Code (UPC) in the food-marketing industry. This code, some say, provides an excellent analogy for what can be expected with EFT. For years, consumers received computer output in the form of bills and monthly bank statements; but in UPC, the computer and the consumer confront each other. The result is nonpositive. The UPC itself, now printed on nearly all packaged items sold in supermarkets, seemed harmless. The idea was that the code could be read automatically at the checkout station. The clerk would simply sweep the code block over a scanner, which identifies the product, rings up the price, maintains the inventory status, orders new stock as needed, and prints out a detailed list of the items included in the total price of a consumer's purchase.

With all these advantages, why wasn't UPC widely acclaimed by consumers? Aside from the advantages to the store, the consumer would find his order checked out much quicker and would end up with a much more useful sales receipt. It was never clear, however, whether the store would reduce the number of checkers simply to maintain an acceptable queueing pattern. The fatal flaw in the system, consumer groups insist, was the supermarket industry's attempt to reduce staff by eliminating the stamping of individual prices on each item. Instead of individual item pricing, computer-generated shelf tags carried the price. A consumer would check the shelf tag, but once he picked up the item and walked away, the price was not available again until it flashed on a computer display or appeared on the detailed cash register slip provided as a receipt after he paid for his order. This irritated consumers. Some pressure groups insist that in the context of existing pricing schemes, there is little or no reason to believe the consumer will find electronic funds transfer systems in his interest.

How can consumers be convinced that EFT is beneficial? Under current circumstances, a restructuring of pricing arrangements is the only way the problems discussed above can be addressed. For the checking account customers, the introduction of explicit pricing ends the cross-subsidization of low-balance, high-activity customers by other customers. The customer must be given incentive to economize on the use of the entire payment mechanism and to reduce the amounts of transactions from checking accounts to temporary havens, either in savings accounts or in money-market instruments and back. Further, the customer must have an incentive to use electronic payments; that is the cheapest, lowest, explicit-charge method of transferring funds. (Of course, the customer gives up the "float" in all these transactions; in return, the payment of interest offsets the loss of that benefit.) Finally, there are incentives for all concerned to seek out the cheapest technology and economize in the use of the overall payment mechanism.

In the current legal and regulatory environment, it is impossible to move in the direction outlined above. All of the topics discussed are interrelated, and reform should take a "systems approach" to avoid the problems and risks associated with piecemeal change. This has not been the case in the past, and even now is perhaps too much to hope for. Ignoring the problems associated with current implicit pricing arrangements, however, will make it much more likely that innovations and technological change will not proceed rapidly.

TRENDS IN THE FINANCIAL INDUSTRY

The consumer must be informed about developments. He must be trained in the use of the new services and given confidence in the cutting edge of technology, the way it affects financial institutions. This trend is irreversible, and the earlier we realize this, the better it will be for all concerned.

Bankers, too, should be getting better acquainted with technology. The evolution taking place in the financial industry makes it virtually impossible to do without computer-based, communications-supported services. At the same time, it is becoming clear that it is equally difficult to make a profit on them. We are reaching a stage, leading banks have concluded, where the delivery of EFT services is a condition of doing business. In studies, three reasons for this state of affairs have emerged:

1. Transaction accounts bearing interest are becoming a reality, legislation notwithstanding. Movement to these services is a logical extension for the have-nots (savings and loan institutions and credit unions) to capture the customers of the haves (banks). To the have-nots, the "getting" is sufficient justification for developing the services.

2. The intense competition for the retail customer dollar is causing shifts in the competitive balance among institutions. Sears' recent announcement that it will accept credit union share drafts is an immediate opening to national banking, independent of regulation and legislation. This type of move can do nothing but force bankers to aggressively counter with new services just to protect their customer base.
3. Most importantly, management at some financial institutions seems to have missed a key point by concentrating on low volume. The point is that those customers who use the services like them very much. This has come about in spite of the limited reliability and usefulness, from a customer standpoint, of some systems. Even if volumes rise slowly, then, a base of desirable customers who like the services is being developed. These customers want the services, and they feel cheated if they are removed.

In the case of EFT, a claim is being placed in an area, so that the presence of the bank can be established in the market. The payback might not appear for a number of years. However, the alternative—being frozen out of the market in the future—is reason enough to move aggressively.

Let's return to the origins, noting that the first solutions to computer-based funds transfer were of the giro type. The example I gave of the French bank fits well. Early application required considerable clerical processing, and, cost aside, the delays that resulted often inhibited consumer usage. The newer authorization listings offering consumers the ability to make most, if not all, of their payments began in 1971 with *Bill Master*, a franchise service by Bank Business Systems, Inc., which was offered through such banks as Marshall & Isley in Milwaukee. This service used a computer listing of payments for the previous month, on which the consumer noted the payments to be made for that month. Authorization listing services store payment data for individual consumers in their data-processing systems. Although only a few years ago, the storing of consumers' payment data in a computer system would probably have been too costly to consider for a low-priced service, the continued lowering of the expense of the computing capability makes such a feature possible today. Then the service itself developed.

The *Supercheck Payment Order* used in the *Phone or Check Bill Payer* offered by PATSI illustrates an improvement, since the consumer can either "value date" each payment for the exact day the payment is to be made, or he can make all payments on the same day. Debits against consumer accounts are furnished to participating financial institutions in the ninety-four character National Automated Clearing House Association (NACHA) format. Payments are made to merchants or corporate payees daily by the issuance of checks with listings of the individual consumer accounts being paid. Conceivably, in the future, both the debits against consumer accounts and the credits to all selected corporations could be handled through EFT networks transmitting batched data. A key requirement regarding the various types of consumer-initiated bill payment services is that low-cost, efficient methods be used. This will enable payment instructions from consumers to be captured inexpensively in machine-processable form.

PAY BY PHONE

Initiation of payments by telephone began in 1973 with the introduction of "In Touch" (terminated in 1974) by the Seattle First National Bank. The service was repurchased from the bank by Telephone Computing Service, Inc. and offered as "Pay by Phone," with installations at such institutions as Farmers and Mechanics Savings Bank in Minneapolis and the People's Savings Bank in Bridgeport, Connecticut.

Among the telephone payment services being offered today are: IBM, a system initially developed almost wholly by Commercial Federal Savings & Loan Association, Omaha, Nebraska; Periphonics, Long Island City, New York; Financial Industry Systems of Hartford, Connecticut, which markets "PIPS (paperless item-processing system) by Phone"; Telephone Computing Service, Seattle, Washington, with "Pay by Phone" developed from the "In Touch" service; and University Computing Company, Dallas, Texas, with its "Bill System." Several of these services (for example, "Tellerphone," offered by Greater New York Savings Bank, and "Phone or Check Bill Payer") use a serial number to identify the sequence of the consumer's payments.

Telephone bill-payment services are similar to the newer, authorized listings services, in that the consumer advises his financial institution of the payees and gives the institution his account number at each payee. This process of establishing the payment data to be stored for consumer initiation is generally done by using a merchant's listing and a unique identification number. Most services require that the consumer use the unique number to initiate a transaction.

Bill-payment plans generally contain verification lists showing the consumer's account numbers to be paid in the future by the particular service. Notification serves to verify that records are correct. Prenotification records are sent through automated clearing houses (ACHs) before real dollar transactions are handled. Consumers can initiate telephone payments via Touch-Tone telephones for automatic data capture through audio-response units, or they can do it by voice. Voice initiation can be to an operator at the bill-paying organization or through a voice-activated recorder. Such devices as "SoftTouch," selling for under $20, can replace the usual telephone mouthpice, converting a conventional telephone to Touch-Tone capability.

At present, some bill-payment services (for example, People's Savings Bank) submit payment data in machine-readable form to such high-volume users as utilities and department stores. For payments sent through ACHs, the receiving financial institution submits the individual payment data to the billing corporation, in addition to handling the transfer of funds to the corporation. What is the future of ACH?

Electronic Funds Transfer Function

10

In spite of the technical challenges and consumer reaction, the future lies in automated banking through electronic funds transfer. Therefore, it is no wonder that in its recommendations, the EFT Commission, consulting the President of the United States on new banking laws, called for state and federal laws governing branch banking to be set aside when terminals, rather than brick-and-mortar buildings, are involved. The commission would allow banks to offer debit services anywhere in the United States through terminal systems, and would permit the immediate expansion of deposit-taking services statewide, then across contiguous state lines to serve logical market areas. In other words, users with a Debit card from a New York City bank could use the card in New Jersey if the New York bank had a terminal there. A New York bank could expand its deposit-taking activities into places across state lines (in marked contrast to current laws, whereby most banks are limited to doing business within their home state) if these were construed as "natural market areas" for the bank.

Automated branch banking has become feasible because of "intelligent" terminals, data communications, minicomputers, and microcomputers. This is a new horizon in banking. MoneyOne, the excellent network of the First National Bank of Boston, is not just another application; it is an "intelligent" banking strategy. It is the *future*.

The new systems can be made more secure than those used today. Having studied the area of security, the EFT Commission played down customer concern about their financial records in EFT systems. It did, however, recommend that state and federal regulatory agencies develop uniform security regulations, and that all state and federal regulatory financial institutions consider joint solutions to common security problems.

A new era in banking has begun. As expected, implementing broad new services creates some anxiety. The earlier the psychological barriers are overcome, the better it is for all concerned.

WHAT IS EFT?

Let us first establish a definition. Electronic Funds Transfer is the generic name of a market which includes several fields of opportunity. They range from international financial transfers (for instance, SWIFT) to automated clearing houses (ACH), cash dispensers (CD), and automated teller machines (ATM).

Many of these services are like a gyro. An example is the initiation of payments by authorization listing. The customer notes the amount to be payed for prelisted payees, and the execution takes place through computer media. "Super Check," "Multicheck," and "Quick Check" were among the early services in this field. At the consumer's bank, payment data is generated for transmission through the payment infrastructure. The receipt to the customer would be a video presentation with local storage capability, a printed form or a periodic descriptive statement showing payment identification, name of beneficiary, and the amount debited for each payment.

The three American examples of funds transfer services between banks are:

The *bank wire*—a method of communicating the information necessary to transfer funds among correspondent banks.

The *Federal Reserve wire network (Fedwire)*—also used for funds transfer, it also has a settlement facility for immediate debiting and crediting of accounts.

CHIPS—an automated clearinghouse system among New York City banks, in which a clearing account is also debited or credited, as opposed to simply transferring information.

Leading American banks to which I have spoken over the last three years, indeed, regret that SWIFT did not tie up to one of these networks, to gain from their experience.

Of the total transactions taking place in the American economy each year (estimated at between $200 and $300 billion), only fifteen to twenty billion are executed at the request of corporations, including banks. But the significance of corporate payments is clear when reference is made in terms of dollars. Of the estimated fourteen trillion dollars transferred annually in the American economy, eleven trillion dollars are corporate transfers. Because of the large amounts involved, many bank-to-bank transfers are being handled in an automated environment.

Not much electronic communication takes place, however, between a bank and its corporate customer. Most transactions done today come from the corporation via mail or telephone. In different terms, although magnetic tape interface services are being offered, by and large, any electronic communication between corporations and banks is done via common carriers. No wonder more important banks are anxious to create more convenient payment facilities for their customers that will capture a large share of the corporate payment flow. All this can be summed up in one message: "There is a need for money transfer systems." Computer experience, however, also suggests the wisdom of thorough study and preparation. Investment in the development of new money-transfer systems in banks should be based on:

(A) The requirements of corporate and correspondent bank customers for improved transfer services.

(B) A desire to reduce money-transfer-processing errors and to improve money-position managment within a bank.

Automated money-transfer systems benefit the customer by accelerating accounts-receivable collection and by providing better information and control of the scheduling and timing of disbursements. Although the banking industry as a whole may lose cash balances as a result of these new systems, individual banks can capture a greater share of corporate payment flow and the benefits from fees and related service offerings.

In larger American banks, several departments initiate or receive hundreds of funds transfers per hour, making it impossible to manually maintain same-day information on the money position of the bank or its major customers. Yet it is necessary to provide same-day information to support money management. The need for effective, internal, information systems becomes more urgent as more corporate customers become accustomed to making funds transfers late in the day.

Just because an international, or even interbank, computer network is difficult to get off the ground, some major banks are developing what is becoming known as an "internal switch," a computerized system that supports money transfer within a bank and which can be extended to connect the corporate customer with the same system. One example of the internal switch is *Citiswitch*.

CASH MANAGEMENT

To work constructively, we must have a concrete image of the specific operation to which we address our efforts. Bankers, however, do not have a clear idea of the basic economics of automated funds transfers, of the risks and opportunities. Clearly, guarantees, regulation, security, and experimentation with new services cost money. Until the image of bank operations is upgraded, avant-garde financial institutions face the formidable task of discussing cause and effect with other banks that subscribe to the nothing-or-only approach. Still, sufficient evidence exists to suggest the deep change now under way in banking.

Take cash-mangement techniques as an example of how change affects the corporate services offered by financial institutions, albeit at a slow pace. The discipline itself was first subjected to automation only some three decades ago, when RCA introduced the lockbox. Rather than having remittances mailed to corporate headquarters or a designated branch, RCA asked customers to forward remittances to post office boxes in each region, where they were emptied several times a day by local banks. Basically, this first optimization of cash-management techniques was no more than an extension of current practices. Lockboxes were strategically placed near the mailing addresses of major customer bases. The results were positive, and this simple, pioneering plan was widely adopted as corporations realized that "mail float" could be reduced while remittance crediting was speeded up. Corporate treasurers reaped the benefit.

The next milestone was the time-consuming determination of where and how much cash was actually available for use, either for short-term investments or to reduce borrowing. This brought the computer into the cash-management equation, and computer-based solutions transformed the management of cash into a discipline in its own right. Computers and communications became prerequisites to sophisticated cash management.

Progress has, of course, been made step by step. An early step in the growth of computerized banking services was a one-dimensional system for daily cash management. The most common example is daily balance reporting for corporations, so they know exactly how much cash is on hand at a given time. Adding such planning tools as target-compensation and -execution capabilities for funds transfers, we reach such advanced levels of computerized cash management as EFT. The benefits are obvious. We have already discussed them: improved speed, increased accuracy, and reduced administrative costs for corporate treasury operations. This level of service is being offered by a growing number of money-center banks. The next step expands the dimension of time to cover not only daily functions but short-term funds management as well. Automating such operations as portfolio managment, cash forecasting, and the management of securities movement, a move is made toward a broader, better integrated, more responsive financial management-information system.

Benefits are improved, including return on assets through higher portfolio yield and the use of forecasts. This level of service is presently offered by only a handful of large banks. While it may be meet all the needs for large corporations, the technology is available, and it can lead to an era of greatly expanded electronic money mangement.

A SERVICE TO CORPORATE SUBSCRIBERS

A specific example should be helpful. Chemical Bank, a poineer in corporate EFT services, had one of the first computerized cash-management offerings, which is still billed as one of the most sophisticated in operation. Corporate subscribers to *ChemLink* instruct their banks across the country to phone in deposit information to the time-sharing computer in Rockville, Maryland any time after the close of a business day. Early the next morning, the corporate treasurer can turn to a terminal and in a moment get a printout detailing the status of his bank's balances.

This way, corporate treasures can make documented investment decisions early in the day—while the yields in the New York money market are still at their peak. Furthermore, should they find they are in deficit at one location, they can wire money from a location where there is a surplus. The transfer is accomplished in seconds. The top benefit ChemLink and similar computerized services offer to corporate treasurers is time.

In addition to balance-reporting and money transfers, ChemLink provides an array of other corporate services, including balance histories, target balance projections, short-term rate reports, and foreign exchange reports. The system is modularly structured so that corporate clients can pick and choose from the modules only those services they desire or can pay for. And the cost is quite reasonable. The average corporate ChemLink customer pays about $350 a month, which includes balance and transaction reporting as well as a significant number of wire transfers during the month. (The bank charges fourteen dollars for the first Chemical account and $1.50 for each account thereafter; balance-reporting costs fourteen dollars per month, and wire transfers are performed free of charge in an effort to encourage volume usage. Depository transfer functions, including the reporting and preparation of the check, are billed at sixty-five cents per item, a charge that is levied monthly. Foreign exchange reporting costs a flat $100 per month.)

I should add that this is not the only money-management system in operation. Since 1974, Morgan Guaranty has been operating a highly successful system worldwide called *Mars*. Data transport is assured by satellites, and the corporate treasurer can be sure to find all financial data concerning the financial operations of his firm both by topology and in a consolidated statement.

Chemical is presently soliciting the participation of other large banks in what it calls BankLink, a nationwide corporate information network. Management says it already has commitments from several regional banks around the country to join the program. The idea is that a standardized nationwide information system can reduce the reporting burden of banks that presently complain of the plethora of requests from corporations to report data to a growing number of different bank computer services, none of which uses the same reporting format. A nationawide system could broaden the availability of these systems to more corporate customers, providing a bank-operated offering that would ensure uniform services for a golden horde of corporate transactions eventually to be wired into the bank-corporate computer channel. Securities movement and foreign exchange purchases and sales are other possibilities.

The trend rather than the single application, the interest of the whole banking industry rather than that of the single institution, are what is important. The same is true of several important advances made over the past decade, for instance, automating and broadening the quotation and tracing phases of securities operations. Such systems as computerized stock-quotation terminals, the consolidation of off-board market data in major stock exchange quotation tapes, and the more recent development of electronic quotation and execution systems for government and federal agency securities are among the major developments that have occurred in the trading area.

Within the broad, money-management perspective affecting financial institutions and their clients, important changes have taken place in regard to the custody and settlement of many types of equity and debt securities. The paper crunch that threatened to close down stock brokerage offices and bank transfer offices, and which nearly paralyzed stock trading in the late 1960s, has been effectively dealt with through depository systems in which paper securities are immobilized and transfers of interests are effected by bookkeeping entries, without the need to move underlying certificates. Computers have been crucial in these improvements.

THE NEXT VITAL STEP: PROFITABILITY

The next step will, most likely, be a nationwide link owned and operated by banks for their corporate relationships, which could free corporations from the need to develop their own systems. The benefits of a generalized solution will be standardization in reporting formats, as well as the consolidation of information. The nationwide network could also satisfy corporate, geographic banking needs.

Indirect benefits could eventually prove as instrumental as direct benefits. The latter will make both corporations and banks appreciate that information flow is almost as important as money flow. The timeliness of information has been the very reason corporations asked banks to provide cash concentration and disbursement services in the first place. When better, more accurate information can help corporations reduce their excess balances or working capital borrowings (or increase the yield of short-term portfolio), then we are talking about P+L, something every corporate treasurer understands.

Whether we talk of retail banking—and hence, of the Debit card—or of corporate banking and cash management, EFT is a form of cashless society. The fine tuning is coming. The "cashless," "checkless," "less-check" society has been discussed for more than a decade, and serious questions about the willingness of consumers to give up a known system, with its benefits, for a new system have been raised. As the benefits become apparent, though, first corporate and then retail banking will be on the move.

Let nobody think of "free" services. The electronic funds transfer system clearly will call for massive investment in development and implication. The success of such investment will require a high volume of activity to take advantage of economies of scale. It also has the prerequisite of a well-directed, determined, steady effort. To date, EFT has progressed at a slow pace, with a high cost. The reason lies in the difficulty of defining control, regulation, opportunity, and responsibility. Technologically, direct electronic credit-and-debit transfers could have been accomplished by 1975. Given the present rate of progress, however, common use of electronic debit and credit systems might not occur unitl 1985 or later.

Viewdata depends on copyrights, fees, regulation, and the able solution to consumer-education problems. We have to realize that we are at least one, and maybe two, design cycles away from anything that could be called full-scale national EFT. What does this mean? Let's take an example. Many bank demand deposit accounts (DDA) systems designed in 1960 were redesigned and reprogrammed by 1967. And many present POS, or online ATM, systems designed in 1975–76 will have been redone by 1982 to incorporate those security techniques and service options that time and experience have shown desirable. Further, many bankers seem to lack an image of how necessary live experimentation is to determining which services are vital and justifiable. Such tests are just as important as opening new accounts. Electronic debit-and-credit operations cannot be widely accepted until people develop an image of themselves as having a computer-run account at a financial institution.

The image of the check as a small transaction device has to be changed. Changing the consumer's image of when and how to use cash and checks is a formidable task. The same can be said of the banker's image and, by extension, of the bank's own internal procedural approaches.

PROCEDURAL CHANGE: A BASIC PREREQUISITE

If banking procedures do not change, electronics can do little or nothing to improve the timeliness or the efficiency of services. Several years after SWIFT began operation, I made a financial transfer from an Italian to a French bank—both SWIFT members. Although the money transfer was electronic, the situation at the money's destination was hopeless. The DDAs were still manually kept by "positionists," with the result that seven days were lost writing in the credit.

Management should have known that, unless the entire network is studied, it is useless to accelerate—at one end or in between—and leave the rest at the paleolithic stage. The old delay will remain invariable, because no chain is better than its weakest link. In this particular case, automation should focus on client position, client order, international transfer, registering, check-up, and the position update with regard to money exchange and client balances.

GYRO SYSTEMS AND MISSING PROFITS

The use of Fedwire to transfer United States Air Force payroll credits was a forerunner of Social Security and other government transfers now being made in the United States. Whether civilian or military, electronic gyro systems have to ensure that payment data is readily available for proving or checking transactions and for correcting erroneous transactions.

In the case of authorization listings, telephone processing, and automated teller machines, payment data for each payment transaction handled are stored in the computer system for initiation by the appropriate method. An electronic debit is generated to charge the client's account for the amount of the payments initiated. For partial payments, customers would note on each individual bill the partial amount to be paid, so that the total amount to be paid for all bills could be correlated with the customers authorization.

These are projected as labor-saving applications that promise a good future for EFT equipment. And yet, such equipment has been slow in getting hold of the market; development has been slow, with the ACH the most visible system. The threat of "missing profits" has given some managers second thoughts. A sense of action was generated because of the experiment known as "Hinky-Dinky," named for a supermarket chain bold enough to allow a savings and loan institution to place a branch in the store. A number of events soon followed this initial Hinky-Dinky incursion. A congressional commission was created to investigate the new concept of EFT, and financial institutions began to install hundreds of pieces of equipment.

In a short time, 6,000 ATMs were in use. Check-guarantee programs sprang up. Telephone bill-paying was launched. The ACH movement, however, plodded along. With the first flush of euphoria from those who labored to bring these events into being, there were also great projections of profit. The most confusing aspect of the case concerned the fact that after all the activity, there were still no profits. With the exception of "Honest Face," the volume of transactions was lower than projected. The Honest Face program had many customers—but no profits—because the service was given away. If it had not been, there would have been no customers and thus no profits; it came to the same thing.

In many American banks, particularly, medium-sized ones, management, upon hearing the facts, requested a rundown on what had been done to generate profits. Bank-marketing experts came up with several answers. One expert contemptuously reported that an examination of actual costs had been discouraged rather than encouraged. Another said that the "miracle combination" had not yet been found. There was no tie-in of services that would create a rush to the bank.

A third expert stated that the entire EFT business would be chaotic until all the legal hurdles were cleared away. But the experts agreed on one point: "EFT services are just *not* being marketed correctly. Bankers have not learned how to market these products. All we have to do is to get out there and sell!"

Major banks with finances strong enough to withstand the subsidies EFT called for took a different approach. They directed their staff to gather all the NCEFT reports, ACH reports, and other documentation about EFT. Once that information was available, thorough studies were undertaken, which revealed that (1) EFT is a way, and a very efficient one, to overcome legal restrictions, and (2) that investigators had been focusing on the wrong issues.

The entire effort had focused on profits—and short-term ones at that. Contrary to conventional wisdom, the real issue is long-term trends and the needed understructure for reasons of preparedness. The real issue was missed. Something was being searched for that did not exist.

NYACH

It would be useful to take a snapshot view of the New York Automated Clearing House (NYACH). As one of the two privately operated ACHs (the other is in Chicago), it could hold some of the clues to the ultimate trend of the ACH movement. Like many ACHs, NYACH was organized in 1975 to offer member institutions automated sorting, distribution, and clearing of preauthorized electronic debits and credits. The purpose was to effect savings for members (and eventually consumers) by eliminating several manual steps in the current payment process.

Consumers would benefit by reducing their need for stamps and time required to pay bills and a lowering of bank service charges. Corporations would be able to reduce their lockbox charges and eliminate the need to reconcile paper checks. NYACH was open to all depository financial institutions from the first day of operation. (According to the officers of NYACH, it was the first ACH in the country to open its doors to all comers.) Two benefits were derived from open membership. First, a maximum number of end points were created, giving potential users an incentive to participate. Second, no energy was wasted worrying about how to keep other institutions out. All thoughts were directed toward making the ideas work.

To carry through the theme of ease of use, NYACH created operating rules and procedures that ensure the greatest possible participation. Costs are low—one-half cent for the receiving bank and one-half cent for the originating bank. To increase security, NYACH requires prenegotiations on every new credit to the system, not just the first time a company uses the system. Nowhere, however, is the effort to make NYACH viable for its members more evident than in the schedule.

The NYACH transmission network will allow members to communicate over data lines. As with Citinet (see Chapter 14), this capability eliminates the need to move tapes around by truck. A major payment development will be to have corporations identify, on their billing documents, the routing and transit number of the particular bank offering the concentration service and the corporation's own demand-deposit account.

Services such as pay by phone presently have the ability to generate data in standard format, although the concentration banking data is not usually furnished except for the largest local billers. Those corporations not identifying their concentration account data would probably continue to receive listings of payments, and the transfer of payment funds would be delayed by the physical preparation and receipt of a check.

NYACH is an interesting experiment in what can be done when members decide to provide services in a fashion designed to accommodate their customers rather than themselves. Their freedom from the constraints of the Federal Reserve has contributed to the innovation evident in NYACH's services, schedules, and procedures. It is a model that could be followed elsewhere. Ultimately, volume will depend on the ability to move data nationwide efficiently, reliably, and on time. But many procedural questions remain to be resolved.

The Wheels of Change

11

It is proper to look into the future of information systems for financial institutions by outlining the criteria that leading banks brought forward in the course of the working meetings I held during the last two years with their management and computer specialists. Because of the fast-moving technology to which I have referred so often, such criteria, while not unchangeable, do constitute a reference point.

The information systems that currently support stations in excess of 1,000 in number are no longer uncommon. Networks of more than 2,000 terminals are in existence. The Bank of America plans for 12,000 terminals online through distributed intelligence. Yet most such networks are still centralized. Few portend the future large-scale online capabilities to be based on local information resources.

The lack of specialists, and the aforementioned slow movement in computer and communications skills acquired by management, are two reasons; insensibility by the providers of products and facilities is another. Computer manufacturers and telephone companies will eventually understand that organizational change at the client company involves much pain and preparation on their part as well as on the part of their clients. The carriers and providers of electronic gear will some day appreciate the need to improve the quality of their products and services, not only in terms of hardware and software but also in regard to the advice they provide to users. Typically, so far, this advice has been too raw, with many banks training manufacturers' specialists, rather than the other way around.

Needed recommendations regarding the improvement of communications networks include dependable line control, efficient line-switching, rapid substitution of a faulty line by another one to reduce the effect of breakdown, automatic line restart, and realtime controllers able to switch one or more telephone lines dynamically. Knowhow in the efficient use of the gear provided by computer manufacturers centers on interactive capabilities, online-oriented operating systems, reliability insurance, online-maintenance capability, computer-assisted programming aids, and the sharing of technology's advances with users (more facilities, lower costs). The manufacturer will need to develop greater sensitivity to diagnostics and service. Generally, the time needed to locate hardware, software, and communications faults is too long and offers too little.

In their own field of activity, even the more rigid, larger banks may abandon their current level of resistance and accommodate change. They may profit from the advancement of technology, convert to exception reporting, and begin to offer new, profit-making, computer-based services.

JOB REQUIREMENTS

Workstation equipment, POS, ATMs, teller terminals, and inquiry stations will be part of the bank of the future. To be effective, they must be chosen on their merits. Several current designs are not highly functional. Particular attention will need to be paid to workloads and job requirements. A bank's online operations change composition in the course of a working day. Present tuning methods are not suitable for varying load levels or job composition.

These and similar developments call for a cooperative effort. Many banks have indicated that they are willing to enter into a continuous dialog with telephone company authorities to help direct research and development toward useful goals. It's an opportunity manufacturers of advanced technology should not miss. Nevertheless, users in general, and banks in particular, aim to improve their relations with the manufacturers of computer and terminal gear—not the reverse. They consider their demands realistic and obtainable. These include: engineering support, maintenance, testing, diagnostic facilities, better software delivery, and improvement in machine operation.

Because changes in procedures, systems, and software and hardware have a long lead time, in most cases good management practice requires that the newsystem coexist with the old. This is a fundamental procedure, followed in other times by using parallel processing. But it also means that double standards must be maintained, sometimes for years. Double standards pose both operational problems and have a great impact on integrity. The question of data integrity is vital for banks. Manufacturers have not yet attacked this subject in an able manner, and neither have the users.

Bankers, for their part, must finally start applying, with information systems, similar criteria to the profit-and-loss and risk-versus-business opportunity thinking they use in dealing with clients. This has not been the case in the past where computers and communications confronted banking management with a curious mix of mysticism and comprehension.

Let's take an example. Computer costs, as stated, have been dropping steadily during the last ten years. This cost reduction has left communications costs an increasingly expensive component. Yet most banks stick to the old, technically inefficient and financially unadvisable star-type networks. Is this merely resistance to change? Or is it failure to calculate computer profit and loss? Becuase the bank pays for the calls, it is wise to reduce the number of calls, to address local databases and use the network capability for exceptions. Statistics from farsighted banks that applied distributed information systems (DIS) demonstrate that only two to eight percent of all questions posed at the branch office concern another DB than that residing at the BO itself. Why not leave the balance (ninety-two to ninety-eight percent of transaction-handling) at the local level—answerable through the local DB?

A DISTRIBUTED ENVIRONMENT

For the coming years, the hottest issue among the leading financial institutions of the world will center on the choice of machines for databasing and for interactive applications. In all likelihood, microcomputers will be the winners in terms of cost effectiveness.

Grosch's law, stated in 1953, says that the power of a computer system increases as the square of its price. This is a good reason for centralizing processing power. Grosch's law was widely accepted until the early 1970s. With the advent of minicomputers and, more recently, microcomputers, the law seems to have been broken. Why? Many information scientists think the reason is simply that Grosch's law never reflected any inherent economy of scale in the manufacturing process but merely the pricing policy of manufacturers—a policy that mini- and microcomputer suppliers declined to follow. Another hypothesis is that certain factors obscure the simple relationship between price and power that Grosch predicted—for instance, the supervisory overhead of an operating system.

It may be coincidental, but the minicomputer appeared at approximately the same time as the general-purpose operating system in mainframes. At the beginning, the market for minicomputers grew slowly. Then it was found that the supervisory overhead of an operating system does not grow linearly, with the complexity of the applications environment, but exponentially, instead. Increasing the power of a processor did not give the user a proportional increase in throughput, but roughly the square root of the improvement in processor power. In other words, not only did the cost benefit predicted by Grosch disappear because of software overhead, but the law itself was inverted.

Experiments which I conducted with leading financial institutions demonstrate that the multiprogramming/multiprocessing environment consumes so much power that it slows down turnaround to the point where it is fifty percent more effective to use, say, two programs on a large machine rather than two large machines working together and, between them, running eight procedures. Indeed, the experiment results shown in Table 11.1 document that, for exactly the same type of large-scale equipment, two jobs run more effectively (at .6 hour per job on the average) than do eight multiprocessed jobs (at .9 hour per job on the average). This was further documented when the transfer of a given job stream from a dual processor to a simple processor actually reduced the processing time rather than increased it (Figure 11.1).

It is reasonable to conclude that Grosch's law applies only to the raw power of the hardware. Once the hardware reaches a certain scope and complexity, the supervisory functions needed to multiplex the system's resouces consume so much of these resources that they leave little of the system's original power for performing production tasks.

As more banks realize the implications of this technical fact, the already noticeable trend toward distributed systems will be acceler-

Table 11.1

TIME EVALUATION (IN HOURS) BILLING (INCLUDING "IOU")

EQUIPMENT	ELAPSED H.	ELAPSED %	CPU H.	CPU %	I/O H.	I/O %
DUAL-PROCESSOR; *DAY SHIFT* 8 JOBS + TS	3.88	100	0.60	100	1.41	100
MONO-PROCESSOR; *DAY SHIFT* 1 JOB + TDS	2.34	60	0.54	90	1.26	89
MONO-PROCESSOR; *DAY SHIFT* 1 JOB + TDS	2.40	62	0.53	88	1.21	86
MONO-PROCESSOR: NIGHT SHIFT 1 JOB	1.30	33.5	0.51	85	1.22	87

NEARLY EQUAL

ated. How *distributed* can systems get, though? Does the word have different meanings in different circumstances? Or is there a conceptual unity underlying all seemingly disparate ideas?

Let's look at the fundamentals. The phrases *distributed systems* and *distributed processing* are used interchangeably in the current literature to denote various types of computer systems, ranging from microcomputer to minicomputer and multicomputer networks. At the most basic level, a distributed system may be a dedicated microprocessor designed to serve a given function. At the next level, a distributed system may consist of interconnected dedicated functional microprocessors. Still higher up, it may consist of multiple programmable microcomputers cooperating on a single job or on different jobs. At the highest level, a distributed system may contain general-purpose minicomputers as processing elements, which are physically separated but which communicate through data links and protocols. Change the minis to mainframes, and you change the complexity of the jobs being handled; functionalize the minis, and you obtain database and communications specializations.

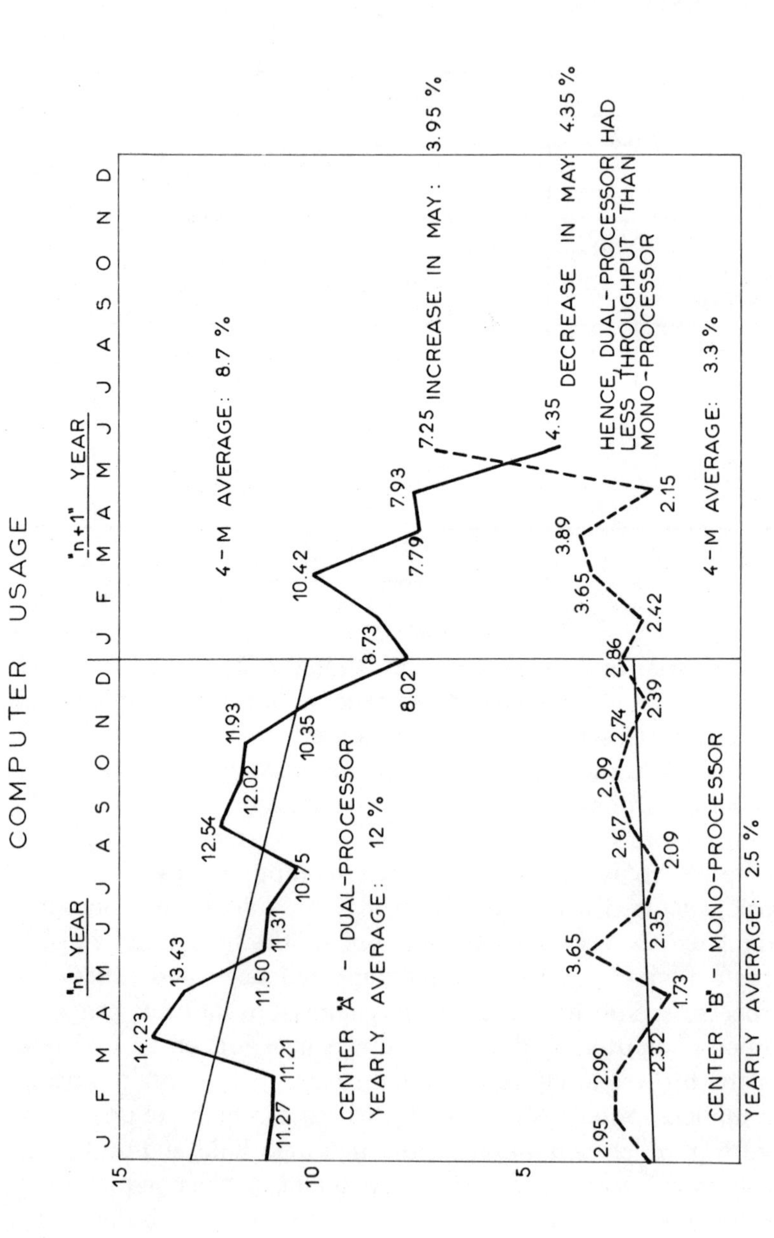
COMPUTER USAGE
"n" YEAR
"n+1" YEAR
J F M A M J J A S O N D
J F M A M J J A S O N D
15
10
5
11.27
11.21
14.23
13.43
11.50
11.31
10.75
12.54
12.02
11.93
10.35
8.02
8.73
10.42
7.79
7.93
7.25
4.35
2.95
2.99
2.32
1.73
3.65
2.35
2.09
2.67
2.99
2.74
2.39
2.86
2.42
3.65
3.89
2.15
CENTER 'A' - DUAL-PROCESSOR
YEARLY AVERAGE: 12 %
4-M AVERAGE: 8.7 %
INCREASE IN MAY: 3.95 %
DECREASE IN MAY: 4.35 %
HENCE, DUAL-PROCESSOR HAD LESS THROUGHPUT THAN MONO-PROCESSOR
CENTER 'B' - MONO-PROCESSOR
YEARLY AVERAGE: 2.5 %
4-M AVERAGE: 3.3 %

FIGURE 11.1

Functionalization is no mere academic interest. Basic economic factors underlie it. Heavy supervisory overhead and other drawbacks of a centralized mainframe facility were accepted in the past because of the high cost of processing power. The overriding necessity was to keep expensive computer systems fully utilized. Now the economics have changed.

FLEXIBILITY, RELIABILITY, AND SERVICEABILITY

The semiconductor revolution makes the distributed option not only feasible but economically attractive. Dispersing the processing power into a number of minicomputers and microcomputers, each dedicated to a specific function, helps structural implementation, flexibility, reliability, and serviceability.

The impact of the resulting ease in structural implementation is felt both in the starting up of new applications and in the simplicity with which system modifications can be achieved. The distributed-design approach permits expansion of the system over a wide range of sizes tailored to an application stream. It also allows *failsoft* (graceful) degradation when modules are not in use (time out).

Flexibility and simplicity in making changes enhance reconfigurability. In a distributed system, it is possible to restructure the processing, databasing, and datacom elements to suit applications on a dynamic basis. Reconfiguration of the modules is also needed to tailor the system to the applications environment as it evolves, as well as when system modules fail. It is evident, therefore, that the distributed-design approach provides a more reliable system, one that is continuously available despite component failures. It is possible to detect and isolate faulty modules without disturbing the entire system.

Restructuring to suit an applications environment also means that we can: increase throughput by expoiting parallelism, decrease response time by replacing certain software functions with firmware, and tailor the system to the actual requirements of a specific application. Such flexibility allows a distributed system to be used efficiently in a wide range of applications. Because a distributed system is modular, we can provide growth potential without redesigning the entire system. This helps reduce development time when a new system must be built to meet a changed applications environment. Furthermore, because multiprogramming is excluded, programs can be written faster and more easily.

Another benefit of the distributed approach is a reduction in communication costs. Economies are achieved by the reduced amount of traffic necessary when remote sites have their own local intelligent subsystems, by the ability to store until later (when cheaper, off-peak transmission costs are in effect) data that does not need to be sent immediately, and by the reduced cost of physical cabling necessary to interconnect local and remote sites. Greater functionality is available with the distributed approach because of the advent of low-cost microprocessors and of architecture design.

The first major challenge is knowhow. Ninety percent of the analysts and programmers today are from the mainframe era, and the majority are still oriented toward mainframes. It will take courage to turn this orientation toward micro- and minisystems. Such a reorientation will require much training, coaching, and practical examples.

The second major challenge is also a result of past practices. One obstacle to the widespread acceptance of distributed systems is the present heavy investment in conventional computer technology—particularly in applications software. A change away from maxicomputer usage will necessarily involve the development of *new* libraries. This is costly and it cannot be done overnight. Such references suggest that mainframes will survive as long as existing software continues to be operative.

THE SEARCH FOR COST EFFICIENCY

The Swedish PK Banken offer a precise example of how open-eyed management attacks head-on the technical requirements of the job. Figure 11.2 exemplifies this solution, on an interactive, DIS-supported basis. At location "I," the DTE poses questions A and B. Question A is answered locally. Question B is channeled, say, to a global directory.

Figure 11.3 repeats the basic design principles and presents the whole organization, including central functions, interactive minicomputer approaches, installations at the BO, cash dispenser units, data-collection centers, and the PTT terminals system for remote batch. Notice should be taken of the wide range of activities supported by the minicomputer at each branch office. This explains the size of disc memory at the DIS level. The median memory size is 150 megabytes. As a median, it is impressive. "By doubling the DB size, cost increases only fifteen percent for reason of mass economy," said the PK Banker

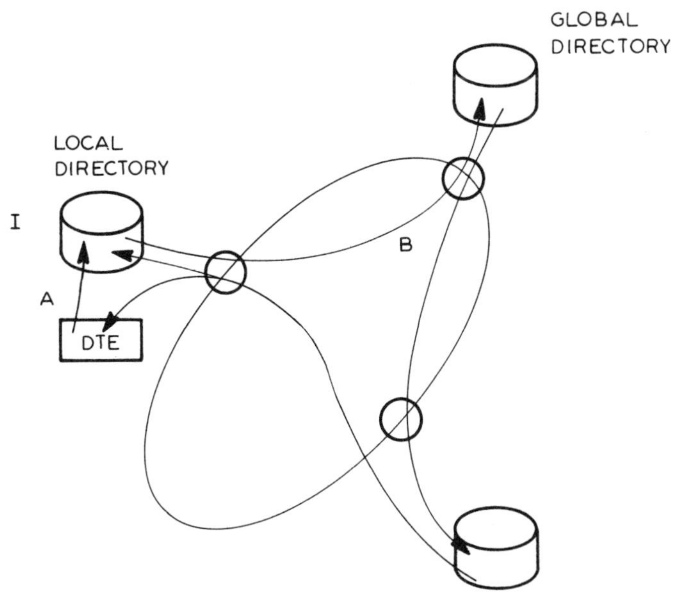

SIMULTANEOUS ACCESS MECHANISM

FIGURE 11.2

executive who was in charge. Thus the decision was made to implement more and more local functions, to take advantage of what technology had to offer. Figure 11.4 identifies the projected yearly workload of the distributed information system. Notice that:

—Central processor-based transactions will be *less than* ten percent of all transactions involving the BO.

—Ninety percent will be handled at the BO minicomputer.

—Data collection, a major problem, will be concentrated in seven centers, then exploded and expedited to 140 BOs.

To bring data collection into the proper perspective, it should be pointed out that the load comes from the postal service, especially those services that are not online to computer resources. Some 450 PTT offices are in this category (Figure 11.5), and another 800 have terminals.

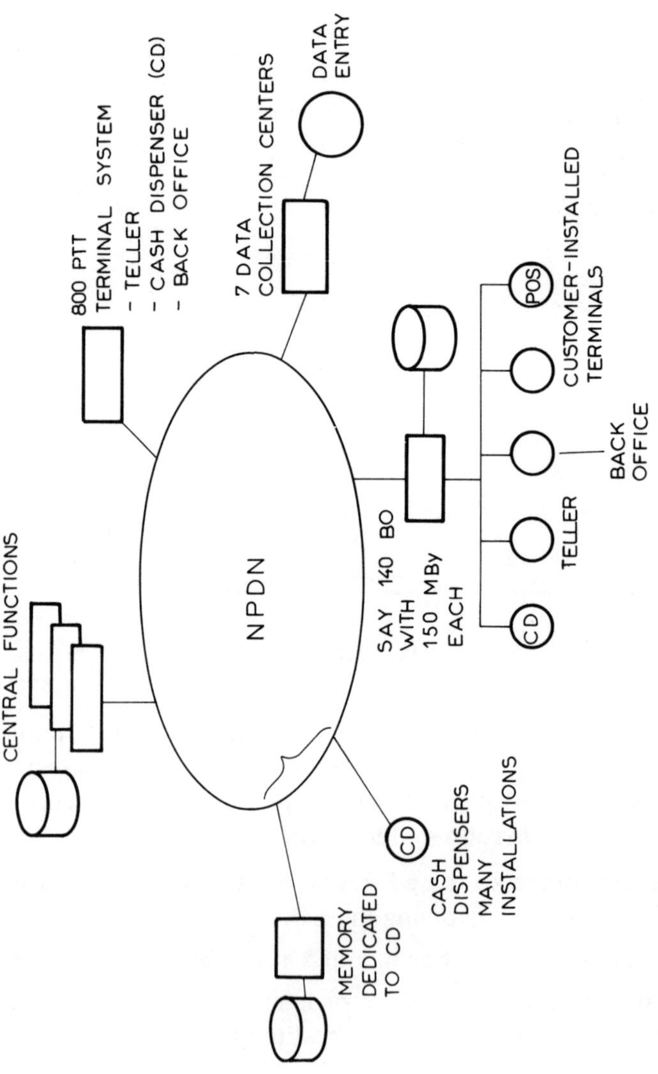
CENTRAL FUNCTIONS
800 PTT
TERMINAL SYSTEM
- TELLER
- CASH DISPENSER (CD)
- BACK OFFICE
7 DATA
COLLECTION CENTERS
DATA
ENTRY
NPDN
SAY 140 BO
WITH
150 MBy
EACH
CD
TELLER
BACK
OFFICE
POS
CUSTOMER-INSTALLED
TERMINALS
CD
CASH
DISPENSERS
MANY
INSTALLATIONS
MEMORY
DEDICATED
TO CD

FIGURE 11.3

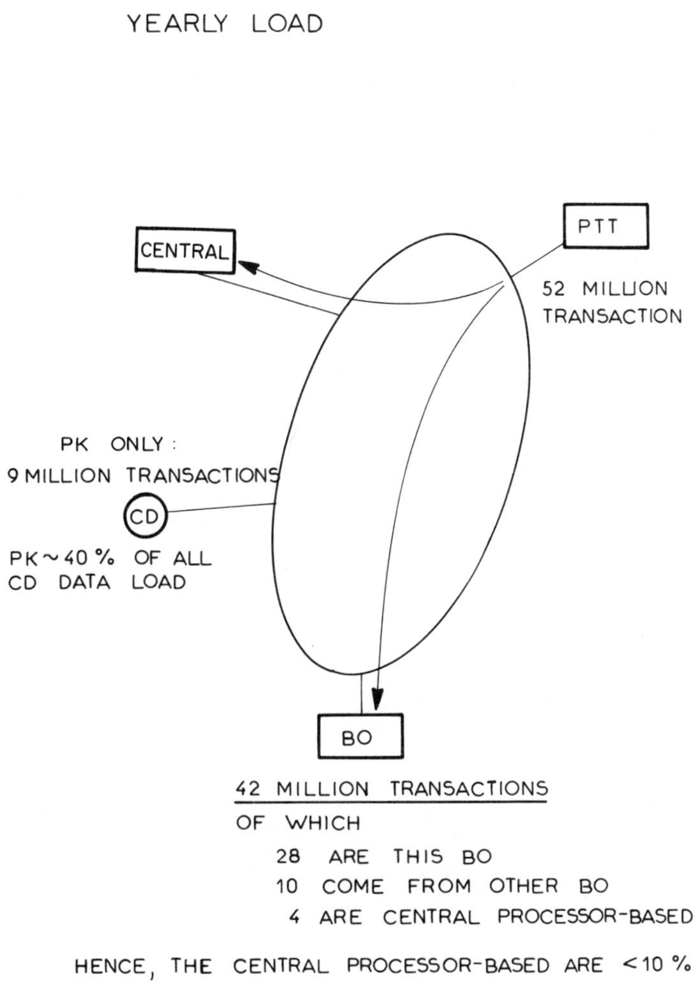
YEARLY LOAD
PTT
CENTRAL
52 MILLION
TRANSACTION
PK ONLY :
9 MILLION TRANSACTIONS
CD
PK ~ 40 % OF ALL
CD DATA LOAD
BO
42 MILLION TRANSACTIONS
OF WHICH
28 ARE THIS BO
10 COME FROM OTHER BO
4 ARE CENTRAL PROCESSOR-BASED
HENCE, THE CENTRAL PROCESSOR-BASED ARE <10 %

FIGURE 11.4

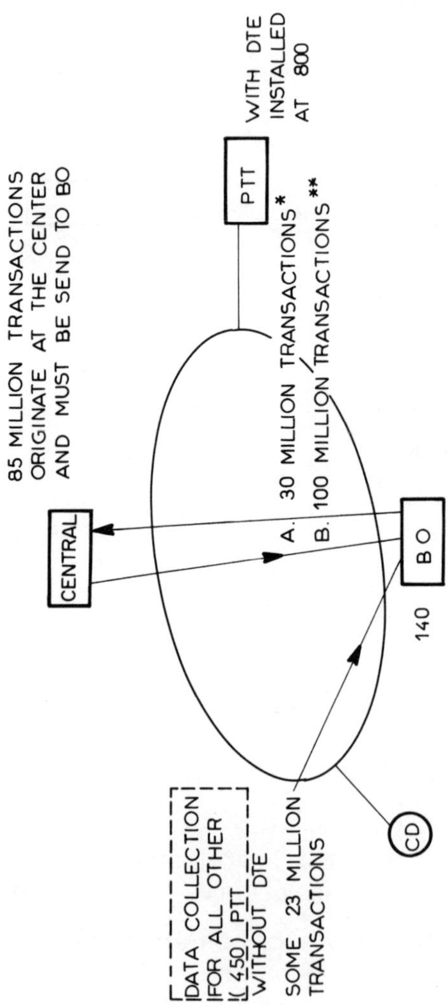

* IF ONLY SUMS ARE SEND - PROJECTS SUGGEST THIS

** IF ALL TRANSACTIONS ARE SEND

FIGURE 11.5

Regarding BO-to-center transmission requirements, the data load is estimated at thirty million transactions if only summaries are forwarded, or 100 million transactions per year if details are also communicated. The forwarding of summaries assumes the establishment of local intelligence, in which details are stored and retrieved when necessary. This is the solution proposed by specialists in making management decisions. Note also that a detailed system analysis made by PK Banken documented, to the maximum extent possible, the need for data collection at the point of origin.

Another problem to be brought into perspective is that of handling radically changing data. By the mid-1980s, data-entry equipment, along with unit records and printers, will either disappear or lose its identity. Before 1985, key-to-tape disc and stand-alone data entry will be replaced by multi-function terminals and POS. More than ninety-five percent of data will be captured at point of sales and point of transaction.

New systems will be designed that include the normal cycle of source-data treatment, but without creation of intermediate paper documents. New systems will also be designed for bank teller stations, the production floor, sales locations, in general, and for all point-of-origin transactions.

MESSAGE SYSTEMS

Communication within the banking environment will be by exchange of messages. The same is true of databasing. A *message* is a file in a database that is accessible by another terminal device, such as a video, printer, or computer. The end user or a program stores the message in memory and processes it as requested.

During the 1980s computer-based message systems will have as great an impact as the telephone had over the past century on the way business is done. Conversation to this new way of banking, however, will require much preparation. Merely because files stored in memory and messages transmitted over wires are the same thing, we cannot any longer afford to store in memory useless data, as we have done in the past. A serious study is necessary, which should lead to a three-part classification.

1. Vital data—should be available immediately at all times. The data should be selected so as to ensure that skeleton opera-

tions chosen for their ability to guarantee performance of vital functions of the bank will be performed at all times, even when most of the available information resources are down.

2. Necessary data—management should have data whose transmission can be delayed without interrupting operations.
3. Merely useful data—which, if need be, can be skipped.

Barclay's is an example of a successful study along these lines. The bank's management defined four levels of information-system functioning: full, or 100 percent; reduced to seventy-five percent; further reduced to fifty percent; and skeleton operations, at twenty-five percent of capacity. Each level of reduction in data processing was studied for its effect on operations, and action plans were established to ensure that basic functions were not affected. The importance of preparatory steps is evident.

Similar studies done by American banks, which introduced COM (computer output to microform) reporting in an effort to reduce the sprawling paperwork giant, provided useful statistics on effectively handling paperwork without losing valuable information. One study classified all paper records into three categories: (1) those of a legal character, which had to be kept on paper for x number of years (they were converted to microfiche for day-to-day use, and actual paper records were stored outside New York City); (2) useful records that had to remain operational, but which could be converted easily to computer-processed microforms without having to print on paper again; and (3) largely redundant and useless paper records, which were eliminated. Joint committees of operational people and legal experts were organized to sort out the mass of documents. Not surprisingly, categories 1, 2, and 3 represented, respectively, five, twenty, and seventy-five percent.

On the basis of such evidence, we might add that a fourth category looms on the horizon, that of unnecessary daya, which, indeed, contains most of the records. Eventually, these records will also be broken down into two classes, those of data to be put on microforms (or other low-cost devices) and those to be thrown away.

It is redundant to underline the need for the planning and timing of all vital data. The same is true of procedures for recovery. A carefully worked-out plan for *after-catastrophe* conditions is part of this approach. Because the change in message flows will be strange to many bankers, it is wise to emphasize the need for drills. I hope I have made the point (which many systems studies in financial institutions have overlooked) that an online, computer-based environment with interactive capabilities desperately needs an understructure. Unless this understructure is provided, the system will limp along through delusion to failure.

Application studies are necessary, inasmuch as applications are the primary factor in determining the type of data communications system needed. Currently, the prominent message-type application areas are credit inquiry, banking operations, EFT, electronic mail, and stockbrokerage information. The proper applications environment, however, is a superstructure that rests on a solid understructure, and that is procedural. (To complete this list of transaction applications that, in one way or another, may interest banks, let me add travel reservations and scheduling, point-of-sales data collection, sales-order entry and inquiry, inventory control and reordering, production monitoring and control, general accounting and finance, management information and decision-support systems, document cataloguing and retrieval, hospital and other medical information, and the home.

What does the bank want to get out of a message-intensive environment? It wants to simplify clearing—by sending only via electronic media the data to be transmitted and by keeping all paper where it has been deposited. This means that the BO, where checks are deposited, must input the amount, date of issue, date of transcription, bank and BO number, and provide a time stamp and running number, as a basis of retrieval, for handling and in case questions are posed by clients.

This is an example of applications. The understructure will include: communications capabilities (for transmission, switching, storage, and forwarding); terminal equipment and networks capable of ensuring device independence, interactivity, software services, journaling, statistics, and billing; access methods (transport control and session and presentation control); and other properties encountered in data exchange, such as interfaces and concentrators.

Communications media must be tailored to the job. The software impact in communications must be studied (it will exceed that of computers). Also, the resources to be provided by a computer system must be examined on a functional basis instead of in terms of hardware, software, and firmware, independent of each other. The essence of this approach is its emphasis on function. For the banker, the important aspects of any system or system component is *what* the system does, not *how* it does it. The chief executive must ask: "What is the top subject of the early 1980s?" The answer is simple: a long, hard look into the future, at both client-oriented and management-intensive tasks. Only such an approach can ensure that the institution will remain competitive.

Networks, Computers, and Communications

12

I have said that the computer system must be viewed as an integral part of personal and professional life. The same is true of communications and networks. The telephone lies at the center of all banking business activity today, yet in my siminars for the banking industry, I see many executives surprised to learn that within a few years, the telephone as we know it today will be virtually obsolete—and redundant.

Telecommunications is merging with computing to such an extent that it will soon be impossible to distinguish one from the other. An impressive number of sophisticated word processors, wideband channels, satellites and waveguides, intelligent terminals, fast facsimile units, and other communications devices undreamed of as recently as five years ago are now available. Not everything is, of course, streamlined. Many of the devices I have mentioned use incompatible designs and protocols. Even where the same protocol is used, data structures, codes, and so on often differ. Most disquieting is that the difference starts at the source.

In banking, the source is the word processor. In their fundamentals, intelligent word processors can be divided into mini- and microcomputer-based word processors, which include devices able to handle, at the top level, electronic mail, and at the bottom, simple text-processing; and maxicomputer-based processors for publications management. The latter category is appropriate for users with heavy publication requirements. Boeing's 747 flight document manual, for instance, contains 750,000 pages! In the typical financial institution, however, particularly at branch offices, the equipment needed for office automation will depend on microprocessors.

Automated branch offices will not be able to exploit their potential if their equipment is not linked through an information utility that allows data to flow freely from one end to the other, to serve the needs of both management and clients. This is the role of the network. As network experience among financial institutions has grown, so has the range of use to which networks are put.

COMPUTER-BASED ACTIVITIES

Advances in technology are creating a business environment that fosters a management information system which goes beyond the old boundaries of data-processing. In the United States today, financial institutions have more computers outside the data-processing department than inside it. It is, therefore, important for management to recognize what is happening and to direct the ensuing evolution.

Word-processing and telecommunications are part of the communications-information network. Why not align them functionally with other related elements, to integrate information management with printing, mail, memos, and, generally, with document distribution? In Europe, Japan, and the United States, leading banks are actively involved in building computer networks linking their computer-based distributed-information systems. Typically, these networks include a packet switching discipline*; a transport protocol at the user level; applications-oriented solutions for virtual terminals, file transfer, and so on; and a certain amount of interactivity between the terminals and the applications they handle.

Two financial institutions have been the avant-garde in this effort, the Bank of America and Citibank; but others have followed quickly. The aim of these early accomplishments is twofold: first, to develop a general concept, using increasing levels of terminal functionality; and second, to analyze fundamental protocol mechanisms (i.e., negotiations, data-exchange synchronization, and attention-handling). As always, pioneering efforts undercut the general building effort. Although a variety of approaches have been tested—and, in some cases, adopted—the fundamental issue remains: the interaction between remote processes communicating via the computer network and the challenges posed by the dialog between people and information.

---

*See Chorafas, *Computer Networks for Distributed Information Systems* (Princeton: Petrocelli Books, 1980), and Chorafas, *Data Communications for Distributed Information Systems* (Princeton: Petrocelli Books, 1980).

Technically, this boils down to interaction between an operator at a terminal and an application available in a connected host. In terms of systems architecture and design technology, however, it involves much more. Unlike batch-type applications, where the user feels remote or even alien to the data-processing job, online, interactive solutions intimately involve the user. Thus we have the severe, penetrating problem of user education.

Within the computer and communications networks that are coming, there will be three levels of understanding: (1) the ultimate user; (2) the level pertinent to the system architect, who must build up the applications spectrum; and (3) the network architect's domain, which will involve all sorts of challenges. Not only should the network architect project the grand design of the computer and communications, he should study databases and data exchange mechanisms as well. The architect should choose protocols, apply standards, and provide gateways and interfaces. Gateways and interfaces are necessary because of the well-known heterogeneity that characterizes the terminal market. Heterogeneity raises a compatibility problem, however. Interfacing has to be performed whenever a new type of terminal is to gain access to an application already running on computer-based equipment.

It should be added that, within the framework of the conventional starlike systems made of local and remote terminals connected to a single host, it is conceivable, though not necessarily rational, that a different adaption for each type of terminal connected to the system should be kept performing. But this is unthinkable with the modern, horizontal-type networks dedicated to the transport function, as opposed to the old transport-and-processing mix.

Although the mechanics of building gateways and interfaces are of no particular concern to the senior management of a bank (they can easily delegate the job to specialists), management must become involved in the overall design. Typically this concerns:

productivity measure (to be enhanced by such solutions as teleconferencing);

document distribution (for reduced costs and greater efficiency); and

the *integration of data, voice, and image* in one network.

The integration of voice and data, for example, can be of major importance in terms of overall cost reduction in computers and communications. Both managerial and technical problems are associated with real-time communication over switched networks. Protocols are needed to support this application. Other issues must be accounted for, too, such as data control, device independence, and performance monitoring.

Major managerial problems must also be faced. These are related to objectives. Many leading banks have put, as the overall management objective, economies of scale through the creation of a single facility (Figure 12.1). The following guidelines can be helpful in establishing management objectives in the domain of the new information services. The guidelines should:

(1) be achievable through planned effort

(2) be directly related to the problem requiring solution

(3) be feasible and acceptable in relation to the cost involved

(4) be compatible with other objectives, providing a unified basis for planning

(5) be measurable and concrete

(6) represent a decision, not an alternative

(7) fit into the hierarchical structure of the organization.

In setting objectives, we automatically imply that choices must be made; for choices to be made, alternatives must be developed. At the senior management level of decision-making, choices will involve both the overall structure of the document-voice-data system to be developed and the question of "make or buy." Should the bank build its own private network, or should it adopt an existing one that is already in operation?

Experience at the Bank of America

The larger financial institutions have opted for private networks. As data-communications utilities develop from coast-to-coast, the smaller banks will undoubtedly use public networks, an option made more attractive by the offering of such privacy-protection mechanisms as closed user groups. Yet, since nobody wants to reinvent the wheel, early experiences are—and will remain—the guide.

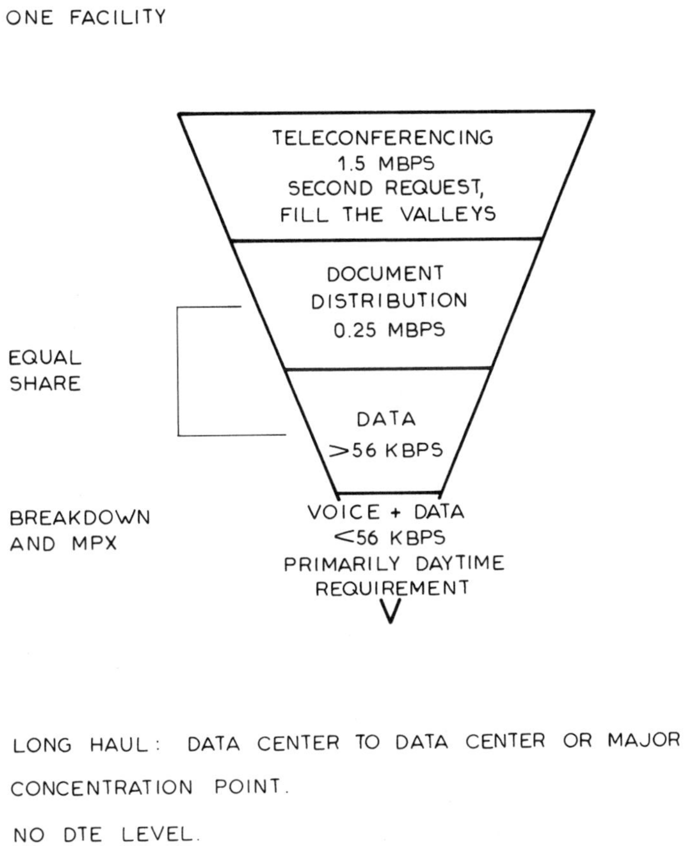

FIGURE 12.1

The network the Bank of America projected in the early 1970s had many aspects which have become standard in a distributed information system. We can distinguish three levels of increasing sophistication:

- distributed data processing
- distributed databases
- a network architecture supporting peer-to-peer communications.

Bank of America went straight ahead to meet the requirements of the second level. This was a giant step at the time when it was undertaken. While the minicomputer environment I will describe in the following pages is now aging (and may soon become obsolete) it remains an excellent reference in the evolution, design, and implementation of computer-based systems among forward looking financial institutions.

The Bank of America started out with minicomputers running segmented databases, installed at such central locations as Los Angeles and San Francisco. The modules working on demand deposit accounts are allocated to branch offices by topology; others are dedicated to a single application, and serve all branch offices. (In Bank of America jargon, a module comprises four "minis", two for frontending and two for rearending, taken two by two for reliability.)

The handling of loans and of the BankAmericard is an example of the functional allocation of some modules. Whether functionally or topologically oriented, modules can be either centralized or distributed. The centralization of the resource, even if only temporary, does not result in the savings in communications costs that decentralization offers. But the Bank of America thought the cost reductions realized at the central location merit adoption of this solution.

Before deciding to switch to minicomputers, management examined the alternatives. Four maxicomputers (two to be installed at each central site), with all the storage and peripherals they needed, ended up costing millions of dollars for hardware alone. The same service, rendered by minicomputers, with a higher level of reliability, resulted in a saving of up to sixty percent, according to some sources. There was also a significant reduction in the cost of software.

"The applications are easier and faster when our staff is familiar with data communications and [when it] works on small-scale systems," said a senior executive during a meeting I had with him. Although the Bank of America did not elaborate on the software savings, there is reason to believe that they exceed those of hardware. Some organizations have given me startling statistics. Ciment Lafarge, for one, impled that, job for job, the software costs of a minicomputer are lower by eighty to eighty-six percent than those of a maxicomputer—depending on the job. A New York bank official stated that software written for minicomputers typically takes up to six months, in contrast to two to two-and-a-half years for the same job programmed to run on mainframes. Even if one allows for a much lower ratio—say sixty percent, one comparable to that of hardware—the cost reduction is impressive enough to justify keeping it in mind. And the resulting minicomputer software is also more robust.

Such news has had an impact on the banking industry. "We must change our equipment and improve our methods," was a concept once advanced by avant-garde bankers. Today, it is spreading like a bushfire. Cost-consciousness is the driving force. In many banks, DP costs are increasing at the rate of eighteen percent a year, while the volume of data-handling grows at a rate of only six percent.

There are operational reasons as well. *Every time we move paper, we lose data (including increasing the probability of error); hence, we lose money*. This is the prevailing view of management. Furthermore, the online solutions now projected, with hundreds or thousands of terminals, cannot be handled efficiently through centralized solutions.

It is interesting, therefore, to review the way in which the Bank of America pursued the distributed environment applications since the early 1970s. Three problem areas must be treated to an extent sufficient to assure understanding of the application. These areas are: module, network, and database.

The structure of the module reflects the frontend and rearend approaches. Frontend machines to handle communications and relieve the central processor from that part of the load were developed in the mid-1960s as a result of experiments at Dartmouth College. Some computer manufacturers adopted them outright; yet it took nearly a decade for frontend machines to gain general acceptance. The network is the transparent mechanism. Its object is to carry data from any data-terminating equipment (DTE) to other such equipment. A DTE can be a computer, a terminal, or a device running the database. The database is the bank's storehouse of information. All computer-run data kept in the computer system can be addressed by authorized computer specialists and bank executives for updating, interrogating, or general data-handling.

Data are a corporate resource, and they have been declared such by several forward-thinking organizations. In time, they will become even more vital to financial institutions.

MODULES AND DATABASES

A module comprises four minicomputers (Figure 12.2): two message-handler (frontend) processors and two database-management (rearend) units. Each pair of machines, one frontend machine and one rearend

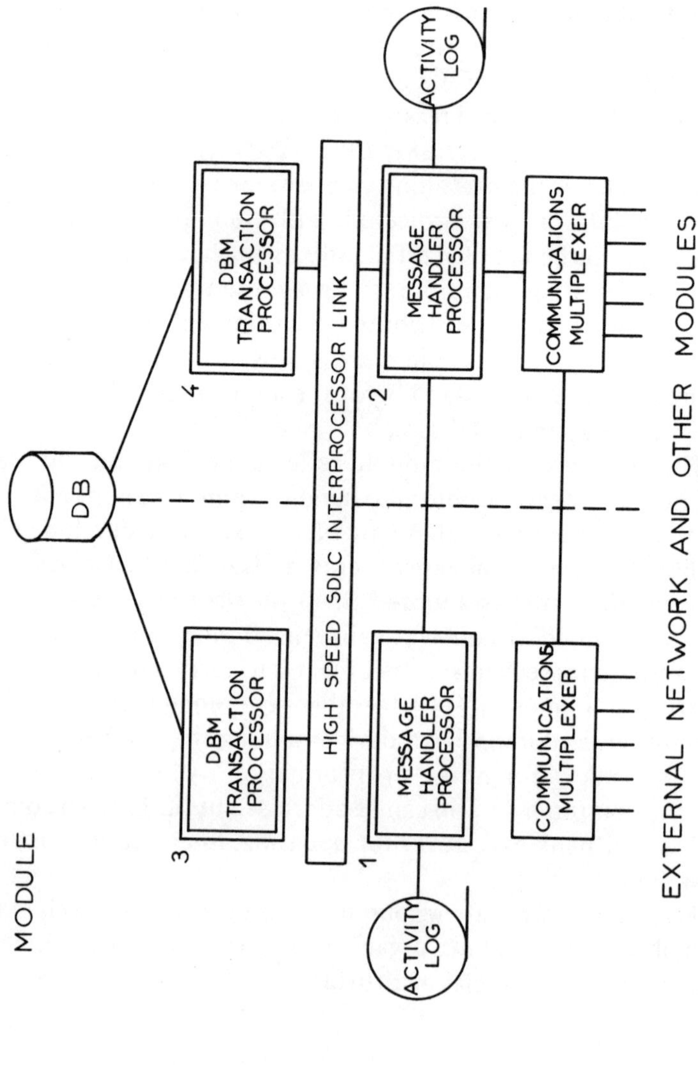
MODULE
DB
3
DBM TRANSACTION PROCESSOR
4
DBM TRANSACTION PROCESSOR
HIGH SPEED SDLC INTERPROCESSOR LINK
1
MESSAGE HANDLER PROCESSOR
2
MESSAGE HANDLER PROCESSOR
ACTIVITY LOG
ACTIVITY LOG
COMMUNICATIONS MULTIPLEXER
COMMUNICATIONS MULTIPLEXER
EXTERNAL NETWORK AND OTHER MODULES

FIGURE 12.2

machine, can handle all the message traffic allocated to the module. Thus significant reliability is assured—from concept to application. Note that this duplication of resources is far more efficient than having two mainframes back to back. The failure of one maxicomputer could reduce, in a stroke, fifty percent of the available resources.

Frontend and rearend processors communicate through a high-speed interprocessor link working on a modified SDLC, packet-switching principle and using microcomputers to ensure up to 2.5 MBPS (10^6 bits per second = 1 MBPS). A future version, though, may involve fiber-optic links and reach 40 MBPS. Each module has a portion of the database. Access to the DB is localized; the data is put where it is used. The network is the link. Figure 12.3 shows the interconnection of the modules with the two locations. All communications are packet-switching (SDLC). In the overall design, the architects took care to reduce the amount of data transfers among modules. Routing from module to module is assured by the network operations center (NOC), which keeps statistics on traffic flow, for example, on routing, monitoring, and operations. It also establishes when traffic becomes excessive. Also, every other module has a table that helps maintain the routing path. A transaction enters through the external network. The first operation at the frontend (the message-handler) is an error check. Logging is done on tape and disc. If the processor fails, its functions are switched automatically to the other message-handler in the module. Hence, there is no interruption of normal operations.

Designers have made sure that the frontend throughput is greater than that of the rearend machines. This is a necessity, because incoming messages may, where applicable, be switched to *other* modules. They also provide balance between communications and databasing. Figure 12.4 presents the database management (DBM) system. All transactions are recorded on a mass-storage device. Memo posting is used in the present version, but the *primary* files are kept offline on the maxicomputer. Should a discrepancy arise, these files will be used to tune the online files. This approach, incidentally, has not been widely accepted. The counterargument is that the preferred location of the primary file is the branch office, where it permits handling all local traffic locally. This approach has been tried in the United States by Citibank, in France by Parisbas, in Sweden by PK Banken, and in Italy by IBI—and it works.

The choice of the proper location of primary files is fairly complex, since it involves organization, systems, database administration,

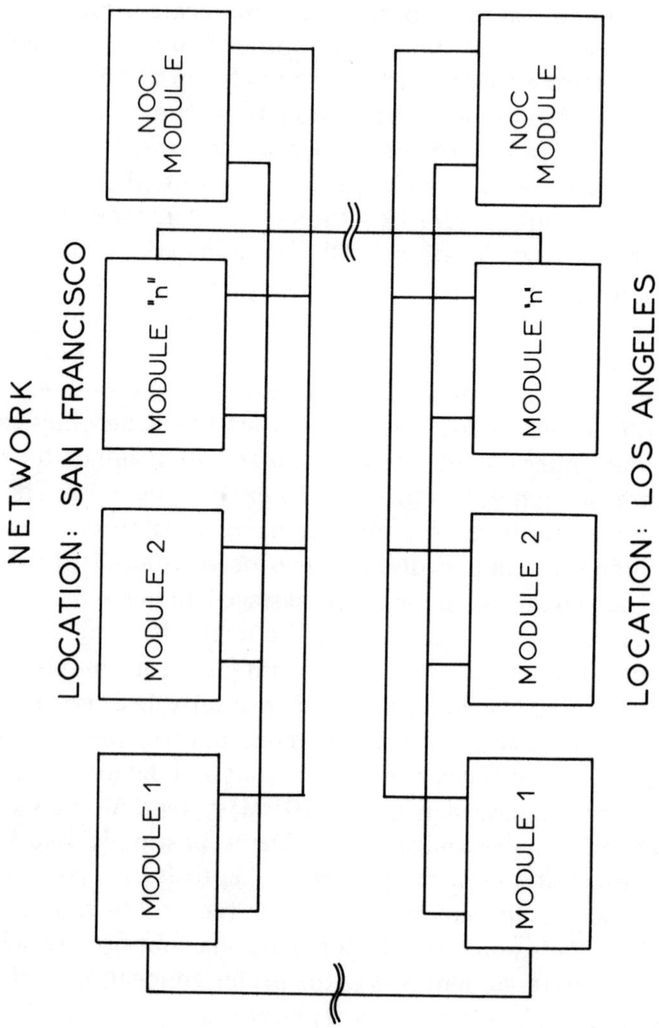
NETWORK
LOCATION: SAN FRANCISCO
MODULE 1
MODULE 2
MODULE "n"
NOC MODULE
LOCATION: LOS ANGELES
MODULE 1
MODULE 2
MODULE 'n'
NOC MODULE

FIGURE 12.3

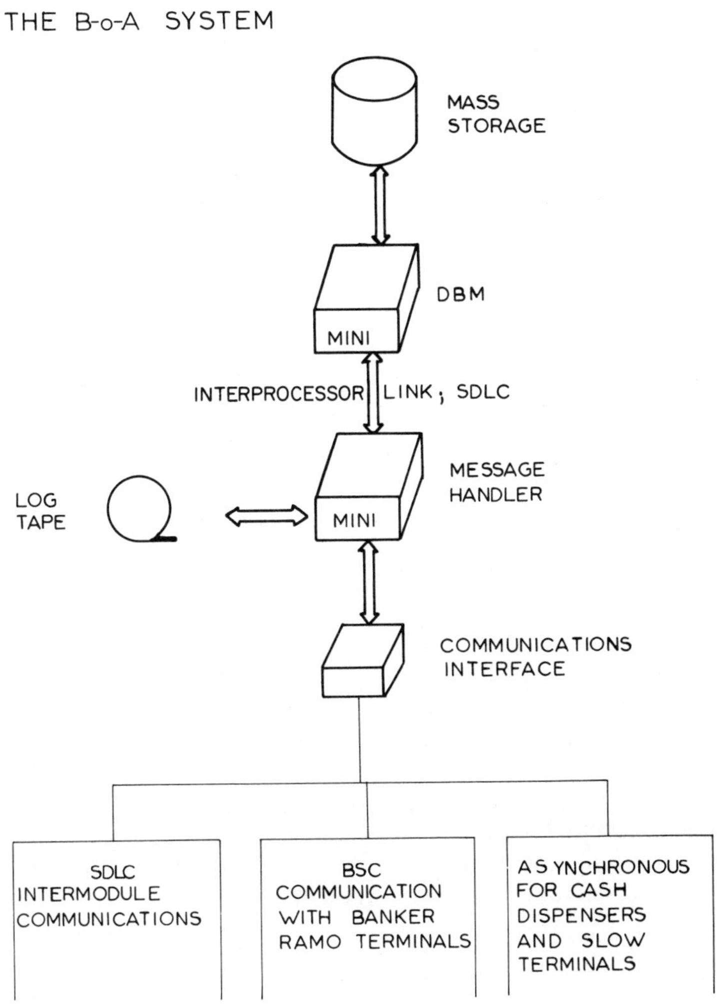
THE B-o-A SYSTEM
MASS STORAGE
DBM
MINI
INTERPROCESSOR LINK ; SDLC
MESSAGE HANDLER
LOG TAPE
MINI
COMMUNICATIONS INTERFACE
SDLC INTERMODULE COMMUNICATIONS
BSC COMMUNICATION WITH BANKER RAMO TERMINALS
ASYNCHRONOUS FOR CASH DISPENSERS AND SLOW TERMINALS

FIGURE 12.4

coordination, security, and control. An analysis of banking activity has shown that about eighty percent of all processing of enquiries and customer-account updates is related to accounts that exist in the same geographic area—for instance, that of a branch office. Consequently, if customer account files are in the same geographic area, about eighty percent of the traffic on the network could be reduced, thus reducing the teleprocessing load. Then it is necessary to return only about twenty percent of the transactions to the central side.

Arguments exist, of course, for both procedures. One solution for a centralized master file has the advantage of simplicity in tuning the database, as well as better coordination. In other words, that way, the unique, integrated image of a distributed database can be better protected and deviations corrected faster and more effectively.

Finally, notice that, although communications within the module are packet-switching, communications can be transmitted from the environment to the module: *SDLC* (intermodule), *BSC* (communications with teller terminals), and *asynchronous* (for cash dispensers and elder terminals). This flexibility is a significant asset in Bank of America's solution.

WHAT IS THE BENEFIT?

Although nodes are usually linked through communications hookups, the database is distributed throughout the network. It is stored, updated, and accessed with minimal redundancy. The Bank of America solution also provides, through NOC, a distributed operation system for maintaining order and logical flow among the units without often replicating the same commands.

Distributed processing and distributed databases make possible the removal of data-handling from the category of *overhead*. Management can then allocate costs to various departments, permiting remote locations to operate even if several of the network's centers are down. This is achieved by dissociating data-processing from data transfer. In addition, traditional DP applications have been administrative in nature, but new applications have had an impact on business at their very heart. Nearly every department of a financial institution depends to some degree on computers, and when these machines breakdown, users cannot do their work. Information-system specialists have to bear the brunt. As a result, they must broaden the scope of their interest beyond its traditional width. Information-systems managers long have shouldered the responsibility for the overall productivity of information systems. Now they must spend more time planning and coordinating computers and communications systems and in becoming the guardians of all the institution's communications and database assets.

Distributed-information systems give rise to the need for increased standardization of communications protocols, forcing both designers and users to cut the cost of moving data. Basic economics must be weighed carefully. As the Bank of America aptly put it, most applications, when compared with the alternatives, are more economical in the distributed mode.

These, in short, are the reasons for the impact we can expect from a distributed environment. By gaining firsthand contact with computers as tools in everyday use, we will generate more ideas. The result may well be a significant change in the way we do business, as well as in our personal lives.

What did the Bank of America gain from DIS? The answer given by management is increased availability; improved throughput; better response; lower investment; modularity and, therefore, expandability; terminal independence; application transparency; easier applications implementation; more effective people-machine communication; and better maintenance. At the Bank of America, the system was created to allow dynamic growth beyond the initial design parameters. A significant feature is the emphasis on DIS as a way to achieve this growth. Clearly, if the system becomes overloaded, it is a simple matter to provide further equipment for handling the terminal population. In the event of frontend congestion, this equipment could be processor- or channel-bound. One way of significantly reducing the processor load would be to off-load polling and terminal-handling onto local concentrators. Solutions could then be found more easily and implemented in a more flexible manner than if a maxicomputer alternative were used.

Needless to say, centralized approaches would not have worked in any reasonable sense with over 1,000 online terminals. What is often overlooked is the far more limited capability of the machine-within-the-machine, the special software needed to handle the enormous amount of traffic. To their credit, Bank of America's specialists never lost sight of this fact. Indeed, operating system (OS) capabilities for mainframes can make a large computer seem smaller than a small one—even if the former costs forty times as much. Some minicomputers today have operating systems capable of handling up to fifty messages per second, whereas some maxicomputers have not yet reached the ten-to-twelve-messages-per-second ceiling. (The maxioperating system takes more time to keep itself running than to handle a user's job. Complexity introduces complexity in a big way, and not merely incrementally.)

OTHER LESSONS

Bank of America's experience highlights another lesson. It is good advice for both management and the analyst starting a DIS project: *Do not use the minicomputer as a maxicomputer.* Forget what you learned about multiprogramming; it will not be helpful.

The Bank of America started the DIS project by bringing together its best analysts and programmers. It sounded logical. But then it was found that they did too good a job in designing and building the minicomputer software. When this lesson had been learned, the programs had to be redone. The second time around, for each the specialists allowed only *one* functional area, across the topology of the applications spectrum.

Functional specialization requires communications, and data communications tend to complicate the problems involved. Don't make them more complex by adding to the problem at the beginning. This vital one-to-one rule must be observed. There is another rule: *assign to each computer only one segment of the database*. Don't give access to one computer throughout the range of files treated in the network. (Recall that in the Bank of America's approach, the reason a DB segment is handled by two minis is reliability.)

This rule not only takes into account systems requirements, but it enhances security and privacy as well. Databases today include much valuable information—in fact, all the files of a company. Terminals access the database through frontend computers. Controls for entry are made there. Once past this checkpoint, an intruder can obtain access to classified data. (Memory-protection algorithms are sometimes used, but they are not failure-free either.) In fact, we are now better able to implement security and protection than we are to solve other problems. Truly distributed databases, with consistent image requirements, pose a simultaneous-update challenge which, in the current state of the art, we do not know how to handle efficiently.

The known approaches to simultaneous update do not guarantee security, although they do tend to generate a sufficient amount of traffic to bring the network to saturation. The challenges encountered in implementing distributed databases and the operating systems needed to support them led the Bank of America to organize on a dual basis. Two projects are now proceeding in parallel: networking (whose mission is to deliver messages), and DDB (with all the local functions necessary). Work in progress and the solutions advanced for efficient software support in solving the problems of distributed databases will have an impact on the banking industry in years to come.

We do know how to optimize local functions, however. The mini used as a message-handler should also perform data-entry clearance. With the falling cost of hardware, we can afford to specialize machines and, just as important, match them to the job to be done. Remember: labor costs, particularly those of specialized labor, are high, whereas machine costs are relatively low. Save the first, pay the second.

Our main concern in using minicomputers should be to match computer power to the problem. Look at the problem to know what it is. As cannot be repeated too often, *do not enlarge the problem to match computer power*. Generally, this is the trap users fall into. That is how, and why, maxicomputers became bigger and bigger: machines outgrew applications, then the applications grew to match the capacity of the machines—but machine capacity grew faster, and we had to move quickly just to keep up in the race for gigantism.

The Bank of America (and other financial institutions with similar experience) had other remarks to make about mini- and maxicomputers. With multiprogramming, you lose efficiency. It takes a lot of code; in its *housekeeping*, the machine eats up power and time just switching between functions. Finally, software needed for the centralized solutions is becoming more expensive.

Then there is the subject of data transfer. Traditionally, communications aspects evolve along equipment lines. This was wrong. Guidelines must be functional. We started out by attaching a cable to input devices, and soon someone realized that input devices could be placed within a few hundred feet of the terminal. Then the cost of a single line per terminal became too expensive, so multidrop lines were invented. Slowly, communication costs came to represent a major portion of the cost of the system. Finally, we had to hire specialists for every branch of activity, and other specialists to coordinate the work done by the other specialists. Personnel costs soared as management, confronted with requests for more people, lacked a basis for making decisions. The question became: "Would you like to leave the very expensive central computers underutilized?" This is a false problem. Now we must rethink our systems, take advantage of the edge of technology, review, reevaluate, and revamp.

Procedural Prerequisites- The Right Way

13

In studying two of the earliest distributed-information systems (Citibank and the Bank of America), the casual observer might think there is a fundamental difference between the solutions they offer. The careful observer, however, will find that any difference that exists is a superficial one, that, in reality, the two solutions converge.

Those financial institutions that present examples of the application of DIS have already gone through the three phases a computer and communications facility desires; philosophize, plan, and organize—prerequisites for making the system work, and work well. Characteristically, and despite what opposed theorists say, none of these organizations has discarded the maxicomputer (and the investment in software that it represents); nor have these organizations changed overnight the way their information systems work. Instead, the change has been gradual. It will take a number of years to fulfill all of its aims. During transition, there is no archtype. Each organization has followed its own plan. If, however, we synthesize the steps taken, we could approximate the following general outline:

1. There is a central background, usually the aging maxicomputer with its applications software. With few exceptions, this machine works offline, batch.
2. Before implementing a successfully distributed-information system, financial organizations have gone through detailed procedural studies of all aspects of banking operations, points at which the impact of computers and communications can be felt.
3. The local minicomputer operating on a decentralized basis manages the local terminals and has database capacity.

4. The terminals themselves are connected to decentralized computer resources, with significant cost economy in comunications.
5. A network is implemented to ensure that data transport is cost-effective.

All this is intended to yield a system that functions according to a design philosophy. Well-established procedures, perspectives, and goals in communications are required. A number of minicomputer systems installed on the periphery do not make a network, but notice that Citibank (the main theme of this chapter) has a privately owned, Arpanetlike data communications system.

Although the leading organizations follow, and rightly so, a step-by-step approach, we should not underestimate the effort that has been invested in making the system work. There is still much to be done, both at the procedural and at the systems level, before tangible results are obtained. In the procedural steps to be reflected in the system design, it must be guaranteed that the distributed information system will correspond to the hierarchical information structure of the enterprise, including general management, regional management, and branch offices. This is much more important and delicate with DIS than it ever was with centralized batch-processing.

With DIS, the people at each site are responsible for systems functions, from data entry to interactive terminals, soft-copy reports, and handling files. The purpose of distributed systems is to achieve increased individual productivity. This can be accomplished only if the task is treated as a management problem and not as a strictly technological one. To demonstrate how this concept is put into action, we shall study the Citibank example.

THE CITIBANK PERSPECTIVE

The first minicomputer was installed in 1968. Within a year, the second had been installed, and then the third, for timesharing, a management information system application. In 1973 another minicomputer was installed for management. Then, when the designers had become familiar with DIS, and had tested the system, the pace accelerated. In 1975-76, two more minis were installed. A Citibank vice-president told me, in a personal interview in New York in April 1976: "The H 6000 installed last January at our center on Long Island is the last 'dinosaur' to enter . . . this bank." By this time, Citibank had about sixty-four minicomputers in various applications.

Results were satisfactory. With centralized, maxicomputer-type processing, for instance, some 25,000 complaints had been received in one year (1974). The service responsible was snowed under, a situation that would continue as long as centralized batch-processing continued. At that time, the computer department employed more than 450 programmers and analysts, but only one or two projects were coming through each year, and even those were behind schedule. With DIS, the system group was sharply reduced; the minicomputer software was simplified, and there was a switch to packages and the farming out of the surplus programming work.

Citibank has consistently followed a package-and-purchase policy. The International Banking Group purchases ninety percent of the software it needs. To paraphrase management, this policy is deliberate. Its purpose is to reduce costs. The internal staff of analysts and programmers has been reduced to a skeleton staff of well-trained specialists capable of attacking systems design, not programming problems. Systems analysis that got lost among the complexities (and perplexities) of multiprogramming is now directed at fundamental areas, where the design effort actually belongs. That is how studies of the need for accessibility and direct control over computer resources has led to the work-station concept and to machines dedicated to specific applications. The guiding concept has been that of a single minicomputer capable of handling all the applications in a given customer group. This may be by geography or by product line, or it may be client-oriented, as is sometimes the case when a major customer account justifies the use of a minicomputer. Running the General Motors account, for example, might take an entire machine.

We need hardly emphasize the preparation this new philosophy calls for. Account integration would be impossible without having thought through what it takes to proceed with integration *after* DIS has been implemented. Account numbers must be redesigned, databases pruned, algorithms developed. The entire approach to account-handling must be changed from top to bottom.

The goal—and one that is feasible—is efficiency. At Citibank, it has been attained by implementing work stations. This minicomputer-based concept integrates product-processing disciplines with a market-driven customer orientation. Citibank has demonstrated, properly, that it is capable of producing quality financial services by making use of advanced technologies while, at the same time, providing job enhancement for the bank's employees. Defying conventional productivity principles, which rely on specialization by function, the work station integrates all transaction-processing activities in a single job. This goal has long been the aim in data handling. I never tire, though, of repeating that it takes a great deal of preparation to attain one's objectives.

As implemented at the Citibank sites, an individual (the work-station professional) is responsible for delivering a service, from the time the order for it is received until the service has been provided. All necessary information for processing transactions and answering customer inquiries is available to the professional at the work station's minicomputer terminal. Usually, a customer's problem can be handled directly by the person who originally processed the transaction. The resulting economy is obvious to anyone who has studied manual data-handling in a financial institution and who has tried to apply cost-control measures.

THE PROCEDURAL STUDY

Each banking operation, whether it is a letter of credit or a transfer of funds, is broken down by Citibank's analysts into independent units. Each unit is assigned to an appropriate segment of the marketplace, where it is defined—domestically, according to industry, and overseas, according to geography. A procedural study is done before an application is assigned to a work station. This enables a service to be tailored to the needs of a particular customer group. The functions are automated, and data is fed electronically to decentralized minicomputers, which then process the transaction and otherwise handle the customer account group.

By following the principles of DIS, we can record and investigate everything required by a transaction at one work station. The staff are trained to perform all tasks for the identified customer segment. The reduction of paperwork and the elimination of many processing steps allow work-station professionals to devote more time to their main function—improving customer services. We should also note that the bank employees are happy with the solution. A job diagnostic survey provided documentation for this statement. (I had a similar, positive reaction with a DIS experiment conducted in mid-1977 at the Bologna branch office of the Instituto Bancario Italiano.)

Citibank employees who went from a functional environment to one involving a multiplicity of tasks were evaluated to determine whether there were any differences in the motivating potential of the new positions. In the new letter-of-credit work station, the motivating potential score of a position was 134.9. This compared favorably with 47.9 for the same person previously working in a corresponding position. Ten reasons were identified by management to explain why it chose a decentralized approach in 1974. By now, these reasons have been validated. They are:

1. Minicomputers are a totally *new* design philosophy.
2. Time scales can be reduced significantly in terms of software development and hardware delivery. Often a six-month period is sufficient.
3. Minisystems can be developed quickly, but a centralized solution requires a longer time scale and more resources.
4. Minicomputers should be used for online applications, not for batching; decentralization serves the purpose.
5. Decentralization puts the operation and control of the information system in the hands of the banker, or user.
6. Getting people to agree on the nature and functions of a centralized system had often been a frustrating experience. With decentralization, the complexity of the task is reduced, while the package policy ensures that the user can't ask for exotic software.
7. With centralization, decisions were very slow; with decentralization, the process is accelerated. There is a direct line. Also, the charges are easier to implement.
8. Placing the system in the hands of the user ensures that the user will be responsible for the system.
9. Because of decentralization and the use of minicomputers, the size of applications must be limited to handling one per machine. This, in turn, makes it easier to purchase the necessary software.

10. Decentralized, independent applications simplify maintenance.

Not only is the policy followed in purchasing packages, but also in hiring a software-maintenance service. Typically, a $60,000 package costs $1,000 a year to maintain. But objectives should be established before purchasing a package, including the setting of boundaries, limitations, and open ends for connection. Each system must observe them; otherwise, it will not pass quality control. This is valuable advice. Each prospective DIS user should say to himself: "First, I must return to the fundamentals. I must study and establish beyond any doubt the banking product my organization offers on the market, and how I wish to market it. Second, I must do a procedural study, and third, a systems analysis." When the system analysis is ready, and has been approved by the management, a systems study, for integration, should be done. Let's divide data collection from database management, as is done by the institutions with experience in the field. Let's train our people. In short, let's get ready.

A CITIBANK APPLICATION

To gain a perspective of applications, it is advisable to look back at the early years, at the first experiences. The following minicomputer applications were advanced in 1974-76 by Citibank as the *new look* in bank information systems. In each application, a dedicated machine was used, and the years of experience that followed justified this approach.

In identifying the current status of a system, it should be noted that many applications involve foreign operations, in which banking profits (and risks) lie these days. Management choices were right; the proper direction was given, and here are the results:

1. *COBRA*—thc "Nostro" accounting system.
2. *DARTS*—the foreign exchange system, covering all of New York-City's operations.

DARTS is quite sophisticated in its design. All the contributing accounting systems dedicated to foreign operations are fed into this system.

3. *LETTERCREDIT*—issues letters-of-credit authorizations (two separate minisystems on separate machines).
4. *CLIPS*—handles loans, acts as frontend and data collector for information to be transmitted to current accounts (DDA), international clearance, and loans accounting.
5. *ALPS*—the loans accounting system for which CLIPS acts as a frontend.
6. *STAR*—an online branch office responsible for overseas branches.
7. *CITISWITCH*—the concentrator and switching system used where all overseas datalines terminate.
8. *ITIPS*—the international transaction-processing system to be installed in small branch offices overseas; an upgrading of accounting-machines applications.
9. *QMIS* (quality MIS)—a quality indicator to help management evaluate employee productivity, error rates, and so forth; a cost-control system run on minicomputers.
10. *IRIS*—a management-information system designed for tracking complaints, mapping investigations, record resolution, and so on.

Each software package has a specific goal to fulfill. For instance, the quality MIS system, or QMIS, monitors production volume, employee productivity, the timeliness of work being done, and the error rate. Citibank is highly cost-conscious, and rightly so. The policy is that unit costs and total costs are tracked through all central departments and branch offices—by minicomputers. Each product, *channel* in Citibank jargon, is priced, costed, and followed up. "We are thinking of the bank as an assembly line," a senior executive stated. Daily reports resulting from QMIS go directly to the manager of a department or branch office. These reports and their summaries are part of a vice-president's monthly book. Frequency of reporting depends on the level of management. This frequency is either daily or monthly, not in between.

Let us now consider another example—IRIS—an application that has been in operation for several years. IRIS is an internal, daily, information-reporting system run in real-time through a minicomputer.

The database, interrogated through visualization, contains the *complaints*, or status of the database. The job of IRIS is to track whatever happens in international operations. End users look it up daily; they can get at a glance all the necessary statistics on customer satisfaction. This system not only tells them how often each file has been investigated or, having been closed, how often it was subsequently reopened because of incomplete or defective handling, it gives pertinent data on the operations.

The output of IRIS used to be on paper. Now it is produced on a video screen. As one director suggested: "We made it very difficult for people to get paper out of the computer. Our experience clearly indicates that a lot of paper—even a lot of microforms—is nonsense. If you want information, ask for it yourself, interactively. Now ninety-five percent of information comes on CRT."

Citibank has been using more microfiche than paper since the mid-1970s. From the beginning, however, all requests have been scrutinized to avoid a microform explosion. In the case of IRIS, direct, online, access availability of the complaint log was ordered by the president of the bank, to ensure that no one hid complaints—an excellent policy that top mangement throughout the banking industry would be well advised to follow.

HANDLING CLIENT INFORMATION

It is to the credit of Citibank that since the beginning of the minicomputer-based era, major emphasis has been placed on client service through the timely and orderly management of client complaints. Delays or errors in client handling can happen in every financial institution. It is the task of management to flush them out, have them corrected, and follow up on corrective action.

As a management-control system, IRIS operates the following way. A *standard response time* (SRT) has been established in advance, jointly set by the organizational department and the responsible operations channel. Client complaints, and their follow-up, are registered as they arrive, and receive the corresponding SRT. If no satisfactory response is given within the SRT, penalties are applied. On the day I interrogated the terminal, the status of complaints about foreign money transfers was:

CURRENT ITEMS:	OPEN	XX
	PENDING	*XX*
	TOTAL	XX

This is the mirror of what goes on *now.*

ITEMS TODAY:	NEW	XX
	REOPENED	*XX*
	TOTAL	XX
WORKLOAD (A + B):		XX

The man at the terminal could then select a file (number call) and investigate its status. Visualization included a *heading* (running number; coded issue; summary) and *columns*. The columns identify the control number, inquiry, amount, deadline, remarks, and agent investigating.

Management statistics are presented through a *resolution timeliness report*, a report that can sort statistical data by channel (the product). *Summary This Month* statistics reflect all the complaints for the year to date and for last montn—all with reference to international operations. The following columns are continued in the *This Month* report:

1. *Report Period*: month to date, last month, year to date, yesterday.
2. *Volume.*
3. *Timeliness*: standard time, forecast time.

Statistics are then given, by *early*, *late*, and on time. This column is repeated twice—*In-Bank* and *In-Channel*.

4. *Budget*: plan; actual.

This column is also repeated twice: *In-Bank* and *In-Channel*.The system observes a hierarchical structure. The timeliness of response and budgetary control are reflected by channel and for the entire organization. Most importantly, the bank president has direct access to the system. A program provides him with the capability to interrogate obstructions and get a swift response.

Security measures have also been taken to protect the privacy of the bank's data assets. To keep informed of who has access to the DB, who is asking for what, and security, each interrogator uses a password.

A NEW PHILOSOPHY IN BANKING

It will be appreciated that this procedure represents a new philosophy in banking and in management in general. DIS is a management style more than a solution that is implemented on a machine. Techniques are secondary; management drive is vital. As such, it implies a number of prerequisites to make a success out of the tools computers and communications provide.

If Citibank is a good example, it is precisely because management was not manipulated by specialists but took the leadership role. Management appreciated interactivity; it endorsed computer resource-distribution. Central planning was forced to make possible unified operations. Interconnection and coordination have been implemented throughout the organization. For their part, the system specialists have done a clean job. Accessibility was assured through proper personnel training. Accessibility should not be limited to data, it should characterize the approach to be taken by the employees, and eventually by the clients of the bank. This requires a new approach to organization, and a different type of thinking and procedural structure.

Interconnection should be technical as well as managerial. It should be assured through the proper design of mini- and microcomputer-based systems. The style of management, accessibility, and interconnection, in turn, bring into evidence an emphasis on central planning, profit-and-loss responsibility, and personal management and accountability. Otherwise, high accessibility is meaningless and database segmentation cannot be carried out; or if carried out, it may lead to disintegration. Let's review the basic steps management should take, as suggested by Citibank's experience.

1. Break the total system into sets which can go from inception to production within six months.
2. Increase accessibility. Put the minicomputer near the people with the problem.

3. Standardize packages; choose an economic aproach to software production and maintenance.
4. Reduce personnel expenditures. Don't add costs; subtract.

Here again, the policy taken by Citibank management, is an excellent example. Since the midseventies, for each $11,000 spent on computerization (including software and overhead expenses) operations must eliminate one job. But cost efficiency cannot be enhanced by computer dinosaurs. The concept of modular design is proof that it enhances reliability, increases throughput, eases maintenance (both hardware and software), reduces the overall costs, and makes possible geographic distribution—which, in turn, improves system responsiveness.

LESS THAN MINIMUM WAGE

Looking at previous chapters, the careful reader will have noted a repeated reference: mini- and microcomputers can work for less than minimum wage; this is a socially acceptable way of replacing clerks. The faster such solutions are achieved, the faster we can benefit from the advances of technology. Minis and micros provide efficient solutions because they were designed to be interactive. If we do not study the applications in an interactive manner, however, this facility will be lost. What lessons can we draw from the examples just given?

First, we wish to gain interactivity, not just substitution of routine jobs. As some avant-garde banks aptly remarked: "Our intent is eventually to have a microprocessor chip in a desk, packed up with a video and the bubble memory necessary to support that particular position." As these institutions are the most cost-conscious ones, management has made clear to each corporate profit center that it was expected to squeeze out a fifteen percent annual growth rate without increasing personnel costs. That may sound a little tough, yet an unambiguous management policy is definitely an asset.

Second, the systems approach must be taken. The term *distributed* implies the passing of information from one computer to another. Communications through data links should be simpler, safer, easier, and less costly than mailing a floppy disc or exchanging a magnetic tape.

Third, transaction aspects must be emphasized. Transaction-oriented data is kept in a database, and users frequently check against the file that interests them. Minis and micros perform transaction-processing very well, and many users like to take this operation off a mainframe.

Fourth, DIS must help to drastically reduce the error rate. Errors are a banker's worst enemy. Numerous corporate studies have indicated the substantial cost of errors. The longer errors go undetected, higher costs rise, and the more client service declines. Verification of entry data substantially reduces the time and material cost of errors. As information is entered, it should be verified for completeness, correct format, conformity to parity, and for agreement with other data in the files. Costly errors must be detected before they are passed on and repeated. Recent studies have shown that correcting an error after it enters the DB costs ten times as much as it would if it were corrected at the source.

Fifth, the implementation of mini- and microcomputers must be carefully studied with all factors given their proper weight. Now, let us examine the "80/20" rule. Looking around his office, the user finds that eighty percent of the information he needs to perform his job is either on his desk or near it. As we stated, if the location is well chosen, only twenty percent of the time will be used to handle data that will go to a central site or that will be retrieved from it.

Sixth, DIS not only benefits the periphery, it can also help headquarters. Distributed processing provides advantages to managers at a central site. The user at the periphery sends in correct data, not errors. The manager transmits only when required. This process decreases the size of the teleprocessing pipeline, accelerates procedures, and reduces costs.

One of the reasons for the existence of DIS is the fact that, in the case of old, large, centralized data-processing operations, things had become so bad that a simple request for information went through a dozen people, and took a dozen days to complete. Now output is produced instantaneously and is available if we take care to implement local databases.

Some banks related that "there were many problems with centralized control. Users were forced to homogenize their requirements to fit the job mix, and system lead time was out of proportion to business needs. Users were were unhappy. Since mini- and microcomputers have all the capabilities of large mainframes, at a fraction of the cost, there's little reason not to use them."

In conclusion, the banking industry is moving toward bringing the power and variety of functions a computer can accomplish out of the machine room and into the work place, where transactional activity actually occurs. This makes computer resources available to those who need them, instead of their being available only to the computer professionals who sometimes made it a hobby to run machines as they saw fit.

Citinet

14

The evolution of a DIS environment indicates a first phase of geographically or functionally developed resources with or without the simultaneous benefit of a backbone network. That is, no online communication capacity can be made available after the first instance, but plans should be made for its provision.

Typically, such a network offers distributed-processing capabilities. It may also provide an early approach to a distributed database. As the number of work stations—and, generally, the number of mini- and microcomputers dedicated to the DIS environment multiplies—there comes a need to interconnect the DDP and the DDB elements. This degree of freedom in the development of the information resources of the bank has come about because of the separation of data-processing, databasing, and data-transport functions. Dividing data transport from the other two activities permits an orderly evolution along each line—always keeping in mind the eventual integration.

Data communications involves the able handling of data transport and, by consequence, the new work phases connected to the deployment of the network. The first is a basic structure of the backbone with its nodes and links. Next is the multiplication of the nodes and links, as the volume grows, to reach all areas of DIS operations. This has been the case in Citibank's experience. To bring the evolutionary steps into perspective, let's remember that, while the minicomputer-based distributed network was implemented, work progressed on developing the physical resources needed to run a company-operated and -maintained data communications network. Management decided that the network should operate on the packet switching principle, along Arpanet lines. It was also decided to incorporate not only minicomputers but the maxicomputers still in service.

In late 1977, Citinet went into operation. It had eight nodes and covered most of Manhattan. The Arpanet software, already in the public domain, has been adapted to meet the logical requirements of Citinet. By early 1978, there was documentary evidence that the maxicomputers operated by the Citibank and a number of minicomputer-run work stations can use the transport facility developed within the banking environment. Work is now concentrated on increasing the number of work stations feeding into the network, rather than continuously expanding the minicomputer installations into new areas of activity.

In the meantime, an extensive applications library has been developed. Within this time frame, Citibank has in operation over 200 minis, each on a dedicated section (geographically by function and task) of a broad base of applications. The first data transport activities concerned Citibank's management information system, and the connecting of various minibased systems developed during the 1970s.

This private packet network uses an RS-232 electrical interface, together with character-stuffing (instead of bit-stuffing) principles. Its data link protocol is based on the HDLC format and the X.25 standard. (Some changes were made to the HDLC protocol for Citinet.) For the first time, the packet network was used for host-to-host data transfers. Terminal-to-host and terminal-to-terminal capabilities are also being considered. Using minicomputers, it costs the bank only $25,000 to add a new processor node to the network.

TIMING MANAGEMENT OBJECTIVES

Citinet is an example of how private networks will apply the virtual circuit switching techniques that have been emerging beginning in the early 1970s. Data transport capacities of the type we will be considering extend the distributed-database and distributed-processing concepts to allow thousands of terminals and hundreds of hosts to communicate, with the most important contributions being on the management side.

As computers were in the 1950s, data communications in the 1970s have become indispensable tools of management action. A bank needs to own neither one nor the other, but modern management can't do without their facilities. Management must decide on the basis of cost effectiveness. Whether a public or private network is used; whether this network extends coast to coast; whether it covers a more limited area such as Manhattan; or whether it is strictly local will be dictated by the business environment. There must be a network, however.

The facilities that data communications make feasible will change people's thinking about banks. This calls for a plan and it takes time. Citibank management consideres that it will take two to five years for the network concept and its implementation to filter through the organization, depending on how well the sales job is done. The product is for the end user. The sales job must cover both managerial and technical highlights. Three points stand out regarding the technical characteristics of one of the first COAM (Company-Operated-and Maintained-Networks). First, Citinet is Arpanet-based. To make use of the Arpanet software, the nodes are HIS, L6 compatible to the 700 which have been used for IMPs (interface message processors) of the Arpanet.

Second, this choice made significant savings possible for Citibank. The United States government spent twenty-five million on the Arpanet operating system (OS) software. The Citinet OS cost $250,000 —two orders less magnitude because management used an established technology rather than developing its own.

Third, the right tone was set from the start. The objective set by Citibank management had been to establish a utilitylike telephone service—for transaction switching and the modernization of formerly classic batch-processing now converted to online batch. The basic interest is the provision of a reliable, cost effective and timely online solution. There are three main poles of activity in banking data processing. The classic is the low deadline hour-long message that characterizes online (remote) operations. Citinet demonstrated its usefulness almost from its inception.

The second, and more modern, class is that of interactive transactions—short messages. This is what a bank needs the most. This timesharing application is expediated by mini- and microcomputers at the user location (topological or functional). As we have said so often, this is the purpose of the work stations. Their incorporation in Citinet makes interactive transactions networkwide.

A bank has to face another type of challenge. Precisely, financial transactions of the interbanking type (corresponding banks and state authorities). If we look into all types of banking applications, we see that they can be broadly classified into these three areas (Figure 14.1).

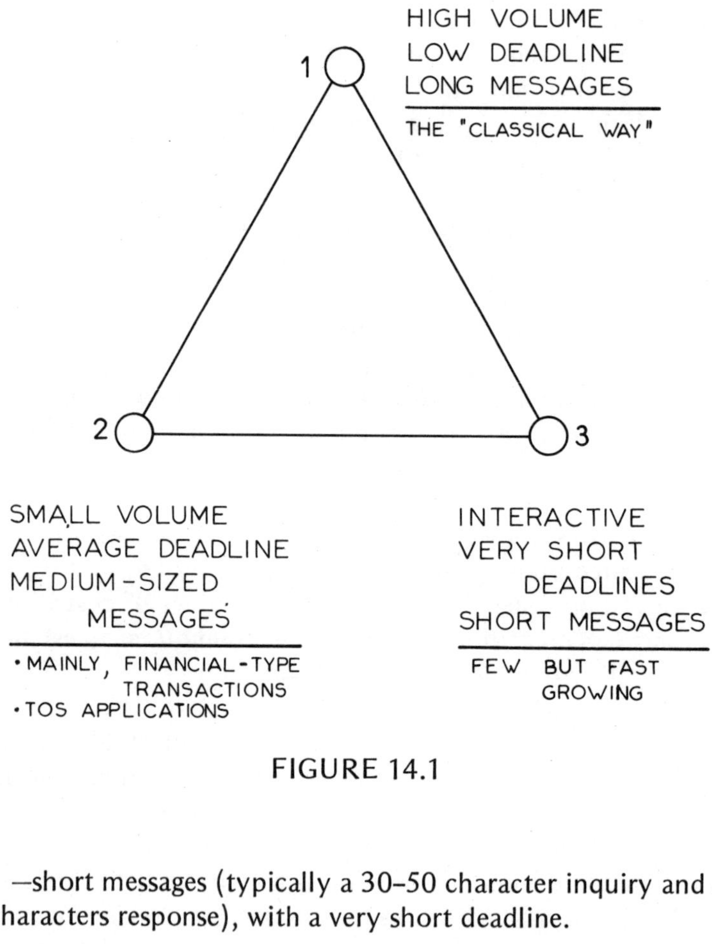

FIGURE 14.1

—short messages (typically a 30–50 character inquiry and a 50–100 characters response), with a very short deadline.

—very long messages with a low deadline—the classical remote batch type.

—financial transactions of the interbanking variety, characterized by medium deadlines of medium length. To handle the latter, Citibank has another network: Citiswitch. Eventually, a gateway between Citinet and Citiswitch will be developed so that stations in one network can access end-to-end stations in the other.

Figure 14.2 presents the Citinet backbone in its current status.

1. All eight IMPs are L6 with thirty-two kilobytes. At the moment, there is no disc storage at the node level.

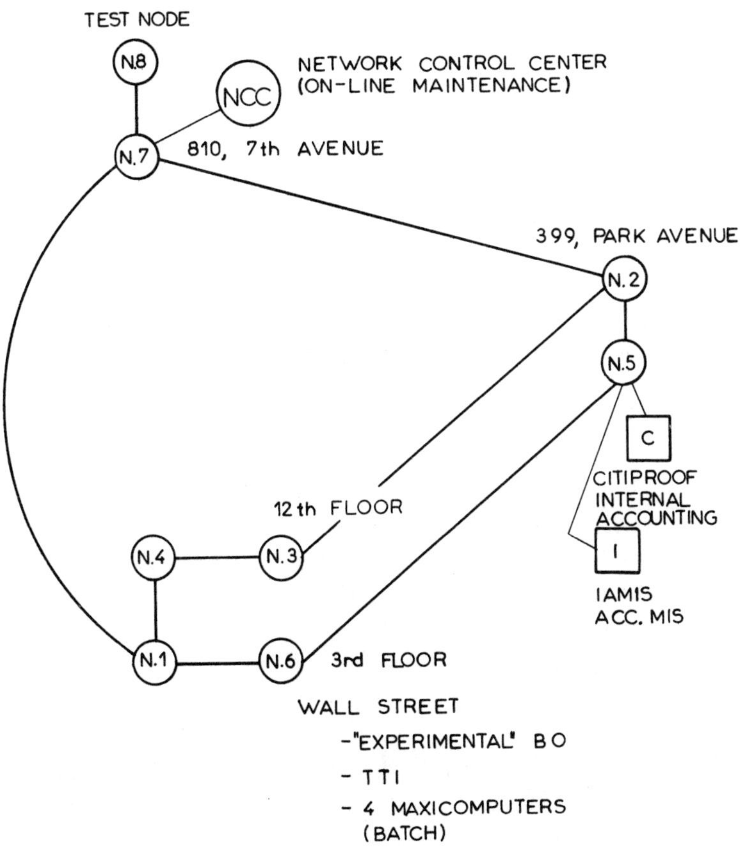
TEST NODE
N.8
NCC
NETWORK CONTROL CENTER
(ON-LINE MAINTENANCE)
N.7
810, 7th AVENUE
399, PARK AVENUE
N.2
N.5
C
CITIPROOF
INTERNAL
ACCOUNTING
I
IAMIS
ACC. MIS
12th FLOOR
N.4
N.3
N.1
N.6
3rd FLOOR
WALL STREET
-"EXPERIMENTAL" BO
- TTI
- 4 MAXICOMPUTERS
(BATCH)

FIGURE 14.2

2. Presently, no store-and-forward facility is provided. This may be available at a later date when transaction-level switching is implemented.
3. Up to four hosts can be connected per node. Currently each host is connected to a separate node.
4. The backbone lines are ninety-six KBPS (kilobit per second). The original tests were made at fifty KBPS.

An interesting example can be made concerning the functions of the Network Control Center (NCC). It reports on all traffic on the network. This involves both accounting and statistics. The NCC also provides a test base for maintenance purposes. The software can perform loop-backs.

Two databases are maintained at the NCC. One registers test results, the other stores quality history from the sensors and provides instantaneous interrogation capability regarding the history and status of all devices in Citinet. Another key subject is the approach taken by Citibank management regarding encryption. A senior executive said: "Protection works only so much. We are looking into the subject of encryption, though if it works, it is questionable that we will implement it systemwide." This is an example of a leading bank ahead of its competitors in terms of a modern approach to information systems that carefully looks at the subject of encryption—evaluating what it takes, what is provides, and what it costs prior to attaching this major expense item head-on.

EXTENDING THE LIFE OF MAXICOMPUTER INVESTMENTS

The Citibank case is an example of how network approaches not only do not contradict a continuation policy with maxicomputers, but also help solve the crucial problem of extending the useful life of the major software investments financial organizations have made for large-scale data-processing systems.

In other words, the introduction of a DIS environment can, and should, be made gently, without interrupting the work currently in progress on large scale systems. The policy should be to stop expanding this equipment by channeling the resources to the work place through mini- and microcomputers. Eventually, this will logically bring new concepts to the end user through a gradual DIS solution. Such conversion avoids upsetting changes and helps develop a new and cost-effective approach.

Here are some of the main applications which Citibank currently has on maxicomputers. Remember that the host processor equipment is now hooked on the Citinet IMPs. In all three data centers, there are:

1. *Consumer Services.* These include DDA, savings, personal loans and mortgage loans. The moving gear is a 370/158. The main work is batch, but there is also some online, particularly the TTI network. This is the answerback system implemented through the very-low-cost terminals manufactured by Citibank's TTI subsidiary. These terminals are installed at the bank's branch offices and at merchant (client) firms. Video terminals for money deposits and withdrawals are other devices on the network.
2. *Investment Management Group*. This group handles all trust applications and securities. It is implemented on a 370/158. The operation is batch with only one large online application.
3. *The Corporate Data Center*. It uses two 370/158's and operates batch with only one exception.

The main applications are corporate check processing, accounts reconcilement, commercial loans, and dial-in by 250 customers throughout the country. Dial-in is a good example of a trend developing among American financial institutions: offering clients long-distance access to the database, under memory-protect conditions, for interrogation purposes. This service is rapidly becoming a competitive advantage among financial institutions.

The examples which we have covered provide good documentation of the way mini- and microcomputers complement each other. While the life of the mainframes is effectively extended through their integration into Citinet, there are currently a significant number of minicomputers that are employed in a variety of applications.

Minis can also be used by a financial institution as an income earner, offering new data-intensive services to business and industrial clients and to other banks. For instance, Series 1 minicomputers have been programmed for *Cititran*. This is a self-standing package developed by Citibank with a view to being marketed among the smaller banks in the United States.

Cititran merits some explanation. It may become a prototype of the small business systems market in the coming years among financial institutions. The idea is simple and marketable: smaller banks do not have the human resources necessary for the development of online applications. But they do feel the pinch of competition and want to do something about it. That is where Cititran comes in.

The package can be installed at the client (bank) site, operated and maintained (software) by Citibank personnel. The client bank will be charged on the basis of processed transactions. This is the basic approach. As it unfolds, it may open an important and dynamic market.

FINANCIAL TRANSACTIONS AND CITISWITCH

At this point, let us examine the money transfer system of Citibank. Known as Citiswitch, this network preceded Citinet in its deployment. Largely PDP-based, Citiswitch has (just as the Citinet) an NCC (network control center) equipped with two minis. Other minicomputers have been implemented for the customer information master and each of the banking groups within the Citibank organization. The following banking groups are directly concerned: WCS, for the multinational operations; IBG, including all overseas functions (except the WCS class) involving over fifteen nations; NBG, oriented toward the small to medium customer within the United States, and also the large customer operating only in the United States.

Figure 14.3 outlines the current Citiswitch application. The gateway to Citinet is necessary, as Citiswitch is not X.25, having adopted a modified solution by Collins linking different locations: NYC, London, Bahrain, Hong Kong, and Miami (for South America). In this sense, Citiswitch provides the backbone for all administrative message-switching and for money transfers.

THE OBJECTIVES OF CITINET

Citibank has duly emphasized that the primary objective of Citinet is to ensure both data transport and interfaces for computers already working on corporate functions, such as check-processing for corporate accounts (any corporation) handled through, among others, WCS, IBG, NBG; account reconcilement (a paying service, extension of the

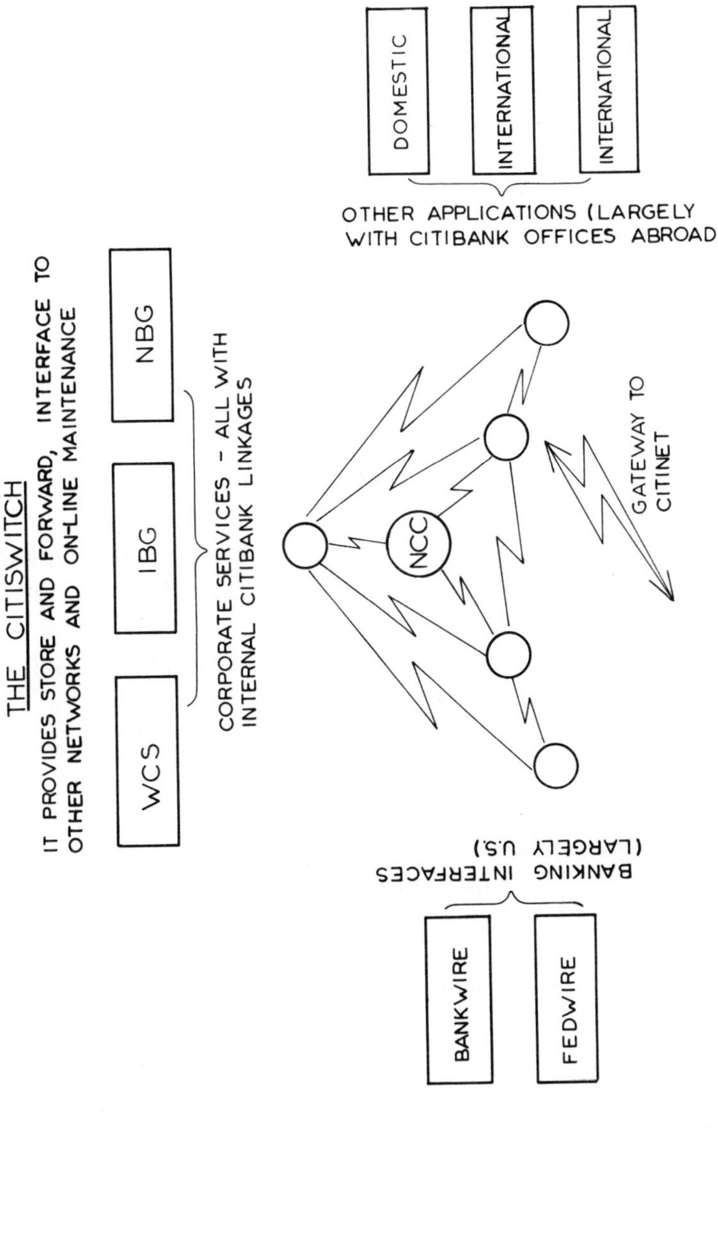
THE CITISWITCH
IT PROVIDES STORE AND FORWARD, INTERFACE TO OTHER NETWORKS AND ON-LINE MAINTENANCE
WCS
IBG
NBG
CORPORATE SERVICES - ALL WITH INTERNAL CITIBANK LINKAGES
NCC
GATEWAY TO CITINET
DOMESTIC
INTERNATIONAL
INTERNATIONAL
OTHER APPLICATIONS (LARGELY WITH CITIBANK OFFICES ABROAD)
BANKWIRE
FEDWIRE
BANKING INTERFACES (LARGELY U.S.)

FIGURE 14.3

preceding one); loans; letters of credit; collections; lockboxes; money transfers; dividend reinvestments; and stock transfer/securities.

Gradually, terminals are hooked up to allow the movement of data among branch offices. This is a great improvement over the past practice of substituting online for manual solutions. For instance, lockbox tapes used to move physically from the mini to the 370 by car; they are now transferred to an online operation through Citinet.

The preceeding reference leads us to the second Citinet objective —but prior to discussing transaction files, let's repeat the goal:

1. *Provide interfaces* for computers already serving corporate functions.

The second goal is copying transaction files for processing as well as for back-up operations:

2. *Ensure the back-up of files.* A senior executive stated, "you can't duplicate everything with so many computers." This is an important goal and it should be given attention. Back-up, wherever provided, is a major headache in the administration of a DP center. File and program copying, done manually for back-up reasons, are often late, inaccurate or incomplete. The demand on employees is too overwhelming. Why not do it by computer?

Another goal of Citinet is to guarantee the needed backbone for online transaction-handling.

3. *Set the groundwork for network channeling of transactions,* both current and future. This is a fundamental issue, one to which Citinet has been addressed. This reference underscores the need for a financial institution to first outline its objectives in the use of minicomputers, thus, subsequent integration serves a concrete purpose. After ten years of experience with minicomputers Citibank is one of the uncontested leaders in the field; it is wise to listen to the advice acquired from this experience.

Ten major points highlight the lessons which have been learned; each one of them applies to an organization operating within a dynamic business environment:

1. Use the minicomputers with online, interactive applications —don't open batch-handling shops everywhere.

2. Organize so that no professional operators are needed. Don't carry the old, centralized, batch experience to the minicomputer sites.
3. Establish Audit Trails from the beginning of the DIS operations. In the old batching, these controls were accidental, not organized. Now is the time to rethink and revise audit and control.
4. Work your procedures out carefully. When you project new operations, don't carry over old concepts.
5. Protect against human error. The more computers are spread around, the more the accidents due to human error. (This situation is much more dangerous in the classic STAR-like RT applications, where quite often the user has not been made accountable for the operation.)
6. Keep the DIS process simple. As with all computer operations, the more complex, the more likely are errors.
7. Centralize both maintenance and development of the software.

This means more than writing the applications programs centrally. It requires taking the compiler-interpreter out of the minicomputer so that users in the periphery cannot assemble. (And, when the manufacturer's special software does not permit this solution, then trancate the *Edit* feature.) It also calls for an infrastructure able to police this rule. To my judgement, the Citibank principle is simple and effective. Keep a central group to undertake changes, and upkeep, then distribute new releases to the users.

8. Standardize the equipment. Have the basic specifications before shopping.

This lesson has a handicap in its applicability. There are not many standards *now* in the computer field, but microcomputers (not minis) will eventually become like light bulbs. The massive numbers of microcomputers to be used in all sorts of applications will eventually force standardization and this reference is just as valid for hardware and software:

9. Look for basic software features (OS, monitors, timesharing routines, etc.) that can reasonably answer the user's requirements.

Don't change the OS releases too often. The software aspect in the standardization effort is as important as the hardware. In both cases, it is the user who pays the bill. A senior executive said: "We press the minicomputer manufacturers to stop making changes to the OS documentation. But many mini manufacturers are also in the hardware business. They do *not* understand the software OS implications."

10. Look into self-maintenance. Project your needs. Train your own personnel.

To do this, it is necessary to control the introduction of different equipment, not only with respect to manufacturers but to models. An executive of Citbank commented, "Self-maintenance can mean savings. With DEC, Interdata and similar equipment we spend three to four million per year for maintenance alone." And there is the possibility of online maintenance. Both Citinet and Citiswitch have Network Control Centers. This is a necessary measure, and also a logical step towards remote diagnostics and eventually self-maintenance.

ADOPTING AN ARCHITECTURE

It should be evident that, for a financial institution, network architecture is a necessary complement to its computer activities. But, how to choose the most suitable? Here are the answers given by various financial institutions with the experience and know-how to discuss announced computer architectures.

SNA. A joint study undertaken by some banks with IBM equipment evaluated SNA's applicability and expected benefit.

As a result of joint projects, some financial institutes stated "this bank spent time educating IBM specialists in the corporate banking business. The project did not lead anywhere."

SNA was generally judged (by the user) as being "conceptually nice" but too expensive to implement; difficult to maintain; too oriented to sell IBM equipment; requiring a long time to put into operation; and very complex. "We had better get rid of system programmers," said cognizant executives in several institutions. "We would rather pay to implement our applications program than to maintain SNA."

DECNET. It would probably reach completion prior to SNA but its developer (Digital Equipment) is not pushing it.

The reaction was this: if the manufacturer is not interested in selling it, there is no point in making a detailed analysis of Decnet. The smaller banks now look towards utilizing the *closed user group* facility offered by AT&T's Advanced Communications Service (ACS) to do the data transport function and link their central departments with branch offices. This frees the bank's specialists to study new approaches to check-processing, account reconcilement, lockboxes collections, and money transfers. Thus, specialists can evaluate their efficiency; automate them; and try to reduce costs.

Interactive Videotex. This is the newest user-friendly networking capability which can be offered either as a public utility or as an inhouse system. Viewdata was implemented in England in March 1979. It was a public offering. One user: Whitbread had by mid-1979 (when I met its specialists in London) two years of experience with an in-house Viewdata system. It was very positive. Barclays used the public Viewdata service to gain experience, eventually launching its own system. So did the London Stock Exchange which by the time this text is written had in the works a private Viewdata network (TOPS) implemented through MODCOMP minicomputers. The advantages are striking. The system is *simple*. It is easy to use and, it uses known technologies: the telephone, the TV set, the keypad. The modified TV set makes color and graphics feasible and still costs about a quarter of the specialized computer terminals.

Why should a bank pay four times more for a complex system rather than using a simple one? (GTE which markets Viewdata in America will, I am sure, be happy to offer the service.) Better put the financial institutes' own system specialists to study and rethink the applications; modernize them and cut the costs. The specialists must consider some basic questions. Which systems justify dedicated equipment? Which can be put on shared facilities? What do we do about the secretarial jobs which the tasks themselves (computing or not) have always entailed?

To return to the Citibank case, the workstation answer will respond to this challenge. In a few words, the response is as follows:

First, attach the mini or micro to the workpost itself. Microcomputer equipment has the ability to perform any banking and/or administrative function in a department. This leads to the next requirement.

Decide on the issue of the primary file(s); establish clusters of BO. Don't centralize throughout this operation. For instance, Citibank worked out seven clusters in the NYC metropolitan area. Hence, CIF is by cluster.

Third, provide for the very important tasks of: journaling; recovery/restart; network supported back-up; and client interfaces. Citibank has worked on both tape and disc journaling. Disc size is eighty-eight megabyte with DEC; 300 megabyte with Interdata.

Fourth, always remember the ultimate objective: linking the workstations to the network and allowing the workstations to communicate with each other. There are also some possible limitations to take into account.

As the applications expand and more traffic is generated (number of clients, volume of checks) the minicomputer may not be able to handle all the work. Growth should be projected from the beginning into the system. Selecting the right minicomputer should also account for the limit on the number of peripherals it is possible to use.

Finally, getting people away from the hard copy is an issue which must be examined. Often, this is a long-term process and requires an able handling of psychological reactions; user training; and conviction by example. This makes the whole DIS field quite complex to implement, and also, quite challenging.

Message Handling in a Medium Size Bank

15

Citinet is a well-conceived and properly implemented network which separates the data transport mechanism from databasing and data handling. Small to medium-sized banks might argue that networks of the Citinet class are for big financial institutions. The risk is always there that the size and cost of modern private networks may discourage research on alternative solution.

This chapter will answer these arguments beforehand and prove that the opposite is really the case. The fact is that transaction systems, from simple dialog solutions, to more complex packet-switching networks, are now offered by public utilities. Still, even if a bank opts for a private approach to money transfers, possibilities exist to implement low cost online/offline solutions.

A current experience with a new data communications system for money exchange and foreign trade payments will be traced from its initial design—to the changes necessary to accommodate new user's requirements resulting from SWIFT (Figure 15.1); the improvements made feasible because of increased internal and external storage capabilities of the terminal devices; the miscalculation of the magnitude of software support necessary (at the terminal level)—and the aftermath; the inefficiencies due to hardware/software trade-offs at the terminal level and the choice of line discipline; concluding with the solution sought.

To set the proper time frame for the experience, this 1976-77 application will be contrasted with an earlier application (1973) on the same subject, but with nonintelligent terminals. (The original reason for the change was the SWIFT formalisms which a nonintelligent ter-

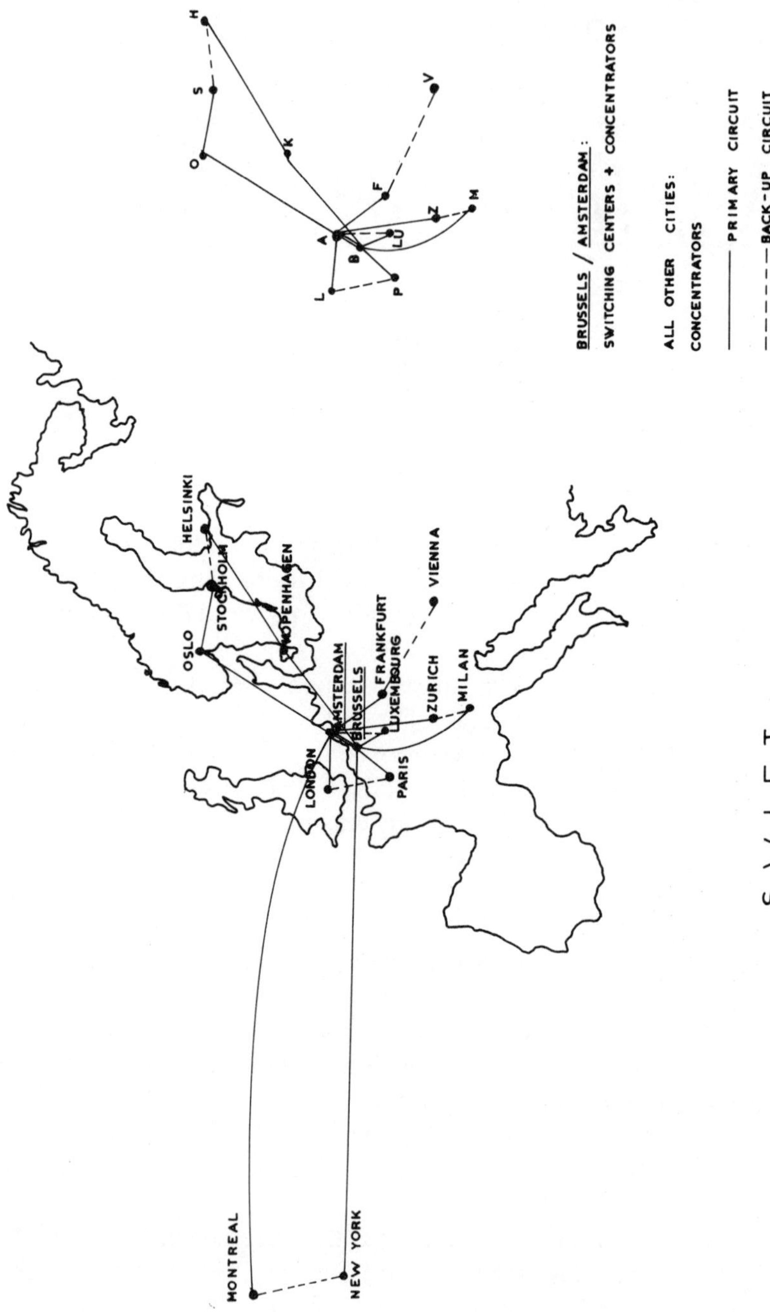

S W I F T

FIGURE 15.1

minal at a remote location cannot accommodate.) We will discuss other improvements, too costly to implement four years ago, that are possible in 1980. Our discussion will carry forward to the frontend reconfiguration which has been necessary at the computer center; restart/recovery procedures; problems that developed and solutions to these problems. Particular attention will be paid, from a user's viewpoint, in terms of the overall logical functions; the procedural alternatives to ease the pressure on the physical facility; the final choice of the physical functions; the accuracy and timeliness requirements to answer the user's demands and, finally, the procedural security measures which proved necessary.

THE USER'S TERMINAL TO HOST COMPUTER

Five objectives highlight the design of the information system for foreign trade operations: (1) data collection of export/import procedures and preparation of confirmation letters to clients; (2) feasibility of immediate error correction; (3) data-gathering for SWIFT (Money Oder) transactions; (4) daily data transmission to headquarters; and (5) daily updating of central files making them available for interrogation on the status of: client accounts, subaccounts, and foreign currency balances.

Prior to the adoption of the procedure, foreign trade operations were handled at branch office level by a typist, who compiled the client confirmation and the original document to be sent to headquarters. This produced a hard copy and a punched tape (Figure 15.2). The punched tape was converted offline to a magentic tape, then transmitted via private telephone line to the computing center. At the computing center, the foreign trade operations were handled in batch. Since client confirmation had already taken place, the main objectives of the process were to update accounts (including client accounts, foreign currency balances, and correspondent bank's accounts); and to prepare error lists. The latter would be sent to the central office (at headquarters), the errors noted, and new data entered on the accounting machine. The punched tape to be produced was sent to the computing center, and the cycle was repeated.

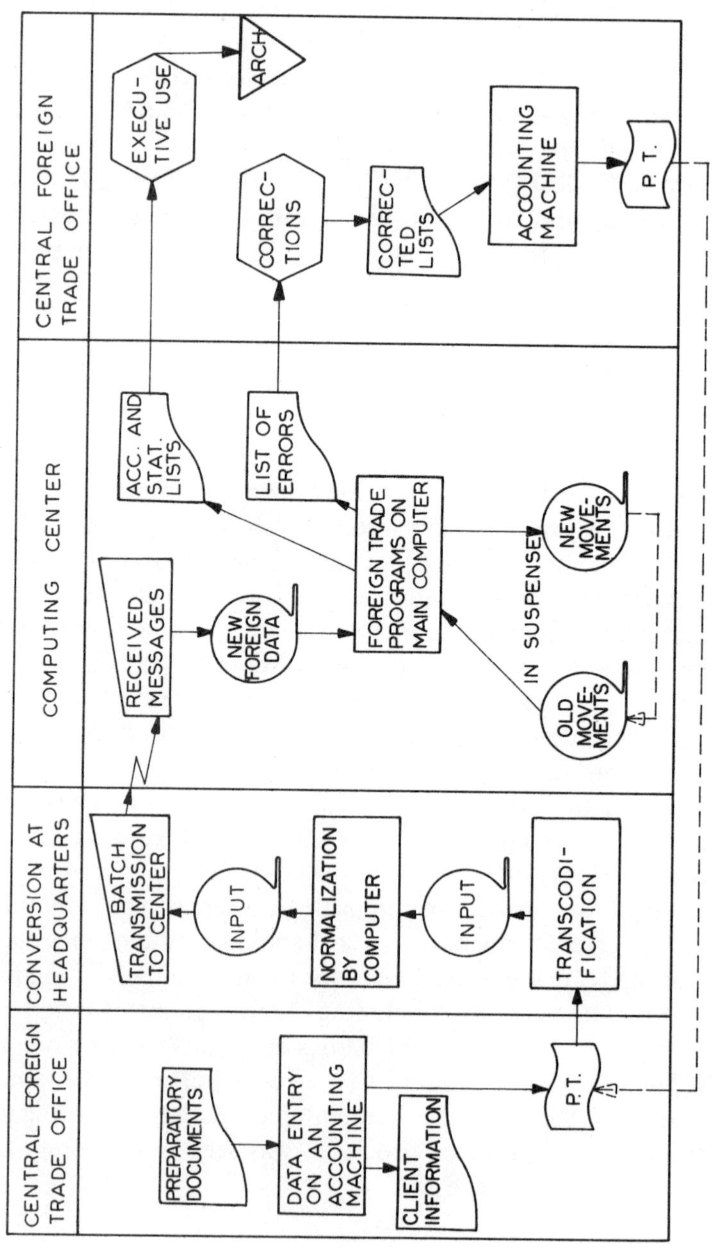
CENTRAL FOREIGN TRADE OFFICE
CONVERSION AT HEADQUARTERS
COMPUTING CENTER
CENTRAL FOREIGN TRADE OFFICE
PREPARATORY DOCUMENTS
DATA ENTRY ON AN ACCOUNTING MACHINE
CLIENT INFORMATION
P. T.
TRANSCODIFICATION
INPUT
NORMALIZATION BY COMPUTER
INPUT
BATCH TRANSMISSION TO CENTER
RECEIVED MESSAGES
NEW FOREIGN DATA
FOREIGN TRADE PROGRAMS ON MAIN COMPUTER
ACC. AND STAT. LISTS
LIST OF ERRORS
OLD MOVE-MENTS
IN SUSPENSE
NEW MOVE-MENTS
EXECU-TIVE USE
ARCH
CORREC-TIONS
CORREC-TED LISTS
ACCOUNTING MACHINE
P. T.

FIGURE 15.2

The following controls were implemented through the batch procedure:

—Validity of the codes (monies, correspondents, categories specified by the central bank and so on).

—Format and length of the fields containing the data.

—Control of the money fields (hash totals) contained on the transmitted information (through a private line).

—Correspondence regarding the client account.

—Control of the profit-and-loss margins assigned to each operation (relative to day of credit/debit, account class, foreign currency, amount, etc.).

—Validity of different subaccounts, created at branch office level, and check-up of their compatibility in relation to the customer account, to which they pertain, and the overall directives given by the bank.

This procedure was the result of years of experience by this bank on foreign operations, and of the influence of central bank directives on record-keeping and controls. As the bank made a hard drive to increase its foreign trade business, the procedure, though valid, became cumbersome. New ways were sought to: automate manual operations; eliminate overlaps; reduce overall costs; and accelerate the time of data-handling. Both realtime and remote-batch solutions were examined to develop an improved method. Two classes of applications were studied:

1. *Accounting Operations*: general accounting; claims (Swift and nonSwift); covering (Swift and nonSwift); proceeds: credits/debits; client information; *cash transfers* (Swift and nonSwift).
2. *Central Information File*: opening of a new client account; opening, variation or closing of a subaccount; blocking or freeing a subaccount; varied client demands in regard to account/subaccount.

At the branch offices studied, the cost and benefit of each solution was examined in detail as a function of the data-load (both present and projected). Cost/benefit suggested adopting at first stage: a solution with local intelligence along with a remote batch procedure. The transmissions for foreign trade operations would take place twice daily.

Simultaneously, foreign exchange operations (Spot, Swaps, Forward, Arbitrage), handled directly by headquarters, were put on a minicomputer. These included data entry, error detection and correction, and interrogation on current and forward positions. All these operations would be made in realtime on the machine.

DECENTRALIZED PROCESSING

The bank chose a small minicomputer to implement a distributed data system for foreign trade operations. It exhibited the following characteristics: A 4K central memory (increased to 16K, then to 64K when technology made this feasible at economically acceptable levels); two floppy discs of 512 KByte storage capacity (changed to a 2.5 MByte cartridge disc). Other devices were an alphanumeric keyboard; a serial printer; and an asynchronous line discipline. The prevalence of asynchronous communications between the periphery and the center in other applications led analysts to choose an asynchronous protocol. This limited the program. The output produced at the periphery by the minicomputer can be divided into four classes:

Accounting Documentation. All account elements, relative to foreign trade operations of the day, are kept on a continuous roll of paper.

Client Information. Confirmations are made on a document, manually introduced through front feed, after accounting operations are executed. The equipment is programmed to retain and repeat the needed data for client information.

Control Listing. This produces a comprehensive list of handling all accounting entries, regrouped by foreign currency, for local management.

Data for Central Processing. This is stored on a floppy disc and comprises details of all executed operations to be forwarded by remote batch to the computing center.

The end results have achieved security, modularity, guides to foreign banking operators, reduction in amount of data entry (reduced client files for frequent clients are kept on floppy disc; the same is true for corresponding banks), and elimination of double and triple transcription of information. As Figure 15-3 documents, introducing this dedicated minicomputer to the branch office, will modernize the overall procedure.

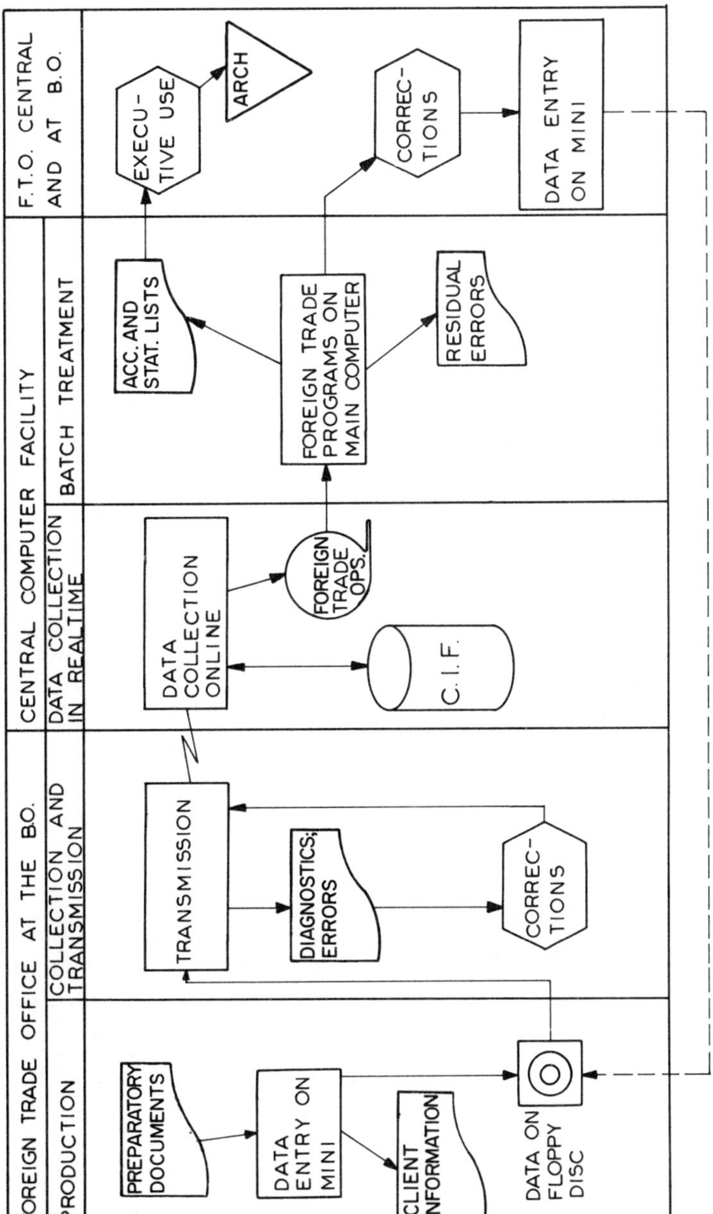
FOREIGN TRADE OFFICE AT THE B.O.
PRODUCTION
COLLECTION AND TRANSMISSION
CENTRAL COMPUTER FACILITY
DATA COLLECTION IN REALTIME
BATCH TREATMENT
F.T.O. CENTRAL AND AT B.O.
PREPARATORY DOCUMENTS
DATA ENTRY ON MINI
CLIENT INFORMATION
DATA ON FLOPPY DISC
TRANSMISSION
DIAGNOSTICS; ERRORS
CORREC-TIONS
DATA COLLECTION ONLINE
FOREIGN TRADE OPS.
C.I.F.
FOREIGN TRADE PROGRAMS ON MAIN COMPUTER
ACC. AND STAT. LISTS
RESIDUAL ERRORS
EXECU-TIVE USE
ARCH
CORREC-TIONS
DATA ENTRY ON MINI

FIGURE 15.3

Specialists attacked two types of problems. The most difficult was procedural, age-old habits on how to prepare foreign trade documentation had to be changed. The formalisms established by SWIFT not only provided standards but also cut short arguments of resistance to change.

The other problem was technical. When this study was done, central memory was still expensive; the same is true of disc memory. The first idea was to use cassette tapes as storage. It was dropped as tests proved that floppy discs were a better alternative. A broader look, however, changed the programming perspectives.

The manufacturer (who also provided the software) thought that 3,000 to 4,000 instructions were enough to handle the problem. But programming finally required an impressive 23,000 instructions (assembler level) to cover the whole range of applications. The floppy discs contain client files, corresponding bank files, Swift formalisms, working tables, counters by foreign currency and product line, totals and control sums, and data to be forwarded to the computer center.

The original central memory capability (4 KByte) had been distributed as follows: resident monitor, 1 KByte (including a buffer of 256 bytes); housekeeping 0.5 KByte; input module—0.75 KByte; operating system, 1 KByte; working memory—0.25 KByte. The equipment is either employed for local input/output or for data transmission, the online module can be used without overlays. The design seemed clean and polished enough to all concerned. Simulated runs gave good results. Problems occurring during tests made with the first applications programs have, however, presented a series of challenges.

TECHNICAL PROBLEMS AND THEIR SOLUTIONS

The near completion of software for foreign trade transactions and the first installation of the experiments which followed it, brought in evidence the need for a coordinated action to face hardware/software inefficiencies inherent to the interaction between the application and the equipment on which it must be run. To explain the problem, let's start with a quantitative example.

The foreign trade message has on the average sixty-five characters—which practically means 650 bits or *roughly two messages per second* in a line of 1,200 BPS. This is the theoretical calculation. When early experiments demonstrated that it takes four to five data communication minutes per average message length the alarm was sounded. In the course of a design review meeting in December 1976, the following suppositions were advanced to explain the observed inefficiencies: polling/selecting; intervening errors; the nonsequential search on floppy disc; issues of normalization.

The first hypothesis is based on the estimate that with polling and selecting on asynchronous lines, it is necessary to make eight line inversions per message (to pass from transmission to reception). Estimating fourty to fifty msec per inversion, the eight inversions mean a lost time of about 360 msec. At a 1,200 BPS line this corresponds to 36 characters, or about sixty percent of the message length. A possible correction was to make a synchronous point-to-point connection. However, there were reservations concerning this solution, because it interfered with other applications on the same central equipment. Furthermore, errors carried by the messages caused delays, as data clearance is done online in the course of data transmission. Even if a point-to-point solution solves some of the problems, the influence of online controls must also be observed. Online controls are the solution adopted today. Let's add that technical approaches taken in the study of one procedure, which may prove significant in that particular sphere, sometimes prove detrimental when the procedure is abandoned in favor of another. The matter is complicated when, in the same banking environment, one or two of the users abandon the old procedure, while another user retains it. For instance, online control, desirable as it is in many aspects, presents buildin delays of its own: transmission is necessarily delayed until each message is checked, and thereafter accepted or rejected. An alternative solution is to dump all messages to be transmitted, have them checked by the computer, *then* return the erroneous messages to their origin. This accelerates the procedure but presents its own limitations. The benefit from such an approach will necessarily be conditioned by the amount of errors in the records. Too many errors will create heavy message traffic. This, too, must be avoided.

Similar considerations are valid regarding the normalization of the message. Here, the analysts retained the option of an online normalization, which has definite advantages when private lines are used, but creates delays and costs in the case of public lines, or the use of facilities offered by a value-added carrier. A system study must focus on the issue of inefficiencies. What they mean in terms of economics can be seen through the example given below.

System analysts calculated, under theoretical conditions, that to transmit to the center, the foreign trade operations from each branch office would need thirty-five min. per day. When inefficiencies occurred the time increased in direct proportion to the inefficiencies—so do the costs. For instance, for a factor six, the time became 210 minutes. The originally projected use of public lines thus becomes unwise—private lines should be rented instead. (This is not a universal standard, but reflects the price structure of the telephone company in this particular situation.) It should not be forgotten that this application required some 23,000 instructions, and software costs are high. Software investments, and the time which they require, should not be lightly abandoned in favor of alternative machines or solutions. After an inherent inefficiency has shown up, decisions for rewriting software packages are necessarily constrained by the policy to apply *Life Cycle Cost*. This has an evident impact on completed software, and on that to be completed.

Finally, the foreign trade application, being the first online treatment of a long list of new applications programs, showed the need for upgrading the frontend to the host processor. The latter must support:

1. Connection of the SWIFT minicomputers.
2. Dialogue with foreign exchange minicomputers.
3. Actual and projected branch office minicomputers for current accounts, savings and general accounting.
4. Administrative and CIF terminals.
5. Realtime portfolio application in the final phases of testing.
6. New current account realtime applications, aimed at putting eighty percent of transactions online.
7. Stock exchange terminals.
8. Other connections in operation due for upgrading in the coming years.

Inevitably, these applications would overflow the capacity of the frontend installed at the computer center. The early results from the foreign trade application were helpful in projecting system availability and evaluating the data-load.

IMPROVING OVERALL PERFORMANCE

Local operating problems and data communicating issues were two types of modifications made to improve the performance of the foreign trade minicomputer at branch office level. The operating problems included procedural aspects to simplify the workflow, the addition of a cancel operation, normalization of messages (an improved version of the old procedure), local calculations such as: counter-value; commission; value-added tax; direct debit foreign currency to a client account; and transit transaction (through local currency).

The handling of these operations at a local level through minicomputers, helped reduce the traffic of messages to the central computer resource. The streamlining and improvement of data communications issues started with a long, hard look at the "2848" procedure. In the early '70s, this procedure was adopted for remote-batch transmission between a nonintelligent terminal and a medium-size computer used at the center at that time. It was kept in operation, though new equipment offered many capabilities.

The normalization issue was relative to the already existing batch programs for foreign trade operations. The record stored on floppy disc does not respect the file structure of batch programs. Normalization, thus, means conformity to the batch input and suppression of blancs, etc.

Experiments demonstrated that the elimination of normalization procedures accelerated transmission time by twenty percent. However, this posed its own problems: keeping copy on nonnormalized messages; linking messages in normalized to nonnormalized form for error search; handling returned messages (from central computer) for error reasons.

The projected improvements at the minicomputer site pointed up the capability of the floppy disc dedicated to data. (The other floppy disc is used for OS and the applications library.) Since the disc does not have sufficient capacity: either the number of messages stored must decrease, or, the machine must convert and reconvert, increasing the error factor. (This problem eventually brought up the wisdom of using larger capacity cartridge discs, when the economics of this change made it advisable.)

The possibility of automatic modems was examined with regard to data communications, as a way of reducing the operator's time in trying to establish a connection. Automatic calling proved feasible: at the modem level, and at the local minicomputer level.

Data transmission characteristics were then examined at length. Particular attention was paid to restart/recovery procedures, taking into account problems that have emerged and the necessary solutions. The design reviews covered the overall logical functions, procedural alternatives to ease pressure at the physical facilities end, and accuracy and timeliness requirements to fulfill the user's demands. These factors are present in all system studies. They have been considered within the overall solution adopted after the first practical results. Data security measures were enhanced, but the most valuable lessons learned from this application were that batch processing concepts are of no particular help to online. Often they confuse the issue.

Designers and analysts soon learned that it was wiser to examine overall requirements before allowing project groups to become involved with important, but different facets of the banking business. This proved expedient given the existing interconnection between different banking applications, even if these involved distinct departments at branch offices.

Today, corrected foreign trade operations have years of online experience behind them. However, with the advent of portfolio management and other applications a significant load has been added to the original realtime perspectives involving current accounts and savings. The branch office ends up with some twelve terminals. The time comes to bring minicomputer-based total intelligence into play. Experience dictates that the modern bank should start the study with *that* issue.

* * *

Questions on where to begin and how to proceed raise other questions, for example; What capabilities and skills should be prerequisites for the project overseer? The following chapters examine these questions, and explore some possible answers. Utilizing a coordinating agency: the steering committee, is one possibility. However, the better option, coinvolvement by top management, discussed in the final chapter, proves to be a more viable alternative.

The Steering Committee

16

Henry Ford once said that a committee cannot drive an enterprise any more than it can drive a car, if all its passengers put their hands on the steering wheel. Urwick added that management by committee is irresponsibility; a committee has neither a soul to blame nor a body to kick. And there is the popular proverb: "a camel is a horse designed by a committee." Yet, with all these derogatory comments about committees, many banks have been running computer policy through "steering committees" since the late 1950s. One can easily follow the results.

As if diffused responsibility were not enough, management by committee has often added to the difficulties by assigning responsibilities to members who know little about computers or who have been left behind by a galloping technology. Many streering committee members fail to appreciate that it is impossible to build adequate information system services without the right knowledge. Proper reorganization is often overlooked. Users must be trained; and the new services computers make possible exploited to their fullest extent. The potential purchaser must realize that the computer is only one (and, usually, the easier) part of a project. To utilize the computer effectively, everything must be built from scratch. This takes time, brains and money.

A second point to consider is that software does *not* improve the performance of hardware. It diminishes it. Hence, a financial institution examining the logical supports to the physical devices it plans to acquire, might logically ask: "How much will software reduce hardware capabilities?" Also: "How much more than the hardware will it cost?"

The often repeated error of signing a manufacturer's contract without the benefit of legal advice, is our third consideration. If you sign the manufacturer's "standard contract," you are lost. You must have the courage to change the clauses of the contract. To do so, you must be prepared: professionally, and in terms of skill and independent knowhow.

Bankers, as well as other potential users, must learn to develop independence through their own abilities. For evident reasons, this type of independence is not encouraged by computer manufacturers themselves. But it is possible to attain it if one strives to reach such a goal. The weak user is willingly weak. He did not assert himself during the initial planning, and, thus, lost control of the crucial issues. With computers, this is the ultimate transgression.

DEVELOPING A BETTER UNDERSTANDING

A basic conditioning for good information processing practice is to understand the nature and impact of information systems and their usage. Though rarely stated, these words must be emphasized; they are essential to financial institutions.

Let me emphasize, at the outset, two types of operations which I consider prerequisites to any investment in information systems. One is the development of new structures; the other the rationalization of personnel training.

The question of cost, hardware and software choices, and the dimensioning of installations, should not precede structure and education. Otherwise, the benefit would be minimal. Money would be lost. A banker should lose neither time nor money. Running computer systems is a management challenge, and as with any management job there are some major points of advice I would give to the users: First, study the objectives; then, establish the procedures; and following this, develop the men. It is impossible to outline and follow a rational information systems policy without the right men. If we have the men, we can do the proper planning for reaching goals and results. As with any management job, the need for planning—and its parallel: the development and maintenance of timetables—is self-evident. Even the optimal change of equipment and software will be of minor impact if we are unable to make and keep a timeplan. Furthermore, the development of cost/effective information systems in an organization depends to a great extent on the maturity of management in that sort of enterprise: "What is the level of maturity?" is a relevant question. Maturity in data processing tells management the sort of risk it might be willing to undertake. Risk and reward are an integral part of automation in banking. Here is a short list of steps taken by a medium-sized American bank to bring the computer subject under control, reduce fianacial outlays, and improve performance:

1. Replace labor-intensive activities with equipment.
2. Purchase packaged software instead of developing applications in-house.
3. Increase the use of computer output to microfilm (COM) in the place of printed output.
4. Survey users every six months and eliminate reports that are not being used.
5. Reduce backup facilities in cases where history shows enough reliability to warrant some risk.
6. Use online verification. Eliminate punched cards completely. Put all input online.
7. Decentralize data capture to the point of origin.
8. Reduce computer reruns. (The bank found that reruns consumed fourty-five percent of production time.)
9. Keep track of programmer mistakes that result in bad production runs.
10. Use a project control system for all systems development projects.
11. Improve computer scheduling to eliminate catchup work on weekends and extra shifts.
12. Implement strict standards for all DP activities that are actually practiced.
13. Implement video terminals and software capable of providing interactive programming.
14. Increase planning on system development projects. Include more non-DP people such as auditors and users.

Once management has provided an outline for developing the bank's information system, the task for the DP steering committee becomes easier, provided that the broader perspectives of a well-thought out policy have been settled. A possible review of and approval on such items as: DP personnel policy; manpower allocations for DP projects; procedures for security and control; research and development studies and the DP budget might be successful.

If the steering committee's responsibilities, and its willingness to take action, do not include priorities among conflicting DP projects (and often conflicting user department requests); if its members avoid considering major systems issues: such as, databases; data communications; organizational changes; and long-range planning, then the impact will be minimal and the result worse than nothing.

RESPONSIBILITIES IN GUIDING AN INFORMATION SYSTEMS POLICY

It is necessary to choose the goal to be reached prior to charting a course. The future of the financial institution depends upon the president of the bank. He must set the goal, not a committee. This fact was highlighted previously.

A recent article on Ludwig's imaginative Jari River investment (an excellent financial operation which has absorbed over $750 million and will probably double that amount during the next few years) had this to say on the executive's foresight: "Often he just sits in his office and thinks three to five years down the road." No better advice can be given in terms of information systems in banking. Ten years down the road is too far. Technology changes so rapidly that nobody, not even experts, can foresee all opportunities. This year, next year, even two years hence is too short. Time will pass by before companies have the chance to implement what has been projected. With information systems, future challenges pose real demands: system implementation; databases; data communications; software development; user training; and keeping the system basically simple. Opportunities for imaginative solutions abound. So do the risk of errors. Take the issues involved with large numbers of intelligent terminals. Changing the software, we must have the ability to distribute the new releases to, say, 800 DTE (data terminal equipment). This emphasizes the need for quality control; distribution procedures; software maintenance, and so on.

Progress in the evolution of services a bank offers its clients would recede without the powerful computer systems and data communications networks a service-oriented society depends upon. But there is a good way and a bad way of using computer power. The solid approach calls for exerting caution in affecting the new information technologies. The work must be clean and well thought out. If so, it will have an impact on the bank in the future. A solid basis means agreements in the use of resources; procedural parallelism; dimensioning of computer center(s) and of the distributed resources; a data communications network for online processing; and the development of applications software which requires a long lead time. Because technology develops rapidly and new products (both hardware and software) are announced all the time, many banks make it a point that up to fifteen percent of their systems specialists devote their time to the study of and experimentation with market offerings in computers, communications and applications. Numerically speaking, the number may seem large. In this case, study and experimentation are the points to be noted.

The late '70s experienced a deluge of new hardware systems, supports, and applications packages. This deluge will continue through the early '80s. These new offerings are changing the basic economies of data-processing. Today, computers and communications budgets are so large and so vital that even small improvements can give significant financial results. The steering committee, or the overseeing authority will face a lot of decisions. Most of them will call for expertise, and will typically include subjects which have not yet been debated and resolved. Nonexperts may find themselves unable to reach decisions when faced with such problems as: the conversion to Cobol 74 (from the Cobol 68 version which most financial institutions have used until recently); the introduction and usage of DBMS (database management systems); the maintenance procedures and policies—given the large amount of human resources needed for software maintenance; the use of mini- and microcomputers (both in functional and in topological locations); and contingency planning.

Management must also focus attention on the vital issue of software maintenance. Using a reference from packages, maintenance consumes on the average of about ten percent of the original investment effort per year. But custom-made programs are not industrialized packages and, depending on their age, patches, robustness, error quality, and documentation, maintenance may rise to fifteen or even twenty percent of the original investment per year. The question is, should banks take independent approaches when considering program maintenance, or would combining forces result in significant financial savings? One solution lies in adopting a package policy and letting specialist firms do the maintenance job.

Finally, the management authority responsible for the establishment and supervision of an information system policy should also get involved with job descriptions and top personnel issues and provide some guidelines in developing personnel policies for data center(s). This becomes imperative as the computer mainframes of today become obsolete, being replaced by minis and micros which spur a radically new generation of computer systems.

Replacing today's mainframe(s) with distributed minis and micros may bring hardware costs down, but *proper care* must be exercised from the beginning to concentrate skills and standardize jobs, to avoid a proliferation of functions, otherwise, staff costs will increase.

Software, as well as hardware, gets distributed. Distributing both physical and logical power will be very difficult to accomplish if management does not change its attitude. Intellectual resources must be concentrated, at least for the next few years until online fully interactive systems become the rule and new structures are in place. Only the physical resource should be distributed.

Within the same complex architectural design of hardware, software and human factors, it is appropriate to add that micros and databases will change the management profession itself, to a substantial extent. Decision-support systems now developing will make many practices now followed obsolete. A new, more sophisticated generation of distributed systems must be installed, at personal level, to strike a dual goal: help the decision-maker and contain personnel costs: throughout the organization; in the periphery and in the headquarters; in the office and in the factory; among computer professionals and computer users.

SOLUTIONS TO APPLIED PROGRAMMING

The chapter introduction pointed out that if you buy a computer, you buy practically nothing. The real challenge is not the equipment but making the programs which will run on it, turning a general-purpose machine into a special-purpose one, able to handle the job requirements. As many computer specialists and some bank management personnel have learned, applied programming standardization is a fundamental issue, its importance grows with systems complexity. It involves a number of subordinate subjects such as central software development organization (even geographically distributed); the possibility of online system analysis, programming and documentation; a central software maintenance capability; and online software diagnostics. Given the vital importance of the subject, it is advisable to study it in some detail. However, let's focus on a peculiarity that distinguishes minis and micros from big computers. Minicomputers call for simple software. This is an attractive point encouraging distributed-information systems (DIS). Micros use (or at least they should) packaged programs—preferably made of solid-state software. Maxicomputers (mainframes) have fairly complex programming libraries. The reasons are historical rather than real.

The Steering Committee (or the policy-making authority in the bank) faces the challenge of ensuring that past mistakes are *not* repeated. With minis, the software must be simple in origin—no multiprogramming; just one application on one machine (evidently, depending on machine size and cost). A careful language choice must be followed—for instance, mini Cobol, proper for this equipment; or Pascal—no sophisticated or complex solutions. Furthermore, software design must ensure unattended operations in the periphery, another reason software must always be simple. The proper directives should be given to ensure homogeneous procedures. If 120 installations are made, we should definitely *not* multiply by, say, "120" the software support. For 120 installations must be *one* release; centrally supported. Definitely a number of criteria enter into this equation. Software must be designed for online diagnostics, and the proper routines made or bought, to support online procedures. After settling these issues, specialists retained by the steering committee should look at the subject of machine selection. Past procedures dictated the exact opposite. Decision-making bodies should not forget the other crucial factors of: cost; compatibility; and survival assurance by the selected manufacturer. Will the chosen manufacturer have the capabilities to support your installation in the "future fronts?" For how long? A year? Two years? Ten years?

Investments, timetables, people (and their training) are all key factors influencing information systems in the bank; these call for policy decisions and able solutions. With a good manufacturer, the machines can be easily guaranteed. Much more difficult is to find or develop the right people. Keep in mind that the new information systems represent a great deviation from the past. There will be change. Great change.

In our plans and enthusiasms over new technologies we should remember one primary fact about change. In almost all people change elicits one response—fear. We must train people, including specialists, to accept change. We should also teach the information systems specialists how to get out in the field to the branch offices and talk to the people with the problems. The operators in the field may not be brilliant or intellectual, but more often than not they know what they are doing.

In planning for the new system, members of the policy-making body of the bank must ask themselves: What are the problems? What's the *salient* problem? How can we solve it? How can we help our people (and ourselves)? What are the future problems?

THE FOREMOST STUDIES

I have said that the steering committee as a concept and as a practice has aged; if retained, it should be revamped. Studies should be undertaken to ensure that the bank's information systems (and services derived thereof) are managed properly. The following paragraphs should be given careful consideration. (Let me add that these are I.S. management studies, they are not the applications requirements which constitute a different subject altogether.)

First, the orientation toward new systems concepts based on distributed intelligence, to take advantage of the developing technology and maintain the bank's competitive edge should be a consideration. This includes both the devices (hardware, software, applications) and their effective usage for controlling the bank's operations and market-share. In turn, this involves two things: new client services and management information concerning the development of a branch-oriented planning; and selected data to help in structural studies, as well as in competitive evaluations per subsidiary and functional area of operations.

The second subject the senior bank authority should address is *operating department collaboration*. A policy is necessary in man-information communication which, as it develops, permits the user direct access to the database in an interactive way. What are the advantages? Making the user responsible for his computer-oriented work; sensitivity of the user to capabilities and limitations of computers; *timeliness* in giving the obtaining data; reduction in modifications and in transcription errors; reduction in development time; a smaller but more precise volume of output; exception processing, rather than mass printing; flexibility in reactions; and functional competency; better exploitation of the information resources. These advantages will not evolve, on their own, as standard operating procedures. Problem descriptions and, subsequently, problem solutions often require quantification. This has been the broad domain of operations research, and simulation studies in management, since the early '50s. As I discussed previously, many banks practiced it but few have had a policy regarding it. The same repeats itself now, with interactive systems. Within this broader applications domain, studies now conducted by typical American financial institutions, include *system design* and package selection criteria. Standards are being established with provisions for input, output and communication between data-processing, the user and the audit department. Bank authorities also study the enforcement of these standards.

An integral part of the foregoing reference is *programming procedures*. Standards in this area include items such as naming techniques; common subroutines that might be used in various applications; programming control and editing procedures that should be used in all applications languages.

Fourth, attention is now focused on *database management systems*. Particular emphasis is placed on the advantages to be derived from DBMS, namely: interactivity, to answer the need for immediate data access; integration, to present one unified picture of the bank's data assets; and flexibility/modularity, to ensure that the data-processing system is not rigid; and by being data-independent, the programs are more suited to portability (from machine to machine).

The fifth policy issue is *testing*. This standard should include the specific types of items to be tested; the extent to which they should be tested; a valid testing methodology; provisions for test data; provision for review of test results; retention requirements for test data.

Sixth, *documentation.* This is very important. It cannot be repeated too often, documentation is needed to ensure the continued usefulness of any system. The steering committee must learn the specific items of documentation necessary for operation. Specialists should be asked to improve on them, complementing and detailing such a list.

User Manuals are an important subset of documentation. Good standards should assign precise responsibility and personal accountability for developing the manuals and provide time frames for completing them.

Development of standards is only half the job. Standards must be maintained in a current status. Some steering committees have a subcommittee which reviews the standards of compliance for the guidelines contained in the work program. The subcommittee also reviews specific procedures used to enforce the standards. It evaluates the user manuals against work performed to determine that standards are being maintained in a current status and reflect the actual working procedures.

Seventh, *implementation*. In many American financial institutions management is enthusiastic about implementation programs. The standard should present items that will be contained in the implementation program, including training; operational considerations; schedules; and postimplementation reviews. A timetable is the cornerstone of valid implementation procedures.

Eighth, *disaster recovery*. Several banks have done research in this area. However, more extensive research is needed. According to a study by the University of Minnesota Graduate School of Business Administration, on the average, following steady and accute data-center failures, operational-business activities would suffer a decline of ninety-one percent after ten and one half days.

CONTINGENCY PLANNING

Whether the disaster is man-made or natural, a recovery plan is a logistical process that will provide smooth, rapid restoration of data-processing operations. The plan should be as detailed as possible. This will eliminate much decision-making following a major breakdown in processing. Once the merits of a disaster recovery plan have been established, a senior executive must be assigned the responsibility for creating the plan. This is an urgent task. It should be an integral part of the planning work concerning all computing centers, regardless of the type of equipment used. Once the data are locked into a computer, data cannot be removed unless an advanced plan anticipating failure is ready to go into effect.

Establishing a disaster recovery program must be assigned to a senior authority who can begin to outline a plan. The plan coordinator's first duty is to select team leaders from DP operations and from communications. The coordinator must supply the overall recovery team with up-to-date information about operations, programs, documentation, procedures, files, and supplies, as well as hardware configurations—computers, terminals, modems and personnel.

The user is an essential team participant. He should be involved in establishing priorities, such as what applications are the most critical in case of a disaster. To be easily manageable, the plan can be broken down into functional areas. Each area must have major responsibilities that comprise the whole plan. The essential aspects are: software; hardware; facilities; personnel; scheduling; communications; documentation, and supplies. Processing priorities are a key aspect. Though work in this area is in progress at some banks, it is not preceding at a rapid or far-reaching pace. This is an urgent and important subject. Let me express briefly some advice on what we should be doing, and fast, in this area.

First, we need *risk analysis* of all the sensitive bank information, for example, storage, processing, and output that in some way depends on computers, memory devices, and terminals. The study should involve the user as part of the analysis. The managers of all bank departments, at headquarters and at the branch offices, should be asked to show the analysts what parts of the printouts prepared by the computer are most valuable to them. The managers should also be asked which reports they would like to have in case of an emergency, and which could be dropped altogether. The risk analysis can determine in a factual and documented manner the effects and losses a bank would have in its business momentum, competitive edge, and cash flow, should the DP center be destroyed only if the user is directly involved. The study should also reveal the essential data necessary to operate during an emergency.

To help define, quantify, and put into perspective the major objectives for development of an overall contingency plan, a multiphase approach is recommended. This must be tailored to meet the needs of each bank when resource utilization shrinks as a result of a catastrophe.

Contingency planning would involve establishing objectives. It must provide emergency recovery documentation, preparation of plans for such an eventuality, and a test plan and the phasing of drills. "Drills" means conducting recovery exercises and, then, a post-exercise workshop.

Not only the computer specialists, but the whole staff should be oriented to the possibilities and requirements for contingency recovery planning. We should develop goals and responsibilities, determine scope of activities, and establish task force work schedules. Existing documentation, studies and reports should be reviewed and analyzed. Assemble inventories of files; systems; applications; and other computer related components. Predefine the problems to be presented in a catastrophy.

Guidelines for non-DP requirements such as insurance—legal and auditing—must be specified. We should provide on a solid basis—not just wishful thinking—the offsite computer center as insurance on a "what-if" basis. Remember: Your bank may have to stop operating if a catastrophe hits its computer center and no recovery plan has been established in advance to take care of the situation.

Involving Top Management

17

Technology, the processes technology releases, and the use made of these processes, will judge whether we do our jobs well today; whether we fight our fights with a view to the future, or close ourselves into the past.

Within a banking environment, computer applications must aspire to the servicing of objectives put forward. The value of technological advancement is measured in direct relation to the profit-making opportunities it creates and the number of jobs it eliminates. It must also be added that technology is inherently efficient, but because it has no morals it would indiscriminately eliminate friend and foe.

The principle characteristic of science is that in its work it ignores all judgments of human-oriented values. Aesthetic judgment has no place here. The greatest contribution of science, technology and mathematics to bank management is the assistance it gives us to help avoid preconceived value judgments. Our responsibility is to apply scientific standards and the latest technological developments to efficient use.

Leaders and followers; success and failure in banking; the balance sheet; and the profit-and-loss statement are influenced by the advantage we take from productivity tools and modern, effective technological media. The more formal a scientific approach, the less danger of losing track of the procedures. But also the greater the risk to overidealize and get away from reality. The difference is through know-how and steady training, organized and implemented to increase each man's storehouse of knowledge. It is to this end that computer-based media, like good business sense, become an asset to the decision-maker. Management is still an art, even if it uses scientific tools. But the cutting edge of technology tells what sort of an artist the manager is. The top artist in a bank is its president and chief executive officer. He sets the examples that others must follow.

THE CHIEF EXECUTIVE'S TASK FORCE

It is not enough that top management is simply "inclined towards" DIS. The directives should be given to actively work with a new orientation. Specific actions rather than generalities—clear objectives rather than clichés—should characterize top management decisions.

This goal has been initiated by the president of a leading financial institution. For reference purposes, it will be called the "Alphabank." This systems study has been coordinated by a top-level information systems committee, composed of the president of the board; the general manager; two assistant-general managers; the area managers (main branch office areas); the director of accounting; the director of organization; the director of computer operations, and a committee secretary who is the boss of the DIS Project.

What distinguishes this from other efforts is that all executives have been highly involved in the process of computer and communications projects in general, and of DIS in particular. Furthermore, the Alphabank has an established *information plan*. This plan is updated yearly. The plan involves all work which is to be done, its timetable and its budget. This blue-ribbon committee checks on the progress of the DIS Project, in a timely manner. For DIS purposes it meets every six weeks. For MIS (Management Information Systems) the meetings are held every four weeks. Even if top management participates, a meeting can take a whole morning.

Priorities are also established by this top-management committee. Most important, all systems studies are submitted in writing to its members. Background has developed as a matter of course and of training—often long, rather technical discussions—held between the specialists and the members of the committee. Exactly for reasons of background, the first reports were most explicit on definitions; while rather elementary in technical detail. Tools used to explain the information systems issues included personal interviews, group meetings and lectures. (This helped the DIS working group itself, as it cleared its own ideas. At the same time, top management gained understanding and appreciation of the complexity of issues involved with computer systems.)

The following projects have been submitted to the top-management committee of Alphabank for approval. Their range identifies the level of detail that must involve senior management.

> *Applications-Type projects:* Improving basic procedures; implementing distributed-information systems (nine persons); advancing with management-information systems (seven persons). The latter project includes: cost analysis; cost center definition; branch office productivity; and product cost—among other issues.

Among other projects falling into this category we distinguish: credit management; personnel information system; banking management of programs and terms; foreign trade; and management statistics.

> *Computer Management Policies*, such as planning and control of the computer center(s) facilities; security issues; maintenance and reliability; documentation standards for applications; the choice of programming languages. The line of responsibility between the organization and computer departments designates that the organization is responsible for: still-manual procedures; procedural instructions to branch offices; paper forms; typewriters, copiers and office equipment at large, and the structural issues.

The system analysis and the programmers depend on, and are managed by, the computer services. The same is true of training programs for specialists and of computer appreciation courses, addressed to all levels of the Alphabank.

GETTING THINGS DONE

The most admirable result top-management involvement achieved at Alphabank is a strict adherence to timetables. To appreciate the magnitude of the job and the relatively very brief timescales, Table 17.1 outlines the stratified structure of the branch office network.

Table 17.1

ALPHABANK–THE BRANCH OFFICE NETWORK

No. of branch offices	No. of people per B.O.	No. of Terminals projected per B.O.
25	50	up to 10
30	20–50	about 5
145	3–20	2–3
300	3	1

In the small B.O., the DTE will do all jobs. In the big B.O., DTEs will be specialized. The policy adopted for B.O. with only one Terminal in this: If the DTE is down, then use the next B.O. for data collection on a controlled basis, the number of employees per B.O., and the projected number of terminals.

At the first phase of implementation, minicomputer installations are made on an area basis. Areas with two minis will have one more serving as back-up. All B.O.s will be online; the minis will be linked among themselves with 4800 BPS lines; the DTE will be linked through 1200 BPS lines, five terminals per line.

The technical problems were attacked head-on by a nine-man-working group, split into subgroups. Both users and systems specialists participate in each. The general directive was; get results. The policy, simple and effective; keep the team dynamic; cut red tape; observe the timetable. The time tables for the distributed information system are outlined in Table 17.2, shown on the following page. No detail was neglected, even with the fast pace. All crucial aspects were examined, for instance, what could happen if the machine is down and data are locked in. "We must plan to decrease, not increase the pressure on our employees," a senior executive commented. The criteria for system design have been set accordingly. They include; performance; cost; reliability; flexibility; security; time of realization; technical risks; and organizational risks. Each pointed out the need for careful overall evaluation.

Table 17.2

DEADLINES AND MILESTONES FOR DIS

Deadlines	Milestones
January, Year 0	The DIS project is born
April, Year 0	*First Report to Top Management*: Machine choice of the software company to implement the applications.
September, Year 0	*Second Report*: Basic A.P. choices and their procedural implications.
December, Year 0	*Third Report*: (a) Functional specifications for DIS (b) proposal on network structure (c) personnel development program (d) preparation of the installation sites. These must be developed in parallel with a specific Timeplan.
November, Year 1	Pilot installation. First application: Savings, made in one minicomputer (regional) center.
April, Year 2	All applications to be run on minicomputers, at the pilot installation.
April, Year 3	Development of the full network. All applications implemented in fifteen regional minicomputer centers, all branch offices online with 700 terminals.

FOUR PRINCIPLES

Top management centered its attention on the basics underlying the MIS system, starting with *the principle of milestone control*. The best control comes through identification of critical, key, or limiting points. This makes close monitoring and adjustment feasible. Inversely, increasing the volume of data given to management does not necessarily provide improved control.

Milestone control counteracts the human tendency to focus attention on too many trivial issues; by focusing attention of the effect of control points rather than on their quantity. As able managers known by experience, the corrective action applied on limiting factors (or bottlenecks) often forces changes at other points in the organization that are not being monitored in this particular instance.

The second issue to become a part of Alphabank's policy was *the exception principle.* Routine occurrences and decisions should be handled by the computer system. "Routine" occurrences fall within a structured-information environment. Only exceptional situations should be referred to the manager. To implement this, decisions that can be preplanned should be reduced to an algorithim and subsequently programmed for computer-processing.

Within a structured-information environment, every effort should be made to preestablish the meaning and frequency of exceptions. This is the case with all routine matters and with a significant number of schedule reports.

The application of the exception principle should consider the computer as the subordinate; and man as the superior component—not vice versa. This is often forgotten by men over zealous about automation—but it characterizes the thinking of those who, by training and experience, have reached the "post-automation" phase.

In matters of high-speed performance, memory capacity, and accuracy of operation, the computer dwarfs man. The same is true about conformance to instruction. Computers do not present problems of emotion, fatigue, or rejection of authority. Nevertheless, computers cannot improvise, learn or (so far, at least) benefit from experience.

Third, *the principle of accountability.* An operating executive should only be held responsible for factors that he has complete control over. Accountability can be best applied if the responsible person is providing with timely information regarding the deviation from standards of the factors he controls. The executive also should know what to do when the computer fkashes a danger signal. The management information system must support and enhance accountability. Not defy it. Information for the top echelon in the chain-of-command is not necessarily a sum of what is required for lower echelons. Additionally, control and planning objectives are (generally) not met the same way through the use of the same kinds of information.

Fourth, *planning and control prerequisites.* The structure of the information environment itself changes. This is why planning is a prerequisite. If planning-and-control objectives are handled in a similar manner with day-to-day management, the resulting compromise is very likely to be inadequate in meeting either aim.

As a matter of principle in system design, the choice of information to be reported should be based on its operating significance, rather than on traditional reasons, or ease of obtaining data from the computer. The database organization (and eventual optimization) should reflect management aims. Table 17.3 brings this into perspective.

For database-operating-protection reasons, all precautions must be taken. They involve: *robustness* and operating performance. "One of the basic limits in projecting a database is the operating performance to be obtained," said a senior bank executive. Database management facilities must be examined, and the necessary procedural steps properly outlined: check validity requests; control authorizations; locate data; lock data; order data; unlock data; map data between schemas and subschemas. Evaluation criteria must be announced, including function-positioning and fault-tolerance and control.

Table 17.3

DATA PROCESSING AND DATABASE DISTRIBUTION

Functional level	Ancient approach	Middle program	Modern approach
Top management	no support	centralized DB (Batch)	inquiry timesharing on mini
Middle management	centralized DB (Batch)	some inquiry capabilities	functional DB on dedicated mini
Operations	centralized DB (Batch or Online)	realtime with long telephone lines	geographically distributed DB on local mini

THE COMMUNICATIONS SYSTEMS

One fundamental aspect the Alphabank study did not consider is integrating data, voice and image. In the future the three will be handled through one network. It is, therefore, better to unify responsibility from technical design to actual management, though most financial institutions today have, for historical reasons, divided this function among different organizational lines.

The successful implementation of the new information technologies implies that a long, hard look be taken at the overall *data and voice* problem, including the physical and logical media. Once the key issues have been attacked and solved, the realm of possibilities—including personnel and cost saving capabilities—are great.

Information is used for communications purposes. Today, largely due to standard practices, the least structured (or formatted) is voice communication. The most structured are mathematical models (algorithms), and by extension the man-computer interactive approaches. Other classes of communications systems fall mid-range.

Voice and interactive approaches to a database set aside, there are currently three main classes of business communications systems.

1. *The Telephone*, is the most frequent method of communication, by a wide margin.

2. *The Postal Service*, private couriers and intercompany mail-delivery networks that carry messages physically instead of electronically.

3. *The Electrical Message Systems*: Facsimile; telex; telegrams. And, more recently, Electronic Mail (Teletex).

Here are examples of possibilities: wideband communications would allow a copier to produce a remote image at the same speed at which it produces a local copy. The emergence of such a unit, would make facsimile an adjunct of copying. The unit would be reserved for local copying during the day and would receive only when it was being used locally. At night, a single copier could receive a few thousand pages.

Data compression units, at best, can receive about 800 pages in eight hours. A facsimile transmission that now takes two to six minutes can be reduced, using wideband, to about three seconds. Given the speed of facsimile images, it is likely that electronic mail networks will spring up, which are expected to include, as a first step, the top

200 companies in the United States. By connecting major operating centers, these companies will be able to operate in a communications environment of unprecedented magnitude.

To appreciate the impact of productivity, efficiency and cost-control in this wide field of communications, let's look at the statistics. Some ninety billion pieces of mail move, per year, in the United States; about ten percent are writer-to-reader correspondence. Four billion letters are business mail; interoffice correspondence is estimated between twelve and fifteen billion letters, memos, etc. In addition, there are: 220 to 250 billion telephone calls per year; and 50 million telex messages. The length of messages is interesting. One study shows that:

- fifty-eight percent of management messages are one page or less.
- twenty eight percent are two to four pages.
- fourteen percent are five pages or more.

Electronic message systems (EMS) carry a much shorter text. An estimated seventy-three percent of the messages transmitted are less than 1000 characters. Data communications have been added to electronic message systems since the mid 1960s, this electronic message systems is a rapidly expanding area of communication. Of the total messages sent:

- forty-five percent go to one individual
- thirty-five percent go to more than one individual
- eighteen percent go to groups
- two percent go to a combination of groups and individuals

A study found that: forty percent of a manager's time is spent on mail, telephone and business travel; an additional twelve to thirty-five percent is spent on reading and writing. Another study identified the percentage of working time some professions spent to push paper: it is astonishingly high.

Statistics show that 550 kg. of paper are printed each year for every man, woman and child in America (of these a good share is computer output). The computer was thought to be a means for reducing the paper jungle. It increased it. It is now hoped that data communications will do this job.

Telephone users are steadily increasing. Though the United States has today more than fifty percent of all telephones installed worldwide (180 million) Western Europe is catching up. But data communications revenues have already surpassed those that the postal service receives as a business-to-business message carrier of First Class mail (forty-four percent of six billion dollars). In fact, they represented about 3.5 billion dollars in revenues for 1978.

Looking at the electronic message system, we observe that the messages in this area are normally of higher priority than those in other areas; while communications can be carried out by many different methods.

Data-communications networks are primarily used for financial transactions, order-entry and associated teleprocessing applications. Here is another big junction between paperwork simplification and the usage of electronic media. Document distribution through facsimile systems has found its way into environments which are not computer-oriented. Yet, they constitute one of the pillars of the electronic mail products now in development.

Britain is planning to implement a full-scale electronic mail system over the next few years. The system will operate when the network is not used, from late night to early morning. The Viewdata public utility previously discussed will constitute the backbone of this system. The process of voice transmission will experience a major breakthrough. Voice *store and forward* capability can be developed for telephone use, and, possibly the cable TV network. The sender directs a verbal message to the recipient's in-box. The recipient can call this in-box from any telephone and get his message.

Technological advances to provide a means of coupling the telephone, and the TV set, to offer terminal capabilities to the users for receiving and sending mail are just around the corner: allowing the user to alternate between voice-and-data communications at the flick of a switch. Merging message and voice facilities along packet-switching principles will decouple sender and receiver, so that there is no need for both of them to be online; offer electronic speeds and geographic independence; use of computer technology to aid in composition, storage, retrieval and reading. Such solutions can operate within different environments; exclusive station-to-station calls; primary addressing with copies to other stations; broadcasts, with messages sent from one station to a distribution list; and teleconferencing (group partition).

Further in the future, lies the concept of the "wired city." In an experiment conducted in the Japanese town of Migashi-Ikoma, 300 families participated in the experience of having their newspapers delivered by facsimile receiver; shopping by closed-circuit television; gas and electricity meters read automatically and deducted electronically from their bank accounts; paying for their shopping by electronic funds transfer (without using their cash or credit cards).

Access to a videotape library for reruns of favorite television programs, banking from the comfort of one's own living room, burglar and fire alarms linked automatically to a central computer that alerts the police or fire brigade if anything out of the ordinary is detected—whether the family is at home or not; air/conditioning, electrical appliances, heating regulated from outside the home by shortwave radio links; and educating children by computer-aided instruction over the visual display terminal, are among the capabilities offered by the future computers and communications environment. Such developments will have a tremendous sociological and business impact and we must be prepared. Banking and the paper-intense industry present a much simpler applications case than the "wired city" and benefits can be much more immediate and visible. We have the technology. What is missing is the procedural, and end-user studies to help in projecting, evaluating, implementing and maintaining the systems to come.

TOOLS FOR OFFICE AUTOMATION

Paperwork simplification, cost reduction and evolving office automation are issues that have retained the interest of top management. In the past, solutions to paperwork problems were largely procedural, today they involve intelligent devices, with communications linked to a host, and the host linked to a network. The goal is higher productivity; invariably, this means less paper. Let me add, as a guide, some figures about paperwork costs. A typical office throws away one third of all the paper it receives, transfers another third to inactive storage and uses only the remaining third in its day-to-day functions. American banking data indicates that each inch of paperwork costs between $250 and $300 to produce and $15 a year to store. Most offices waste sixty-five cents out of every dollar they spend on paperwork, and paperwork accounts for ninety percent of all office work.

Most inactive files have too many records; in files that are more than five years old, nineteen out of twenty records will never be looked-up. Thus, there is a double incentive to investigate paperwork savings. There are potential savings in handling *external* paperwork with microforms until the advent of optical discs. This category includes checks, deposit slips, signature cards and customer credit files. Significant savings can also be realized through the use of microforms for such "internal" paperwork as routine correspondence accounts payable and personnel records.

In addition to cost reduction, adopting microforms can bring the bank an intangible benefit: a clearer understanding of bank operations through comprehensive planning which precedes conversion from a paper to a microform system. The insights gained through this planning can result in revised systems and procedures which permit additional savings above and beyond what the microfilm system itself brings to the typical bank.

To implement office automation solutions, we must: think in functional and innovative ways; improve system availability; study how information must flow between people and machines; improve security and assure growth capacity.

Let's return to fundamentals; to the point which must be studied first, the *work station*, a computer-based unit able to handle day-to-day communications. This has been an evolutionary development based on two facts: the advent of the word processor, and the very large share taken by company mail as a percent of all hard-copy typed or printed in a firm. Studies among financial institutions have indicated that seventy-five to ninety percent of all hardcopy produced in a firm is internal company mail. As a consequence, we can ask: "Why print it in the first place? Why not to leave it in the memory of the machine, refer to it when needed, and even have exception reporting (flashes) on a video-screen as the exceptions occur?" The latter would require a significant amount of organizational prerequisites. The keys for the job are procedural. Next to organizational, the prerequisites are the proper hardware and software support. New generations of work stations are aided by the fact that the cost of microprocessors is dropping sharply; the cost of solid-state memory is shrinking even more; telephone technologies evolve and communications costs decrease but not as much as computer costs—personnel costs are steadily on the rise.

Where will this development lead? Within the banking organization it will bring about a *terminal on every desk* equipped with a screen (soft copy); a simple keyboard; and a hard copy capability, which is near *or* remote. But in the larger horizon of the environment within which a bank operates, it will mean a computed-supported network design that is Point-of-Sales oriented (or more precisely point of origin) and actuated through debit cards and a personal identification number (PIN).

Such a network within a banking-and-merchant facility environment will use many point-of-sales (POS) terminals and automated teller machines (ATMs). Communications lines will lead into a frontend and form there to the host computer of the bank. The same route is taken by the messages originating at, or directed to the banking minicomputer at the branch office.

Private systems will be hooked-up to a regional or national financial network, bringing the cashless society so much closer. Workstations will be combined into office information systems effectively supporting the paperless solutions we have been talking about as the *coming environment.* The change will not be easy. Resistance has always in its background past habits. But, as of recently, we have finally come to appreciate the issue of *mental productivity* based on man-information interaction. There is a management axiom: that if we want the job done we must delegate authority along with responsibility. But if we want an outstanding job done, we should also delegate the freedom to apply imagination. And this requires access to information.

Banks hesistant to undergo the radical rethink of their internal structures that's required for the effective introduction of technology, will find the greatest roadblocks in their way. Now, more than ever, those organizations are able to survive that:

- have clearly defined business goals
- are action oriented
- simply organized
- have lean staffs
- view people as the key to productivity
- utilize operational autonomy
- emphasize the company's strengths and correct the weaknesses

- have a few tight, clearly defined controls but
- allow considerable flexibility in other areas.

Whether by trial and error, intuition, or design, successful companies have found a particular set of values that make them the leaders in their field; give importance to detail; and, through proper planning, are prepared for every eventuality. "Chance" favors the prepared: and preparation means training the human potential. Automation or no automation, the key job is done by able men.

The advancing technology accelerated the obsolescence of our knowhow and made life-long learning even more mandatory than before. Banking used to be a slow-moving profession in terms of innovation. Yet, today the banker who does not train himself in the new technologies loses half the knowledge he needs for his job in the short span of five years. That time lead is down to three years for systems specialists.

Technology is a demanding partner. Like Alice in Wonderland, we have to run fast just to keep in place. There are also many positive sides. An expanding technology dims the distinction between the "haves" and the "have nots," for those who take advantage of it. By bringing us closer together, computers and communications can help erase the argument that "ninety percent of science and technology has been developed for the rich." A quarter century of practice has turned the computer into a cheap, simple, and easy to use tool for everyone, and we should be ready for the change.

To get ready, we should invest in our human capital through the right training. Automating a clerical function does not necessarily improve productivity, service, or job interest. Success will ultimately depend on the human beings who use the system; and the better trained they are, the greater the results we can expect from our investment.

It is not enough to recognize that information is a marketable product. We must also be in the forefront in heeding some of the educational, social, political and economic implications of the technological revolution. Lessons can be learned from our masterstrokes; and even better lessons from our mistakes. Nothing great will ever be achieved without men—and men are great in their achievements only if they are determined to be so.

Index